Music

& the Making of a New South

Music

THE UNIVERSITY OF NORTH CAROLINA PRESS

Chapel Hill and London

the Making of a New South

Gavin James Campbell

© 2004
The University of North Carolina Press
All rights reserved
Manufactured in the United States of America
Set in New Baskerville and Didot types
by Tseng Information Systems, Inc.

The paper in this book meets the guidelines for
permanence and durability of the Committee on
Production Guidelines for Book Longevity of the
Council on Library Resources.

Parts of this book have been reprinted in revised
form from "Classical Music and the Politics of
Gender in America, 1900–1925," *American Music*
21 (Winter 2003).

Library of Congress
Cataloging-in-Publication Data
Campbell, Gavin James.
Music and the making of a new South / Gavin James
Campbell.
    p. cm.
Includes bibliographical references (p.) and index.
ISBN 0-8078-2846-7 (cloth : alk. paper) —
ISBN 0-8078-5517-0 (pbk. : alk. paper)
1. Music—Georgia—Atlanta—19th century—History
and criticism.   2. Music—Georgia—Atlanta—20th
century—History and criticism.   3. Atlanta (Ga.)—
History.   I. Title.
ML200.8.A56 C35 2004
306.4'842'0975823109041—dc22   2003016295

cloth   08 07 06 05 04   5 4 3 2 1
paper   08 07 06 05 04   5 4 3 2 1

To COLIN ROY CAMPBELL
Pilot, friend, brother

*Science, freedom, beauty, adventure: what more could you
ask of life? Aviation combined all the elements I loved. There
was science in each curve of an airfoil, in each angle between
strut and wire, in the gap of a spark plug or the color of the
exhaust flame. There was freedom in the unlimited horizon, on
the open fields where one landed. A pilot was surrounded by
beauty of earth and sky. He brushed treetops with the birds,
leapt valleys and rivers, explored the cloud canyons he had gazed
at as a child. Adventure lay in each puff of wind. . . . I decided
that if I could fly for ten years before I was killed in a crash, it
would be a worthwhile trade for an ordinary life time.*

    Charles A. Lindbergh, *The Spirit of St. Louis* (1953)

*You know I love to fly and I love, love airplanes.
I really want to be a pilot.*

    Colin Roy Campbell, age twelve

Contents

Illustrations

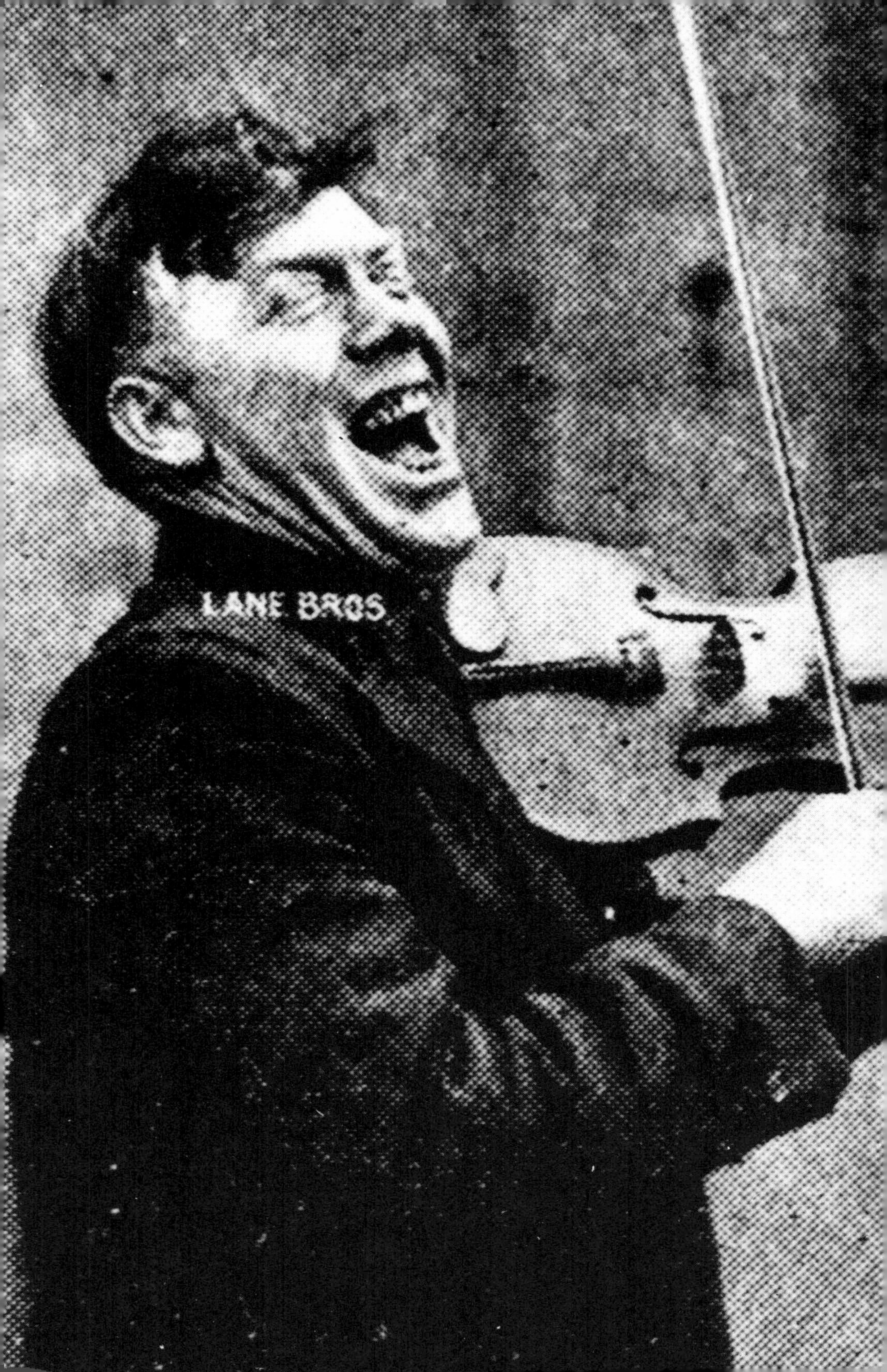
LANE BROS

Acknowledgments

The only thing more pleasurable than finishing this project is publicly thanking the people who were indispensable to its completion.

My initial scholarly debt is to a pair of teachers who, each in their own way, opened doors that forever changed my life. At the University of Kentucky, Schuyler Robinson taught me a clutch of Bach preludes, fugues, and chorales that convinced a struggling (and ultimately failed) organ major that music's frustration was offset by sheer wonder and ecstatic delight. Mary Beth Norton, my undergraduate adviser at Cornell University, was the toughest teacher I have ever had and the one from whom I learned perhaps more than any other. She demanded the highest level of intellectual integrity and honesty, and her stern maxims for historical research still make me sit up straight when I go to the archives. Both Schuyler Robinson and Mary Beth Norton were superb models of committed teachers whose influence extends far beyond their knowledge of it.

At the University of North Carolina at Chapel Hill (UNC–Chapel Hill), where this project began as a dissertation, I was fortunate in having the benefit of two advisers who guided this project from its inception. With stunning regularity John Kasson told me what my project was about when in fact I had no clue, and many times I was tempted to toss my notecards into his lap and let him take over since he had all the good ideas. Readers can only lament that he so gently but firmly turned down my generous offer. And how can I adequately describe the contributions of Donald Mathews? From the first day of graduate school he shepherded me through numerous episodes of backsliding, set my feet upon a rock, and established my goings. I admire him beyond description. I am also grateful to Joel Williamson, Daniel Patterson, Jacquelyn Hall, David Whisnant, and Robert Cantwell, each of whom contributed valuable insights and whose different perspectives kept me from getting stale.

I owe an enormous debt to my graduate student colleagues. In particular, Stephen Berry must claim credit (whether he wishes to or not) for occasionally elevating the prose to something that might approach his poetic sensibility. Indeed, a few of the sentences are by all rights his. Our exchanges often revolved around bitter sulking at our sorry plight —a topic of conversation that we frequently brought to the highest state of whiny perfection—but they were indispensable in building up sufficient motivation and hilarity to keep going. Robert Tinkler, whom I was fortunate to count as both a colleague and a neighbor, proved the warmest of friends and confidants. Like two good ol' boys, we spent many an hour nestled into plastic lawn furniture on the front porch of 232 McCauley Street, sharing scholarly delights and discouragements. I owe him numerous debts of friendship that it is a pleasure to contemplate repaying. Both Steve and Robert read this work so many times that they undoubtedly began reciting whole passages in their nightmares. They both, however, kindly allowed me to claim sole credit.

Librarians in both Atlanta and Chapel Hill displayed that remarkable tenacity and patience for which their profession is justly renowned. In particular, the staff of UNC–Chapel Hill's music library accommodated my requests for obscure material with alacrity and professionalism. Similarly, the librarians throughout the UNC–Chapel Hill system, the Atlanta History Center, the Ida Pearle and Joseph Cuba Archives of the William Breman Jewish Heritage Museum, the Georgia Division of Archives and History, Emory University, and the South Carolina Historical Society were absolutely crucial to this work's completion. I am also grateful to UNC–Chapel Hill for several timely dissertation fellowships.

Others who deserve special mention include Steve Goodson, who early on shared with me his own excellent work on public entertainment in Atlanta; Bryant Simon for getting me a crucial story from the *Atlanta Georgian*; Cita Cook for letting me borrow her Atlanta apartment while doing research; Bruce Baker for some last-minute trans-Pacific bibliographic assistance; the dissertation writing group who pounded sense into my prose; Philip Mulder, whose companionship and sense of humor made graduate school just that much more fun; Yoshimi Matsuura for making my job and life so much easier; Stevie Champion, who wrestled obstreperous footnotes into pliant submission and quietly shuffled offstage a host of embarrassing gaffes; Ruth Homrighaus, for tracking down the photos; and David Perry of UNC Press for his attentiveness throughout the publishing process.

Family members have proven essential in giving this project meaning. My parents, Norma Prendergast and William Campbell, along with the wonderful people they subsequently married, have supported me through every twist and turn. Their unwavering confidence buoyed me up, and their capacity to love so completely has never ceased to humble me. I greatly admire my brother Bill for his unswerving commitment to justice, and I hope that in some small way I have emulated that virtue in this book's conclusions. In ways they cannot know, my in-laws Fred and Esther Ohr have shown me the meaning of generosity, courage, and perseverance.

My greatest debt is, of course, to my dear wife. Tamara Ohr-Campbell has been my heart's companion for more than ten years now, in which time we have gone from Mark Grace and Ryne Sandberg to Asashoryu and Takamisakari. It has been a hell of a ride, and I am glad she bought the ticket. The influence of her wisdom, her talents, and her wit are everywhere in this book, and, more precious to me, everywhere in my life. Thank you.

Finally I wish to acknowledge and to honor Colin Roy Campbell. For more than twenty-five years he was my closest friend and, fortunately for me, my brother. Alas, in 1997 the plane he was piloting disappeared into West Virginia's foggy mountain thickets. It remains a devastating loss. I still miss his awkward hugs, watching crummy, midafternoon, made-for-TV movies together, buzzing to and from small Kentucky airports sampling barbecue potato chips and RC Colas, or just getting a call for no other reason than to see if he could stump me with some question of historical trivia (he invariably succeeded). I miss him so terribly much, and I consider dedicating this book to him a slight and sadly late recompense for the brotherly love that binds our hearts forever, regardless of the grave's call.

Music

& the Making of a New South

Introduction

The "Atlanta Spirit"

Henry Grady was dead, to begin with. There was no doubt whatever about that. Only two days before the Christmas of 1889 the silver tongue of the New South's most renowned prophet lay shuttered inside the dead man's mouth. In his brief thirty-nine years, Grady had preached the South's coming economic and industrial resurrection with such righteous conviction that he converted not only a number of Yankee moneychangers, but countless white men and women of his beloved Southland as well. His Atlanta neighbor William Lawson Peel, for one, proudly counted himself a Grady New South man through and through. Though saddened by Grady's untimely death, Peel nevertheless understood that no private tragedy could derail the South's regeneration so long as he and his colleagues took up the cross. For the next thirty-eight years William Lawson Peel assumed the burden, dedicating his life to the making of a New South.[1]

Born in 1849, William was the third of James and Elizabeth's six children who clustered on a southwestern Georgia farm in what was then called Kinchafoonee County. (The county's name excited such a barrage of giddy ridicule that local politicians renamed it Webster County in 1856 to honor the New England statesman.)[2] The Civil War came and went with young Peel, like Grady, on the sidelines, too young to participate in any but a vicarious way. Though he could not march with the Webster County Invincibles or the Webster Rifles, the nearby town of Preston provided virtually all the excitement any noncombatant could require. Patriotic orations, flag-raising ceremonies, and constant military drills punctured the monotony of Peel's farm life, while breathless reports of success and failure from the front lines quickened the pace of young Webster County boys anxious to lend their teenage brawn to the Cause. The arrival of Yankee soldiers devastated these hopes, and bluecoat patrols through Preston, not to mention the meanderings of freed slaves, made surrender and its consequences starkly palpable.[3]

The war savaged Webster County's farm economy. Corn production declined precipitously from 190,000 bushels in 1860 to a paltry 86,000 bushels a decade later. All told, the cash value of the county's farms dropped by over half a million dollars in the five years following the war.[4] The Peels could claim no immunity from hardship, and they joined their neighbors in a desperate and futile bid to revive their fortunes. The war's trail of economic wreckage severely blighted whatever charms a modest Webster County farm held for the teenaged William.

Even a town as plain as nearby Americus seemed to promise better things. Compared to a lifetime of chopping cotton, tending livestock, and enjoining recalcitrant freedmen to work, the chance to clerk in a dry goods store seemed like great fortune indeed. In 1869 young William Lawson Peel determined to master his future instead of helplessly gliding along the current of events that had swept his aging father through prosperity, secession, war, emancipation, and penury. Like countless others of his generation, he began white-collar work with little doubt that this humble commencement was merely the first rung on a ladder of success whose pinnacle stretched out of view. S. H. Hawkins, president and founder of the Bank of Americus, must have agreed, for it was not long before he asked the enterprising Peel to abandon dry goods for finance. Peel accepted. In so doing, he discovered two passions that would dominate the rest of his life: banking and Atlanta.

At Hawkins's urging, Peel enrolled for a semester in the Atlanta Business College. Classes introduced him not only to the intricacies of business methods, but also to the city's exhilarating spirit of wide-awake get-ahead (and stay-ahead). Though Peel returned to Americus at the conclusion of his brief studies, he could not get the Gate City out of his mind. In 1876 he decided to make Atlanta his permanent home.

The Atlanta of Peel's earliest acquaintance was a city still dusting off the ashes of destruction. In 1865 William T. Sherman's Yankees had laid fiery waste the city's infrastructure, and the earthworks still surrounding the city in the 1870s stood mute watch against their return. By the time Peel arrived Atlanta was a strange commingling of ruin and renewal, with a thriving business district hemmed in by garbage, animal carcasses, sewage, charred buildings, mud, and the inconveniences of incessant construction. Large sections of town—places where his shadow never moved—experienced poverty and misery unbounded. Black men and women, who, like Peel, came looking for something better than dull agricultural labor, found themselves mired in lowlands of muck and sewage, poverty and filth. But even these impediments to life's pleasures

Intersection of Marietta and Broad Streets in Atlanta, 1891, William Lawson Peel's New South in the making. Courtesy of the Tracy W. O'Neal Photographic Collection, Special Collections Department, Pullen Library, Georgia State University.

failed to dim the city's charms for the scrappy entrepreneurs who saw only opportunity. They spoke of Atlanta as a living thing, not an agglomeration of buildings and streets. The "Atlanta Spirit," they called it, and they knew from experience that neither fire nor invading barbarians could repress that collective spirit once animated. Atlanta was going places, and only the most indolent would fail to move with it.

Atlanta's reputation for opportunity in an otherwise prostrate region lured thousands of new residents. Peel's arrival contributed to a population boom that increased the number of residents by more than 15,000 between 1870 and 1880. In the next decade 28,000 more arrived.[5] Though the doors of opportunity never came unhinged by the crush of these new migrants, they nevertheless let a large number pass who, without Sherman's incendiary retribution, would have found the entrance clogged by an established antebellum elite. Indeed, the city's respectable residents looked on with alarm as a new breed of men and women from "plebeian parentage" and "void of any of the virtues and refinements of persons of gentle birth and decent instincts" threatened to overwhelm the city. These new "dudes" paraded Atlanta's streets conceiving of "no pleasure higher than a vulgar show of their purses."⁶ Yet for ambitious young men from modest backgrounds like Peel, the astonishing wealth they both produced and consumed provided tangible evidence of their own power to transform a society of "gentle birth and decent instincts" into one "free from the domination of *caste*."⁷

The postwar generation of Atlanta businessmen minimized their ties to the Old South's plantation aristocracy, and many, like Peel, were too young to have risked their lives in war for its perpetuation. "There is nothing of the Old South about it," one visitor wrote of Atlanta in 1886. "There must be old regulation Southerners in this region, but they have either died untimely in despair or they have drifted into the current and moved on with the world around them." This rising generation did not scoff at the region's antebellum civilization, for certain, but they were clear-eyed enough to see that its destruction was permanent. In its place they envisioned planting a New South in the ashes of the Old. "Instead of discussing the old plantation times 'before the wah,'" the visitor continued, "they talked about railroads, factories, the tariff, the schools, the increase of crops, and the growth of wealth and trade."⁸ They courted railroad executives and Yankee investors, correctly surmising that both would transform the city from a regional curiosity into a national economic powerhouse. The result was countless new industries and businesses ranging from confections and agricultural implements to terra cotta wares and fancy carriages. The Old South's day was past. This New South now awake and thriving would not rebuke its ancestor, but neither would it content itself with languid sighs for bygones. Its residents were poised on greatness and they were determined to seize it.

Trying to put his finger on what separated these new Atlantans from their fathers, Henry Grady explained that they had "fallen in love with work."⁹ Grady's newspaper, the *Atlanta Constitution*, profiled some of these new men in 1880 for the benefit of readers. At thirty-one Peel was still too green to yet catch the editor's eye (that would come a few years later), but he could read with swelling pride of the civic leaders whose humble rural origins he shared. Despite their early obscurity, the larger world now snapped to attention when confronted with "self-made men" like C. W. Hunnicut, who had moved to Atlanta "a poor country boy," or with Judge Logan E. Bleckley, who began his life "on a pitiful salary," or with James Watson, who as a youth drove a lowly dray. Even discounting the pleasant exaggeration Grady employed for promotional purposes, Peel could feel nothing but commingled awe and self-satisfaction when comparing their lives to his. Their success, like his, derived not from "accident of inheritance" or from a "capricious turn of luck." These men, like him, had "wrought their lives with their own hands."[10] Putting aside his newspaper and setting to work, William Lawson Peel counted himself fortunate to live in a place and time with men as these. He, too, was in love with work, and his rising fortunes in the banking profession granted him membership in the ranks of "self-made men" building a new Atlanta and a New South.

By staking his own personal fortunes on those of his native region and adopted city, Peel made his personal ambitions a patriotic service. Like other New South men, Peel did not distinguish between his New South and himself. "My interests are now and will always be in Atlanta," he declared at one point.[11] Every rising downtown building, every blossoming financial report, every burgeoning manufacturing census, every heaving steam engine, measured his power and swelled his pride. Nor were personal triumphs cordoned off from evidence of regional advancement and prosperity. Peel's mansion at the state's most prestigious residential address, his membership in a clutch of distinguished clubs, his meritorious record of public service, his climb to banking eminence all reflected credit upon a city and a region that could adequately compensate the contributions of such an illustrious man. As his life neared its conclusion in 1927, he could reminisce along with the dwindling number of his contemporaries about the impediments dismantled and the obstructions overturned. War, emancipation, depression, poverty, and political turmoil had buffeted but not shattered them. Peel could accept with the requisite grace the highest accolade the city could bestow when Henry Grady's old paper, the *Constitution*, labeled him "an embodiment of the 'Atlanta spirit.'"[12]

A "White Man's Problem"

Peel and his colleagues liked to think of themselves as men of action who bent the times to their will. They wanted everyone to conclude, as did visiting journalist Ray Stannard Baker in 1906, that "the white man is in full control of the South, politically, socially, [and] industrially."[13] They cultivated this image in their wardrobes, in their entertainments, in their architecture, in their laws, and in their panting

William Lawson Peel, circa 1925, "an embodiment of the Atlanta spirit."
Courtesy of the Atlanta History Center.

booster propaganda. In subtle ways, however, they guardedly confessed the limitations of their power and the difficulties they faced in making a New South that was theirs alone. Ulcers and high blood pressure were inescapable.[14]

For one thing, they feared that an infatuation with the promise of constant growth would lead them to fancy the "New" more than the "South." In letting fall slack the reigns of duty imposed by southern history and identity, they feared falling prostrate before grubby, Yankee merchant values. In 1902, for instance, members of the Pioneer Citizens' Society of Atlanta chastised the postwar generation for letting itself become so "engrossed by the empty pleasures or insignificant transactions of the present age" that it was certain to "neglect to treasure up the recollections of the past."[15] Eleven years later, the *Constitution* described the formation of the Country Collective Society, whose members devoted themselves to perpetuating "the old country conditions of Georgia." Its initial meeting attracted fifty "of Atlanta's country-bred" folks who sat around a hominy pot "and told of the days gone."[16] In a land where old times were not supposed to be forgotten, Atlanta's New South seemed mesmerized by talk of the future and of change. To shake off the spell, men like William Lawson Peel insisted that their New South avoided the pitfalls of easy sentimentality promoted by the Old South's defenders. Instead, their New South bundled hardheaded pragmatism together with the region's more durable and flexible traditions.

One regional trait they wrought with considerable care was crafting a style of race relations suitable for their New South. Conscious that in making a New South for themselves, blacks would necessarily create their own New South as well, whites did all they could to tone down the era's regenerative possibilities for blacks. They codified racial encounters with a careful measure of segregation ordinances, voting restrictions, inherited customs, and brutality. Nevertheless, African Americans refused silent dismissal into inferior quarters and unceasing toil. Whether in the raucous energy of Decatur Street bars and brothels, in the dazzling refinement of Auburn Avenue shops and homes, or in the stimulating classrooms of elite black colleges, black life moved with striking vitality. Mounting white hostility slashed at the sails of African American life and culture, but the vessel moved inexorably forward.

Indeed, whites hardly knew what to do, alternately embracing and repelling the blacks in their midst. The further blacks went in the separate direction whites pushed them, the more whites feared losing control over blacks. What exactly happened in places like Pig Alley, Beaver Slide, The Bottoms, and Campbell's Row remained beyond the capacity of most whites to know. "We see them every day," an agitated journalist reported in 1881. "They are about us and work for us, and at night go to their homes; but what these homes are and where they are, and the little picture that each hearthstone presents, we never think of." He concluded with the startling admission that "by far the largest proportion of Negroes are never really known to us."[17] "We do not know what the negroes think," the editor of the *Atlanta News* echoed twenty-five years later. "We don't know what the negroes say when the whites are not present."[18] Ironically, by insisting that they "knew" blacks best because they had always lived together, white southerners had deflected many northern racial moderates from taking a more active role in securing black civil rights in the South. Pondering within the quiet of their hearts, however, white Atlantans gave voice to a corroding fear that their knowledge of black people, and thus their ability to control them, was far more tenuous than they cared to publicly admit. What they *did* know, and what implicit admission segregation rested on, was that the power of white supremacy was most secure when not tested by constant interracial jostling. The New South structures designed to enforce racial hierarchies were, therefore, an admission of white supremacy's fractured successes. Blacks were always ready to point out the logical inconsistencies and to press the limits. It was one more aggravation for those white men reportedly "in full control of the South."[19]

White supremacy's primary target was the black community, of course, but its effects necessarily encompassed whites. White Georgians of a New South persuasion had already tackled a formidable challenge from members of their own race when the 1890s Populist movement opened up startling possibilities for cross-racial economic and political alliances. The possibilities of labor unionization at the city's textile factories in the new century kept these anxieties simmering. Jim Crow laws and customs helped shunt potentially destructive class animosities into less threatening channels. As one famous black Atlantan noted in 1925, "Jim Crow legislation was not to brand the Negro as inferior and to separate the races, but rather to flatter white labor to accept public testimony of its superiority instead of higher wages and social legislation."[20] Yet much to the surprise of those confident in white supremacy's power to knit a New South together, the diversion of working-class white resentment created problems of its own. In 1906 rumors circulated that

Atlanta's black men were sexually ravaging white women virtually by the score, causing the city to explode in a vicious carnival of white-on-black violence. Suddenly white Georgians found themselves at the end of a chastising rod as thunderous denunciations rained down upon them from concerned Americans outside the region. Though whites high and low had responded to the bloodlust, elite Atlantans feared that the racial unrest would forever keep their New South in the nation's backwaters and fretted lest negative publicity rend the veil of boosterism that promised that theirs was a progressive New South. Consequently, they censured the city's white working class for stretching white supremacy's logic too far. Their waffling response to racial and social unrest was most decidedly not the secret conspiracy of Machiavellian New South elites spun out in gilt phrases or whispered with the smoky breath of backroom deals. Rather, it proved yet another example of their tenuous authority. Constructing a New South of glittering success, they knew little how or where to incorporate the region's oppressed and broken citizens. White supremacy offered one solution, encompassing in its promise all but the most degenerate whites. But white supremacy meant different things to different people, and so it opened up possibilities of various interpretations and various styles of enforcement that could and did clash.[21]

While white supremacy promised uneven results when applied to class, it seemed to have even less effect on women. The rapid growth of women's clubs, which refused to quarantine their activities to recipe exchanges and polite lectures, challenged the claim men placed on directing a New South. These clubs and the capable women who staffed them insisted on having their say in the new structures of power and privilege, ranging from public sanitation and child welfare to educational reform and female suffrage. Citing the dictates of domestic duty, they insisted that theirs was not a New South of bland complacency any more than it was for their husbands, fathers, brothers, and sons. Instead, their clubs gave them a voice in pursuing their own vision of a New South and the stamina to advance onto territory that men like William Lawson Peel were accustomed to occupying alone. Moreover, the astonishing growth of the white female workforce further threatened to dramatically alter the balance of power between men and women. Just what this might mean in practical terms remained open to contentious review.[22]

Amid these challenges to their masculine preeminence, Atlanta's men liked to think that they were not, as one observer put it, "dawdling,

The residential palaces on Peachtree Street, 1895. Courtesy of the Tracy W. O'Neal Photographic Collection, Special Collections Department, Pullen Library, Georgia State University.

pale-faced, soft-handed effeminates."[23] Yet Peel and other men of his generation could not help but wonder whether surrounded by the comforts of their Peachtree Street palaces they had begun to lose touch with the kind of masculinity that had occasioned their rise in the first place. Their lurking suspicions received chilling confirmation when the popular press throughout the nation began foaming about "feminization" and "overcivilization." Shrill articles warned men that the snares of urban comforts were sapping their virility. Women's consumer wants, aesthetic tastes, educational interests, and values were inexorably crushing the masculine world, and city life offered no relief. Jobs that required no physical stamina and leisure that required no energy drained virility at a time when men needed it more desperately than ever. Not only did black men supposedly lie in wait, eager to exploit weaknesses among white womens' protectors, but also white women themselves probed for holes in masculine vigilance through which to advance themselves. "Feminization" and "overcivilization" were, therefore, more than popular but empty buzzwords. They gave voice to a creeping fear that gender and racial imbalances might send the entire New South project careening down some unpredictable passages.

In sum, Atlanta did indeed suffer from what one journalist labeled a "white man's problem," but race was not its only or even its most significant manifestation.[24] The white man's problem was a besetting series of fears and anxieties about the future and direction of this New South they supposedly controlled. In part they had no one to blame but themselves. They set before themselves an enormous task and one that had no conclusion. They would never reach their "New South" because it was a process, not a destination.[25] As a result, they could never rest on a mountain of accumulated laurels to survey their handiwork. They pushed forward, each accomplishment opening up possibilities of future greatness. Hence, for men like William Lawson Peel, who arrived in Atlanta when it was a smoky ruin and who helped transform it into a smoggy metropolis, the New South was a steady whirlwind of activity and change. Much of that change he could quantify, make logical, and, in that way, understand: population growth, building construction, banking statistics, and so on. Yet other transformations, though in some measure orchestrated by men like Peel, defied their ability to control, manage, or manipulate. Building a New South from the Old South's shattered fragments was a display of both stunning power and awesome impotence. Though Atlanta's men of empire constantly talked about building *the* New South, they were really only fitfully able to fashion *a* New South.

"More Than Merely Providing Entertainment"

Music is one of the most intriguing ways of studying a New South in the making. Atlanta vibrated with a jangling cacophony of guitars, organs, fiddles, cellos, pianos, banjos, harmonicas, bassoons, and voices, and the musical creativity the city helped foster spread rapidly to remote corners of the New South through travel, radio, and phonograph. In fact, Atlantans like William Lawson Peel promoted music as an essential part of the region's resurgence. For more than a decade he almost single-handedly organized the annual visits of the New York Metropolitan Opera Company, attempting thereby to demonstrate the South's growing cultural sophistication. So if it were indeed a New South, music could claim a rightful place alongside numerous other exciting signs of regional transformation.[26]

To write about music and the making of a New South, however, propels us beyond chronicling the innovations and the musicians that made the era such a creative one. It means stepping back to consider a wider definition of "music." We must be sensitive to the rituals and the rhetoric that audiences used to explain the meanings of what they heard. We must understand how the concerns and contexts of their lives shaped their musical enthusiasms. We must take seriously the observation printed in the *Atlanta Georgian* that the city's musical events were "more than merely providing entertainment for a crowd of city folks."[27]

This study does so by examining how middle- and upper-class Atlantans both white and black—and how Americans more broadly—crafted a musical culture at the turn of the twentieth century that gave voice to their notions of who they were and who they wished to be. Rather than surveying the overwhelming range of musical offerings that Atlanta boasted, my analysis focuses on three annual events in the period between 1909 and 1925 that consistently attracted thousands of spectators and reams of publicity: the Metropolitan Opera season, the Colored Music Festival, and the Georgia Old-Time Fiddlers' Convention. Begun within four years of each other, these events captivated many middle- and upper-class residents; each became an important part of the city's cultural identity. In part, the music provided a delightful complement to the normal rounds of everyday life, and the performances were as good as could be heard anywhere in the nation. At the same time, Atlantans derived pleasure from opera, slave-era spirituals, and old-time fiddling because the music spoke powerfully to a number of anxieties and desires they felt about the society in which they lived.

Describing how Atlantans created social, cultural, and political meanings from the music they listened to should not make us deaf to the aesthetic power they heard. Without question, the performances deeply moved many in the audience in ways they found difficult to articulate. "In 'Rigoletto,'" one thirteen-year-old girl wrote in her diary in 1915, "there was one Quartet that thrilled your whole body and, oh, it was - - - - no words can express the way music sometimes makes you feel, so I don't need to search my vocabulary for something that is not there."[28] It would seem patently obvious, then, that the reason audiences flocked to hear spirituals, old-time fiddling, and opera was simply because they found the music deeply moving.

Such a conclusion, however, stops much too short. It is not enough to say that Atlantans enjoyed the performances because the music was so good, or that audiences were drawn by irresistible aesthetic impulses common to all. If music merely has to be aesthetically enriching to explain its popularity, why did, say, blues, shape-note singing, or ragtime never come close to the civic acclamation bestowed on the opera season, the Colored Music Festival, and the Georgia Old-Time Fiddlers' Convention? The power that certain musical forms exercised over others, then, must be understood within the historical and cultural contexts that gave their performance meaning. The making of a New South is, of course, one of those contexts. But by broadening the scope beyond Atlanta and the South, we immediately realize that Gate City residents were hardly alone in their enthusiasms for opera, spirituals, and old-time fiddling. In fact, Atlantans interpreted the music they patronized within a framework largely supplied by critics, intellectuals, and popular journalists from outside the city and region who also found themselves drawn to the same musical genres. Such remarkably widespread interest in opera, spirituals, and old-time fiddling at a particular historical moment cannot be explained solely as evidence of their aesthetic power. We must be attentive to the ways audiences found these particular forms of music useful in engaging the broader cultural currents that moved through the South and America.

Taking such an approach does not mean that the scholar's task is to expose cynical cabals that manipulated music to advance their own interests, nor does it dismiss as sadly deluded those struck dumb by *Rigoletto.* Instead, it simply insists that the complexity of music's appeal and the fullness of its meaning are more readily appreciated when we understand how they are negotiated in the context of debates about the distribution of political, cultural, social, and economic power.[29] Thus, opera, spirituals, and fiddling outdistanced other equally pleasing music in civic popularity not only because they proved so entertaining, but also because audiences found them malleable enough to answer some of the most fundamental issues in their lives. By studying the language of speech and gesture that Atlantans and people throughout the nation used to communicate their enthusiasm for opera, spirituals, and old-time fiddling, we can more clearly see the ways in which music simultaneously enriched and impoverished the region and the nation these New Southerners struggled to create.

Grand Opera

In 1909 construction workers painted the last beams and installed the final light bulbs in Atlanta's most impressive civic monument yet, the new Auditorium-Armory. The enormous building housed the 5th Georgia Regiment of the National Guard, and a six thousand–seat arena that was, as one later mayor described it, "ideal for nothing" but that could "accommodate anything."[1]

In good Peach State fashion, the building's inaugural event featured a "Georgia dinner." Organizers could think of no one more distinguished or more qualified to relish the delicacies of the state's farms and fields than President William Howard Taft, who even had the grace and the appetite to appreciate the evening's culinary coup de grace: possum. Shortly after the president stowed his napkin, a handful of blustering city boosters arrived at both a more lasting and a more noble tribute to this monument of "patriotic citizenship [and] indomitable energy."[2] Members of the newly formed Atlanta Music Festival Association schemed to launch "the greatest music festival in American history" by luring to the city some of the most accomplished musicians of the day.[3] Violinist Albert Spaulding, pianist Germaine Schnitzer, soprano Geraldine Farrar, and the entire Dresden Philharmonic Orchestra all signed on, but their appearance meant nothing next to the announcement that tenor Enrico Caruso, by far the most widely hailed operatic star of the age, had himself been seduced by Atlanta's charms. "He realizes," one paper assured readers, "that Atlanta is one of the great cities of the country."[4] Although Caruso was forced to cancel at the last minute, sending the festival board into a "Caruso emergency,"[5] the Great Southern Music Festival nevertheless turned a profit of over ten thousand dollars, proving Atlantans financially and artistically capable of appreciating what dozens of articles called "good music."[6] Predictions of wild success, a necessary corollary to any Atlanta endeavor, seemed borne out by evidence.

Assured that they would not be financially skinned by similar efforts in the future, the Atlanta Music Festival Association's board decided to invite the entire New York Metropolitan Opera Company as the sole attraction for the 1910 festival. Sensing profits in a region flexing its newfound economic muscle, the Met's business director agreed, and beginning in 1910 Atlanta hosted an annual weeklong "season" of opera, with only World War I disrupting the pleasant springtime ritual.[7]

Few events on the social calendar inspired greater civic excitement than opera week. The newspapers covered the week's festivities in numbing detail, never failing to overlook a single minute that opera stars spent in public and covering with breathless fascination their appearance, hobbies, opinions, and manners. Long before they arrived in town, their pictures ate up acres of newspaper space, and the operas they were to perform in underwent minute scrutiny. Local merchants whet consumer appetites with irresistible bargains on everything from soda water to diamonds, and the parties for which their products were destined received stupefying press coverage.[8] Whole neighborhoods gussied up their streets and storefronts, encouraged by enthusiastic opera fans who motored through the city sporting small red pennants that urged residents to "clean up and paint up."[9] In short, the parties, club functions, shopping expeditions, picnics, housecleaning, newspaper publicity, and musical performances made opera week one of the most thrilling and most reported on fêtes of the year.

For all of opera week's carefree grace and glamour, however, the auditorium proved an enormously frustrating and contentious place. Rather than burning away the fog of confusion and allowing a temporary respite from the New South's dramatic transformations, the Met's visits seemed to further inflame the audience's anxieties and give them ever more cause for concern. Whether it was sorting out gender roles, promoting Atlanta and the South, or debating the place of blacks, the audi-

"Everybody Is Operatic This Week," 1911 Atlanta Journal *cartoon illustrating
the widespread excitement the yearly opera festival stirred up throughout
much of the city. Courtesy of the Atlanta History Center.*

ence spent much of opera week advancing its own particular ideas about
a New South and trying to tamp down competitors.

One of the most insistent problems that Atlantans confronted when
the opera came to town was the changes in gender roles that the New
South's urbanization and industrialization had thrown into confusion.
Without question, the urban world that Atlanta's men inhabited differed
markedly from the farms so many of them had left behind. Rather than

becoming manly captains of fate, an image that had lured them from the rural world of their fathers, they often found themselves mired in midlevel office careers whose unromantic, unrewarding, and unremitting boredom rejoined them with stinging provocation. Combined with the increasing treble of women's clubs, woman suffragists, and women workers, the fields of masculine endeavor seemed increasingly hedged round about. Searching for new ways to define and to assert their masculinity, men seized upon city building. In Atlanta, the most recognizable form of this masculine civic identity was the "Atlanta Spirit," a slogan under which relatively anonymous, powerless men fused themselves together into a mighty machine of prosperity and regional advancement. "We build up the man," wrote one Gate City patriot, "at the same time we build the city."[10]

At first glance, however, music hardly seemed the fitting place to "build up the man." Across the nation, men ascribed music to a feminine sensibility, and they argued that music, especially classical music, led to "feminization." It was a word that had crept into everyday vocabulary, and articles in leading popular journals—entitled, for example, "Music and Manliness," "Is Music an Effeminate Art?," and "Why Do Not More Men Take Up Music?"—revealed that of all the culprits in this dangerous trend, music had much to answer for.[11] Even simply patronizing classical music necessitated cautious restraint. Afraid lest their attendance at concerts and recitals expose them to ridicule among their colleagues or leave them vulnerable to the botulin of feminization, they publicly declared that domestic duty had compelled their presence and that they were utterly bored and confounded by the whole exercise.[12] At the same time, however, men in Atlanta pursued music with an avidity that belied their caution. Tying their patronage to civic and regional advancement, they used opera week to inject an element of primitive vigor into their rather placid lives. Opera merged the construction of a new masculinity and a New South into a single project.

The city's women, no less than its men, thrilled to live in so exciting a place and during so fascinating a time. Yet rather than welcome in the construction of a New South, they found themselves confined to a narrow circle of domestic concerns, expected to watch and to cheer, but never to lay their shoulders to the wheel. Atlanta, like the other New South cities, would honor masculine endeavor. Though frustrated by their exclusion and confinement, at the same time they worried that a deeper engagement with the wider world might compromise their own identity as women. Thus, they struggled to arrive at some fitting mixture of civic engagement and feminine duty. Music balanced the ledger.

While some were cheered by a rising cohort of professional female musicians in the early twentieth century, far more women used their local music clubs to redefine and expand the range of feminine endeavors. Their efforts at fostering innumerable civic orchestras and concert seasons throughout the nation aimed at adding a spiritual complement to the materialistic, masculine bent of city building and supplied tangible evidence of women's presence and power in a civic landscape that otherwise slighted them. At the same time, club members armored themselves against criticism and self-doubt by describing their work as logically extending the time-honored proscriptions that made the sexes distinct.[13] After all, few gainsaid that music's emotional appeal more properly suited the feminine than the masculine sensibility. Thus, women found in music a public voice that gave their opinions and talents greater influence and that realigned older notions of what was appropriate for women to do and to say. "It is as though the now emancipated feminine voice," one woman wrote excitedly, "would proclaim its destiny only through melody."[14] But because of music's long-standing associations with genteel domestic accomplishment and moral uplift, it made that realignment seem relatively benign and natural.

In large part, the gender anxieties aroused by an evening of opera in Atlanta differed little from those experienced in the northeastern cities where the Metropolitan Opera had grown accustomed to touring. But the presence of over fifty thousand black residents and an increasingly determined campaign to segregate the races gave Atlanta's opera season an added significance for its white citizens. Never once did whites relent in the face of repeated requests from the black community for even segregated seats. The city's opera season celebrated white culture. It gave form and sound to concepts of white supremacy that often had little clear referent. In particular, white Atlantans exploited the long-standing symbolic affinities between music and women to fashion opera week into a holy communion of white civilization.[15] For white residents eager to establish Jim Crow as a settled fact, few things better demonstrated the superiority of white over black than this tangible demonstration of white civilization's greatest achievements. Given the ominous saber rattling so commonly heard whenever white men praised white women, it was more than symbolically fitting that the Metropolitan Opera performed before a largely female audience in a building that doubled as the city's armory. Built largely in response to the militia's ineffectiveness during a three-day race riot in 1906, the Auditorium-Armory functioned as both a host to dozens of cultural events and a base "for the military commands which are a source of comfort and protection to the people."[16] Though flowers and perfume might invade the auditorium's every corner during opera week, the bullets and clubs resting quietly in the attached armory reaffirmed the military might that sustained white supremacy. The Auditorium-Armory and the opera it housed, then, reinforced the dual nature of white supremacy, which rested simultaneously on brute force and assumptions of cultural superiority.

The opera allowed a season of carefree gaiety, to be sure, but it simultaneously engaged upper- and middle-class white Atlantans in profound self-reflection. As a civic event, the Metropolitan Opera's annual visits were designed to display a New South before the smitten Yankee press and the gawking admiration of the entire Western world. Able to appreciate and to pay for the exact same operas and performers that delighted New York City audiences, Atlantans demonstrated beyond reproof the New South's economic power and the cultural sophistication of its people. The *Constitution* raved that opera "was a vivid presentation of the prowess of an American city, ashes fifty years ago."[17] At the same time, Atlantans used opera week to join a local squabble about just what tasks men and women should perform in this New South and thus to define more clearly the boundaries between masculinity and femininity. Whereas women insisted that music led to civic uplift and moral improvement, men countered that opera promoted business investment and regional advancement. Neither purpose was irreconcilable, but endorsing one over the other implied certain assumptions about the extent of power one gender exercised over the other and thereby their authority in the city and in the making of a New South. Finally, opera week forced white Atlantans to more carefully articulate the meaning of race. By continually denying blacks access to opera performances, whites came to a deeper understanding of the meaning of their whiteness and gave white supremacy a cultural justification. In short, few civic events inspired greater anticipation and more lasting heartburn than opera week.

"Woman's Work in Music"

Throughout the nineteenth century schools for women emphasized music instruction as a necessary domestic accomplishment. Music's presumed capacity to guide the spirit to higher realms and to provide families with moral guidance made it an ideal pastime for those entrusted with fashioning the home into a harbor of morality and chasteness.[18] Even into the twentieth century, women were still expected to play music in the home to entertain and instruct their families. "Music has a two-fold influence," explained one teacher, "first upon the character of the girl who studies it; and secondly, through her, upon those for whom she makes music."[19]

The advent of female virtuosi on the concert stage in the mid-nineteenth century, however, challenged the domestic confinement of female musicians. Whether it was the singer Jenny Lind, the pianistic wunderkind Teresa Carreño, or the pioneering violinist Maud Powell, women began to expand their music making into professional careers. These early artists inspired a wave of young girls growing up at the turn of the century to see music not as a social adornment, but as a potential livelihood. In addition, the growing popularity and respectability of opera provided women unparalleled opportunities for pursuing music professionally. By the 1920s women had managed to convince large numbers of Americans that, though female performers should not neglect their duties as mothers, it was "not necessary for them to give up entirely their personal accomplishments to care for a home."[20] They had won a permanent place for themselves on the concert stage.[21]

An even larger number of women became music teachers, a profession that seemed merely an extension of their "natural" roles as mothers and nurturers. One music supervisor observed that of the female teachers he employed, "I am certain that not one of them but will be a better mother," and he reassured readers that "they all aspire to be mothers."[22] Women also formed the core of those who took jobs as music teachers in the public schools, though men tended to horde the supervisory positions.[23] Despite such prejudices, women increased their presence in the music profession as a whole so that by 1910 they comprised 66 percent of those the census listed as music professionals.[24]

Though determined to secure a place for themselves in the music world, professional female musicians provoked uncertainty within themselves and hostility among skeptics. "Any woman who wholly rejects the normal fulfillment of a woman's life for artistic or other mental development presents an abnormal spectacle," wrote a prominent music publisher in 1912.[25] Some women feared precisely this trade-off, wondering if artistic advancement would come at the expense of their femininity. "Does teaching and concertizing tend to make a woman unwomanly?"

"Mary Jordan, the American Contralto, in Her Home in New York." Jordan demonstrates her domestic accomplishments. From Musical America, *May 24, 1919. Courtesy of Imaging and Photographic Services, University of North Carolina at Chapel Hill.*

one anxious student queried rhetorically. "That is a serious question," she answered. "Some of the finest women teachers whom I know are at once womanly, aggressive, keen, and business-like; but never coarse and never masculine in manners and dress." The professional woman became like a man, she concluded, "only in this respect—she learns to rely upon herself."[26] Many female performers, especially those who appeared in the pages of *Musical America*, reiterated their adherence to traditional gender roles despite their professional careers. The Chicago Opera's Jane Osborn-Hannah, for instance, claimed that she was "proud to be known as a good mother and a happy wife."[27] *Musical America* frequently ran publicity photos showing noted female performers with their children or in domestic settings, like soprano Anna Case, who "took real pleasure in donning an apron to try her skill at baking a cake."[28] Others, like opera star Frieda Hempel who declared that "I shall never be ashamed of being called feminine,"[29] trumpeted their fealty to traditional feminine roles. Headlines in a leading music magazine offered reassuring sentiments such as "'Woman's Place at Home[,]' Mme Pasquali, Opera Singer, Says She's No Sympathizer with Suffragists,"[30] or "Cooking, Sewing, Scrubbing and Dusting Appeal to Miss Mero."[31] So common were these vows of domestic affinity that a writer for the *Atlanta Constitution* observed in 1912 that "it might almost be called the fashion nowadays among celebrated prima donnas to be devoted wives and mothers."[32] For those concerned that a career would result in some distasteful personal transformations, the new generation of womanly music professionals offered consolation.[33]

Regardless of whether they attempted to teach or perform, women battled skepticism, hostility, and self-doubt. To explain the obdurate obstruction that constantly blocked them, one female musician insightfully observed that male prejudice really veiled deeper fears "rooted in economic competition." So long as women "were gifted dilettantes whose art lent brilliancy to their salon or their court," she observed, men lavished praise. But when women came into "competition in a field in which man had so far reigned supreme," men began inventing restrictions to female advancement.[34]

Though undoubtedly true in important respects, critics far more often railed against professional female musicians as symptomatic of the "feminization" of American society. The campaign to "feminize" America was allegedly carried out on a broad front, of which music was only a part. The victims were a whole generation of young boys who, "under the constant daily influence of women," were having "the lady-like attitude toward life strongly emphasized."[35] "It does not really matter very much to-day whether women do or do not have the vote, or practice as lawyers, or manage businesses," a writer in the *Atlantic Monthly* groused, because "women-trained men" were doing their bidding anyway.[36] Thus, women professionals were not just crowding men out of jobs, they were profoundly influencing aspects of social and cultural life once dominated by men. By stamping everything with their standards and their attitudes, they endangered the fragile balance of masculine and feminine qualities essential to a stable society and culture. Women who took up music professionally, then, were but one part of a wider transformation in American gender roles that caused anxiety even among its champions and outright hostility among its foes.

*"The Tremendous Power That May
Come through Club Organizations"*

Newspaper headlines like "Mme. Sylva Prefers Art to Her Husband" no doubt inspired told-you-so tirades from opponents of professional female musicians.[37] It was impossible, as Mme. Sylva demonstrated, to balance professional demands with feminine duties. Opera diva Olive Fremstad even said as much, explaining to one reporter that she could "get along without [men] and so can any other progressive woman who has her own life to lead and a definite goal to work toward."[38] In the end, however, women's music clubs stretched traditional gender roles further and more subtly than artistic Amazons like Sylva and Fremstad. Though many women would have heartily denounced these two outspoken performers, they joined music clubs by the thousands to register their dissatisfaction with the modern trend "to isolate women in the home." Everything in their lives, one music club enthusiast protested, was designed to turn them "inward—nothing outward." Weary of housekeeping, "an artificial life of cruel etiquette," and "perplexed in the daily and hourly solutions of loving helpfulness, or discipline, or comfort," women were isolated, lonely, and bored. They possessed an intense "longing for more life, fuller life—higher life." Yet men refused to share with women any "of the cares or responsibilities that reach out into national or even civic life."[39] The division between public and private life was, of course, what critics of "feminization" intended to preserve, and it was what music clubs determined to reconsider.

Club life gave members an opportunity to turn their lives into a "new and extrapersonal channel."[40] What this meant in practical terms was that women used their clubs to participate in aspects of civic life normally closed to them. "Do not make the mistake of attempting to make your club a 'society affair,'" warned one member.[41] It was fine to study the arts of antiquity, wrote another, "but do not be content to leave your Greek sculpture and architecture in Greece. Bring it home and make something of it that relates to the here and the now."[42] The Melody Club of Norfolk, Virginia, among many others, took such admonitions to heart. Rather than pursuing music for its own entertainment and edification, the club believed that its efforts were developing Norfolk "not only materially and musically, but in a civic way."[43] Through their club work, women argued that their civic absence hindered the redress of social imbalances caused by industrial consolidation and massive immigration.

"The reason that club women take themselves so seriously," one wrote, is because they understood that "on the threshold of our consciousness there lies a sense of the tremendous power that may come through club organizations, both to the women themselves and to the public."[44] Building libraries, public parks, and playgrounds, fighting for clean drinking water and safe milk, toiling to clean filthy streets, and insisting on broad public access to art, literature, sculpture, and music formed various wings of a unified effort to bring women's unique skills to bear on the causes of disease, chaos, and disorder.[45] For many women, music seemed supremely well qualified to soothe the class antagonisms and ethnic strife that threatened to pull the country asunder. Music, the National Federation of Music Clubs explained, was "a means to civic improvement" because it developed patriotism, encouraged "a higher form of citizenship," and, most importantly, contributed to "the spirit of comradeship—regardless of race or creed."[46] Music's civic function, then, was no less than serving as a "universal language," uniting a disparate citizenry in a common experience despite "great differences of race, culture, position, and age."[47]

Given these advantages, clubs blasted popular music publishers and performers who seemed to cynically cater to the poor's low-down desires, as well as bloated plutocrats who monopolized classical music to satisfy their own aristocratic pretensions. This state of musical affairs, they argued, spilled over into larger areas of civic life, ravaging the nation's moral climate and perpetuating destructive social divisions. To attack these problems, music clubs helped launch a crusade to spread what they commonly called "the gospel of music."[48] By the mid-1920s their ministry included civic orchestras and bands that gave free concerts in public parks, music social settlement houses that acquainted working-class and immigrant communities with "good music," and music supervisors at hundreds of factories, prisons, schools, and armed forces encampments who scheduled daily musical activities for those under their watchful charge.[49] Recitals and concerts, therefore, did more than merely provide listeners a pleasant diversion. They were indispensable in stabilizing civic life and in building a morally righteousness nation. "Music strikes the deep root in building for character, a finer conscience and a finer character in the people," one club member told Congress, "and it makes more for peace and contentment."[50] In short, through their music clubs women outlined their vision for a new American society and culture in the early years of the twentieth century.

The oblique nature of their civic intrusions inspired nearly universal acclaim.[51] Music club members seemed to reject soprano Lillian Nordica's reasoning that "a profession makes a woman independent, and independence is far better than indirect influence."[52] On the surface, they merely continued their traditional nurturing role, using music to alternately encourage and instruct men. Moreover, women deflected criticism by using religious language to describe the nature of their civic work. "Music," reflected one female author, "is in a sense a religion" with "practical results."[53] Social reform thus seemed merely an extension of the evangelistic mission for which their temperaments were deemed uniquely suited.

Yet, using the power and influence granted them as defenders of culture and virtue, they insisted on voicing their opinions on public issues otherwise closed to their participation.[54] For decades women had watched with admiration, one club member wrote, the "onward sweep of man-conceived and man-executed and man-driven improvements," but they had also recognized in ways men seemed blind to that progress often left in its tumultuous wake a roiling sea of human suffering. "The activities of woman," she continued, "shall serve to correct the defects of man's activities." Those activities, however, were intended neither to topple men nor to "feminize" the nation. Instead, they would restore balance in a world too much controlled by the qualities and shortcomings of only one gender. "There has never been so great a need," concluded the same author, "for the full use of the natural function of woman to supplement and complement the functions of man as now." It was "in the care and interest" of life's "lesser things, that the function of woman as conserver and preserver is invaluable."[55] Club life, then, provided unparalleled opportunities for intellectual and civic engagement within a framework that nevertheless seemed to endorse an older, more constricted female role. Music clubs did not challenge the existence of a distinct male sphere, but they did question the logic of its boundaries.

"Captains of Music"

The firm links that clubs established between music and femininity in the early twentieth century inspired critic James Huneker to proclaim "Music is Woman."[56] In fact, evidence abounded that, as composer Daniel Gregory Mason observed, most men were "inclined to scoff" at music lessons, concerts, and appreciation classes.[57] Walter

"He Fails to Take a Friendly Interest in the Great Composers," the expected somnolent response of any man attending the opera, by illustrator Charles Dana Gibson from his 1899 series, "The Education of Mr. Pipp." Courtesy of Imaging and Photographic Services, University of North Carolina at Chapel Hill.

Damrosch, director of the New York Symphony Orchestra, lamented that in America "men are still largely 'barbarians' as far as the arts are concerned," and they did not appear anxious to divest themselves of their savagery.[58] One teacher marveled how commonly one could hear "a man at his club confess that he did not know one note from another — not with the regret of one who deplores a defect, but with a certain touch of swagger."[59] In short, few observers at the turn of the century failed to notice the dominance women exercised over the country's classical music culture.

The trend evinced a great deal of hand-wringing among men in the profession. "Great as has been the influence of women in music, the cause cannot be left to them entirely," they protested. "The American man must be won over."[60] Just as with other aspects of society, politics, and culture under threat of "feminization," it was time to put American musical life "on a masculine basis."[61] Though he intended no disparagement to the women's clubs, which had done admirable work, "sooner or later there comes a time," *Musical America*'s editor wrote, "when to put a sufficiently substantial foundation under this growing musical life, the co-operation of the men is required." A "normal and balanced artistic growth" demanded equal contributions from both sexes.[62] A bully theory, perhaps, but it dodged the more vexing issue: How could men be convinced to risk the esteem of their peers by sitting in recital halls with club ladies listening to Chopin nocturnes? Merely declaring that music is "a man's art" would not make it so.[63]

The "feminization of music," as the Peabody Conservatory's director called it, deeply disturbed those male musicians and teachers who, until then, had comfortably reconciled their gender with their profession.[64] Indeed, into the early years of the twentieth century, music had seemed a noble calling. As a Brooklyn minister told the National Education Association in 1905, "The highest expression of mind and spirit is in music," and, therefore, the musician acted as a mediator between the Divine and the sinning world.[65] Yet such rhetoric failed to resonate among a generation of boys and men enchanted with the exploits of Tarzan and Teddy Roosevelt. Music seemed, if anything, to sap masculine prowess, and some writers cautioned that music was "often the parent of effeminate sensibilities."[66] In a society that increasingly valorized a primitive, "strenuous" brand of masculinity, any number of boys and men were left stammering to justify spending pleasant summer days inside practicing piano scales rather than playing baseball. To conform to new standards of rugged masculinity while simultaneously following a passion deemed "sissy," men needed to demonstrate that music and masculinity were not at odds.

Several critics looked to the past, hoping to find amid the illustrious composers a model for the kind of masculine traits they hoped to cultivate. A 1905 article in *Harper's*, for example, placed Johann Sebastian Bach—"a manly music-maker"—at the pantheon's summit. Just below him came Beethoven, "a genuine man" whose music possessed "something stern and healthy in it." Mozart, "feminine but not effeminate," occupied a middle ground. Haydn, "a nice gossiping old lady," moved into slightly suspect territory, while Wagner and Mendelssohn tripped lightly behind. Chopin represented the dreaded extreme and was dismissed as "morbidly feminine."[67] "The man who surrenders to the spirit of Chopin is lost," the editor of *Musical America* lectured, because "such surrender implies the triumph of the feminine element in the nature of man." Though Chopin undoubtedly "established an extraordinary artistic standard," the editor warned, he "set no great standard of manhood."[68] One critic recommended a steady diet of Beethoven to offset the frothy Polish pianist. "The virility, the magnificent spiritual vitality of Beethoven make their appeal to all manly students," he wrote.[69] Bach and Beethoven provided concrete, historical proof for modern skeptics that music and masculinity were compatible.

Many writers speculated that men did not show much interest in concerts because programs usually included too many selections from composers like Chopin who catered solely to the fairer sex. Men rarely heard music that appealed to their masculine sensibilities. "While it is true that Music appeals strongly to the feminine nature, it is equally true that Music of a somewhat different type appeals just as strongly to the masculine." The problem was that well-intentioned teachers and concert organizers were forcing "the masculine taste to conform in all things to the feminine."[70] Men particularly loved brass bands, for instance, because, unlike the symphony orchestra, which modeled the "refinement, the delicacy and the sensitiveness of the female," the band represented "the strength, the virility and refinement of the male."[71] The great bandmaster John Philip Sousa told a Houston reporter that fans of his music were "strong and healthy" and liked "virile music."[72] Yet men rarely got to hear band music because effete snobs and refined ladies dismissed it as appealing only to "uncultivated tastes."[73] In a similar fashion, schoolboys naturally despised music classes because teachers fed them a steady diet of songs dealing "chiefly with rose-buds, butterflies and sunbeams." They needed "something 'manly' and stirring" like "old college ditties" and songs popular among soldiers, not "sentimental, 'sissy' songs."[74] Because women dominated American musical life, they taught and performed music particularly suited to *their* tastes. To counter this trend, boys needed to "receive their first associations with music through a man—and a real man at that, one who could show them . . . that music is as much a man's job as a woman's."[75]

Of course, many frankly admitted, few "real men" chose a profession so thoroughly sprinkled with what one teacher dismissed as "aesthetic long-haired prig[s]."[76] Harold Randolph, director of the Peabody Conservatory, related a tale about a certain young boy who, despite obvious talent, refused to take music lessons. The boy's sister explained that "he can't stand associating with the freaks whom he sees studying music." Randolph admitted that her explanation "was a bit of a staggerer, for I could not deny that there are, here and there, some pretty sorry specimens among us."[77] Yet Randolph and others dismissed these "specimens" as lingering relics of an earlier era. It used to be, they declared, that the world had treasured artists "divorced from the world" and careful to "neglect, if not to eschew, matters of business."[78] An 1894 article in *Etude* was one of the last of its kind, praising the "true artist" who did not "study for the purpose of making money" and who, thankfully, had "not yet learned business methods."[79] By the turn of the century, men like Randolph had little patience for the coddled genius with flowing hair, dreamy eyes, and erratic temperament. "If you are to succeed in your profession," sputtered a British musician in 1910, "you must devote your energies to it, like a man. . . . Dress like a reasonable human being, and not like people qualifying for the mad-house."[80]

Old prejudices died hard, however, and men in the profession struggled for years to convince the public that, as one teacher wrote in 1917, it was possible to "be an artist and still be a success as a man doing a man's work."[81] To offset their feminized image, male musicians cast themselves as businessmen, promising young men that music careers could reward students with the kind of prestige and financial success so envied in men like John D. Rockefeller and Andrew Carnegie. A 1903 article in *Etude* predicted that within a few short years a new generation of musicians would emerge as "captains of music" who, like the "captains of industry," would "take the lead and stamp their impress on those around them."[82] An organist anxious to recruit new faces made a similarly dazzling appeal, claiming that the neophyte would swiftly emerge "a captain of industry among instrumentalists and vocalists."[83] If opportunity knocked less fervently on the industrialist's door than in days of old, it fairly tore down the entrance for those interested in a musical career.

Perhaps no "specimens of masculinity" received more admiration than orchestral conductors.[84] Like the great industrialists, they controlled large numbers of men with a mere tremble of their hand and twitch of their eyebrow. Theodore Thomas, for instance, was described as "born to command" and as possessing "that extraordinary gift of making men obey."[85] In a similar vein, bandmaster John Philip Sousa wore trim military uniforms, avidly pursued such rugged sports as boxing, shooting, and horseback riding, and wrote compositions aggressively celebrating America's growing imperialistic power.[86] Arturo Toscanini thoroughly enchanted American observers, ably mixing business and warfare; in a single article he was described as both "the commander in chief" and "the man who knows his business."[87] Controlling the orchestra with the force of an industrialist ruling markets or a general commanding armies, the conductor demonstrated that artistry and masculinity were not at odds.

Anxious lest their own virility be overlooked, singers and instrumen-

SOUSA MAKING GUN RECORDS IN THE SOUTH

John Philip Sousa, the Popular Composer and Bandmaster, from a Photograph
Taken in Pinehurst

*"Sousa Making Gun Records in the South." John Philip Sousa takes a break
from music. From* Musical America, *May 11, 1912. Courtesy of Imaging
and Photographic Services, University of North Carolina at Chapel Hill.*

talists often struck equally rugged poses. An awed reporter wrote that
had tenor John McCormack not taken up a musical career, "the world
would have had a perfect athlete." When asked to discuss music, the reporter gushed, McCormack "looked a trifle bored, as though talking
sport were more to his taste."[88] American pianist John Powell likewise

received admiring press attention for his efforts to organize a wrestling club among London musicians.[89] But neither Powell nor McCormack could best tenor Domenico Russo. A tour of his West Side apartment revealed "a veritable gymnasium; dumbbells, ranging in weight from 5 to 200 pounds; indian-clubs, weight-pulls, rowing apparatus, head-lifts, horizontal bars and punching bags being scattered everywhere." To top things off, rumors abounded that he was an accomplished duelist, having dispatched two unfortunates already.[90] He seemed to merely confirm the sentiments of Fred G. Smith, an Arkansas music teacher, who lectured his students that "the *men* who are playing and singing on the Concert stage and in Grand Opera have to be . . . the *physical equals* of the best football and baseball players."[91] In short, as male musicians became self-conscious that theirs was increasingly considered a "feminized" profession, they sought to demonstrate that success required not only a businessman's savvy, but also a boxer's toughness.

Such dramatic appeals to the sterner sex reveal that, despite strenuous efforts, by the early decades of the twentieth century music had fallen distinctly within a realm deemed feminine. For many, "the very thought of attending a concert" gave them "a kind of chill," and they considered the recital hall "something to be avoided, like a fever."[92] They experienced or feigned boredom at musical performances because lacking such a posture brought their masculinity into question. Neither could they justify arduous practice schedules. The director of the Peabody Conservatory related how one boy, awarded a carrying case for his music, never used it because he feared that his playmates would jeer. Another student made it a point "in broad daylight to pull down the shades, close the shutters and turn on the lights," so that his friends passing by would "not discover him in so humiliating an occupation as playing the piano!"[93] Bedeviled by fears of public humiliation, men in the listening and performing public seemed to have generally ceded to women their claims on classical music.

"Unprecedented Daring and Self-Sacrifice"

Yet to a striking degree, men used music to articulate their masculinity. An indifferent or even hostile attitude toward concert music demonstrated a plucky virility, not given to crumbling at the sobbing arias in *La Bohème*. Even more important, music became a tangible symbol of their collective civic masculinity. While they gallantly toasted women's clubs as by and large responsible for the nation's musical culture, they deflected the implications that those efforts entitled women to an equal claim on civic identity. Chivalrous rhetoric aside, man "still furnishes the 'sinews of war,'" as one editor put it significantly.[94] Parks and playgrounds and concerts might ultimately elevate the city's quality of life, but nothing could first be accomplished without men. City building remained an arena of masculine struggle to which women were invited as spectators. The contest with rival cities to lure a federal reserve bank, a factory, or a railroad line pitted men against each other in a battle by turns savage and cunning. Like the maiden's scarf around the knight's armored bicep, women lent romance and beauty to this civic joust. When the dust settled and the victor stood over the vanquished, then was the time for women to play their harps in praise. But they could not share in that initial clash of arms or claim the honor due the champion.

Club ladies thus could posture all they wanted to about refining the citizenry and raising the level of civic culture, but in the end their achievements depended on the wealth that men generated. The *Etude*'s editor pointedly reminded readers that "while it is the women of the family who do the actual practicing, [and] who make the music, it is the men who earn the money to buy the pianos and to pay the music teachers."[95] An editorial in *Musical America* took a similar position. With "due and with glad recognition of women in their indispensable efforts toward the establishment of a musical civilization in America," nevertheless no one could deny that only men could put this development on "a more solid financial foundation."[96] Men paid for artist's fees, advertisements, instruments, recital halls, concert attire, and tickets, and they demanded some recognition for their "unprecedented daring and self-sacrifice."[97] Consequently, they endorsed the performances as celebrations of men's wealth and of men's power. In 1914 the chairman of the Metropolitan Opera's board of directors told a gathering of Atlanta businessmen that "in honoring art, you honor yourself."[98] In short, musical performances became useful weapons in the struggle between men of rival cities for metropolitan supremacy and therefore tangible symbols of civic masculinity.

Civic boosterism played a major role in justifying the investment of male time, money, and prestige in what otherwise seemed a feminine pastime. "It is as much the duty of the citizens of Los Angeles to see that the Symphony Orchestra is supported as it is to keep up good roads and a public library," observed one Californian. "It is the duty of every merchant, every capitalist and every property owner to secure at least one season ticket."[99] *Musical America*'s editor advised women who were anxious to enlist the financial support of local businessmen to appeal to local pride rather than artistic necessity. "Look here, Mr. Smith," the clubwoman was supposed to say, "Podunkville has a big reputation for its [music] festival, and we cannot afford to let [any other] miserable little town get ahead of us." Presumably shocked into seeing the situation in its proper light, the businessman would naturally respond, "No one horse town around here can be allowed to beat us out." Expected to be skeptical at first, the businessman would begin to "see things" once lured by the prospect of financial success. "He needs something big to get him started," the editor concluded. "One would have no respect for him were he not so constituted."[100] Neither the readers nor the editor respected the businessman who would sponsor a music festival simply because he adored attending recitals. Clearly, men were expected to exhibit a breezy indifference to music that only prospects of financial gain or civic vitalization could dismantle.

In sum, though certainly at times relaxing, the concert hall and music classroom in early-twentieth-century America could be uncomfortable places, fraught with competing and sometimes contradictory gender expectations. One perceptive woman neatly summarized the cultural minefield through which both sexes walked: "No one objects to men as composers, for that is thought quite worthy; but the performance of that music is considered more the province of women than men. It is feminine work not worthy of men's serious attention. Yet it is thought perfectly proper that the greatest players in the world are men, and should be men. Music teaching is considered a genteel occupation for women, but for a man to engage in it proves something lacking in him."[101]

Music, then, became one medium through which men and women articulated their anxieties about changing gender roles. Though not satisfied with their own limited role in civic life, women faced internal turmoil, outright hostility, and condescension when as either professional musicians or as music club members they moved into areas deemed outside their traditional sphere. Men, on the other hand, could indulge their passion for classical music only under highly circumscribed conditions. They had to temper their musical enthusiasms with boxing, wrestling, or other similarly virile activities, or by expressing their interest solely as a civic and husbandly duty. Men and women by and large accepted these awkward constraints because they reinforced the powerful belief that the changes so patently manifest throughout American society, politics, and culture had not obliterated the necessity for gender distinctions. What those distinctions would mean and what role they would play in the formation of a modern industrial society remained less certain. Music became one place where women and men struggled to answer these vexing questions and to arbitrate anew the meanings of masculinity and femininity.

"The Vast Forces for Law and Order and Beauty Inherent in the Feminine Sex"

"OATES REGAINS WIFE; BLAMES LURE OF GRAND OPERA," roared the *Atlanta Georgian*'s front-page headline of April 23, 1913. Just a few days before, the paper reported, H. H. Oates's "young and pretty wife" had mysteriously vanished, last seen in the company of a decorator with the dashing name of Quinius Delolons. Suspicions and jealousies aroused, the wronged husband immediately contacted police who began a search for Mrs. Oates and her miscreant accomplice.[102] Hardly had the investigation commenced before it abruptly ended. The paper reported the couple suddenly reconciled and anxious to dismiss the whole incident. Alas, for those hoping Delolons might still have a role in the ruckus, the couple declared him completely innocent. It seemed that a flirtation with music, not with Delolons, caused the marital strife.

"To grand opera," the paper explained, "Oates ascribes the greater part of his domestic trouble and the flight of his wife." A talented vocalist herself, Mrs. Oates took a musician's interest in the impending visit of the New York Metropolitan Opera Company. "She read every word of the advance notices," her husband complained, "she raved over the success of Lucrezia Bori and wept that she had not had the opportunity to make a name for herself on the operatic stage." Nothing—absolutely nothing—could unwrap her mind from the injustice of staying home while friends less talented accepted prestigious vocal scholarships and pursued glamorous careers. Despite stern, persistent prohibitions from her husband, she lit out for Chicago where she planned to live with her brother and take voice lessons, "with the ultimate idea of supporting herself." Not long after setting the scheme in motion, however, she had come to her senses and returned a chastened (and still a chaste) woman. A plucky reporter caught the reconciled couple on a train steaming out of town, leaving Lucrezia Bori and her operatic companions one less woman to bewitch.[103]

As it did for countless women in early-twentieth-century America, music confronted Mrs. Oates with the tormenting struggle between personal ambition and wifely duty. She resented having to choose between marriage and ambition, and statistically the trend was on her side. Between 1900 and 1920 the percentage of white women in the Atlanta workforce rose a breathtaking 276 percent.[104] Admittedly, most of them were single or worked because they had to, and marrying into what the paper called a "well known" family Mrs. Oates could plead neither of these. But neither could her husband deny the increasing number of "respectable" women making their mark on the world. Two years after the squabble, for example, one Atlanta paper profiled Clemmie and Clara Rosenbaum whose success in the millinery business illustrated "the value of the young woman wage-earner, following the vocation which presents itself as nearest to her."[105] By 1922 women had made such an impact on the city's business growth that they formed the Women's Division of the Chamber of Commerce, and women's clubs likewise moved beyond social dilettantism into areas of public policy.[106]

Atlanta's women could scarcely claim to lead these trends, as women across the nation determined to employ their talents in areas of intellectual, cultural, social, and political life traditionally denied their gender.[107] "Slumber not in the tents of your fathers," trumpeted the motto of an Arkansas music club. "The world is advancing; advance with it."[108] Determined not to confine themselves to stooping over cradles and stockpots with the world afire outside their doors, women like Mrs. Oates nevertheless found themselves trapped between a desire for wider engagement and the lure of feminine duty. Yet, like their counterparts elsewhere, women in Atlanta had music and they had clubs which, when combined, gave them a means of balancing their dual ambitions.

Atlanta's white women used music to make their own New South. Though their campaign to make Atlanta a musical city found allies among men, women led the way, insisting that through their musical activities they offered a necessary balance to urban development. "If it wasn't for the women," one newswriter wrote in a common refrain, men "wouldn't do a thing but grub for dollars," and there would be "mighty little going on for the general profit of the community."[109] A symphony orchestra, a music club, and a yearly musical season were tangible evidence of women's presence and power in a city that otherwise measured itself by such masculine monuments as financial statistics and skyscrapers. Yet by insisting that their efforts merely reflected their feminine propensity for order and morality, they could assuage their critics and themselves that they were not meddling in affairs outside their rightful purview. Hundreds of Atlanta women, then, shared Mrs. Oates's conflicting desires, and music seemed a compelling way to reconcile them.

The women who took it upon themselves to direct the city's musical life frequently lamented that they lived among Philistines. The local amateur organizations that had serenaded Atlanta's nineteenth-century residents had withered away by the opening of the new century, and most residents seemed unmoved by their passing.[110] Those left with paltry outlets for their musical interests complained that their city lacked real musical taste. As she would for years, the *Constitution*'s dour music editor Louise Dooly grumbled in 1902 about the "dreary" outlook for Atlanta's long-term musical prospects. Surveying the season just past she muttered that "people who are fond of 'a tune'" had certainly enjoyed themselves, but "those who prefer music in its noble and ennobling phases are becoming embittered or philosophical."[111] Throughout Dooly's career, bitterness always came easier than philosophy.

One resident refused either option, choosing instead in 1908 to create the Atlanta Musical Association. Like Dooly, Bertha Harwood believed that the city was not, as she put it, "musically cultured." For several years she had observed with growing dismay "the spasmodic musical outbursts in Atlanta, which, when over, left very little in the way of permanent musical development." Thus, she started the association and secured a seven hundred–seat recital hall and club rooms on Peachtree Street in an effort to make "Atlanta a truly musical city."[112] Described by the papers with some relief as "a cultured, but not a professional woman,"[113] Harwood made it a point to court members from "the various social walks of life and not least, an equal proportion of men and women."[114] Her organization's inclusiveness reflected a belief that, as one member of the Atlanta Woman's Club observed, "unconsciously, all men have a love for the good and beautiful, the spiritual and harmonious; and, consciously, all men would gravitate toward it, were it not for the false traditions which bind us down and hold us back."[115] For a time, this attitude seemed to pay off. Within four years the association claimed four hundred members and sponsored a civic orchestra, a choral society, music appreciation classes, social functions, and a season of recitals.[116] Yet its efforts reached only a small minority of Atlanta's citizens. In 1911, for instance, the Pasmore Trio played before a sparse audience, prompting the *Constitution* to compare "fine music in Atlanta" with violets because both were "born to blush unseen."[117]

The beginning of an annual opera season in 1910 did virtually nothing to cheer the pessimists. Dooly, Harwood, and others could nod their heads in grim sympathy with *Musical America*'s editor, who complained that before and after such extravagant annual events "the community is often apt to remain in a state of comparative musical somnolence."[118] Thus, rather than a sign of growing musical appreciation, the weeklong opera season confirmed a bleak prospect for true artistic growth. "To be satisfied with one week of music in a year does not mean a musical city," Louise Dooly sniffed. "There must be something else provided for the other fifty-one weeks."[119] The Musical Association's attempt to fill that void by raising money for a new symphony orchestra met a tepid response and confirmed Dooly's darker suspicions. After all, if the symphony formed "the basis of musical development," Atlanta could not consider itself "a music-loving city" until it had a permanent organization.[120] The *Georgian* concurred, wondering aloud, "What is a week of even the best opera compared with a whole season of symphony concerts for the esthetic uplift of the city?"[121] Apparently not much, for despite vigorous appeals the symphony quickly folded, as did the Atlanta Musical Association a few short years after Bertha Harwood left the city in 1910.[122]

Five years later the Women's Music Study Club stepped into the breach created by the Musical Association's collapse, proving more durable, though only slightly more successful. In 1918 the club changed its name to the Atlanta Music Club, reflecting a desire "to serve the men as well as the women of musical Atlanta," but no member of the sterner sex ever signed his name on the club's roster.[123] Like its predecessor, the Atlanta Musical Association, the club sought the "concert salvation of Atlanta" through a variety of programs and outreach efforts,[124] including a children's division, a chorus, a series of recitals aimed at the city at large, another "for the benefit of those who understand the inner beauties of music,"[125] and a new civic orchestra. "Most cities of Atlanta's size and many of less population and less musical material have such institutions, which are thriving and popular," explained the general call for members in 1915. "Since there is a large element of Atlanta people who profess to be starved for good music, there would seem to be a real place for a musical club."[126] Such a prediction appeared to have the ring of truth, for between 1915 and 1921 the membership rolls expanded from thirty-five to six hundred names.[127]

Shepherded for most of that period by Annie May Carroll, a Georgia pianist with European conservatory training, the club stirred only a small ripple on the placid surface of civic indifference.[128] Indulging a hyperbolic pessimism cultivated by years of frustration, Carroll wrote a concert promoter in 1918 that "prior to last season, it was fatal to attempt a concert in this city."[129] With Carroll in the lead, however, club members labored with a missionary's tenacity to save their cultural Sodom. They aggressively courted newspaper publicity, left fliers for upcoming concerts in department store rest rooms and hotel lobbies, offered lectures on the year's operas, reached out to the local white colleges to encourage student attendance, arranged visits of an impressive roster of major concert artists, and generally kept their work "before the public all the while."[130] Nevertheless, they ran into continual difficulties. In 1923 the club tried to revive a permanent Atlanta Symphony Orchestra, but assurances that even before the first rehearsal it compared "favorably with the finest orchestras in this country,"[131] as well as the advantage charter members enjoyed of entering the recital hall through their own separate entrance, could not interest even a modest one thousand subscribers.[132] Like its predecessor, the orchestra quickly folded.

Such disappointments compounded the sense among clubwomen that their work often went unnoticed and unappreciated. Only the annual opera season, controlled and managed entirely by men, attracted the public enthusiasm for music they labored daily to foster. A 1917 article in the *Constitution* provided a bitter reminder of their invisibility, distributing numerous accolades for the city's "musical renaissance" but conspicuously ignoring the Atlanta Music Club. Annie May Carroll boiled over with indignation. She immediately drafted a letter to the author, denouncing him for slighting the work ("and WORK is the word," she wrote) of the clubwomen, focusing instead on men, such as the head of the Atlanta Conservatory. Unlike these artistic "junkers" who were "content to teach [their] music classes and let the public go hang," she barked, clubwomen were "sensitive to the dictates of beauty and art" and felt "more or less impelled by a genuine desire to spread the gospel of beauty to the utmost extent." Laurels, therefore, rightfully belonged alone to those clubwomen "who thought more about art, beauty and

Annie May Carroll, president of the Atlanta Music Club from 1916 to 1921.
Courtesy of the Atlanta History Center.

the spread of music than they did of their own physical comfort and convenience [and who] got out with sleeves rolled up and worked up the stimulus!"[133] The article hit a sensitive nerve. It reminded Carroll and her compatriots not only of the public indifference against which they struggled daily, but also of the propensity for men to ignore the contributions women made to civic life.

Carroll's letter reveals the larger ambitions she and other club members attached to their work. As was true for women in music clubs across the nation, those in the Atlanta Music Club never lost sight of how their efforts contributed to promoting women's interests. In 1919, for example, members passed a resolution endorsing the State Federation of Women's Clubs "in their recommendation of the bill for Women's Suffrage."[134] Among its charter members the club also boasted Minnie Anderson Hale Daniel, who achieved fame as one of Georgia's first female lawyers and as a founding member of the Georgia Association of Women's Lawyers.

Yet clubwomen refused to limit the significance of their work to merely crusading for their sex's own advancement. Louise Dooly believed that the Music Club's aim was "as broadly civic, or more correctly speaking, patriotic, as it is musical."[135] Like their counterparts in music clubs throughout the country, Atlanta women argued that music helped form a better civic society. With anxiety club members looked out their windows onto a city and country riven by vicious competition between laborer and industrialist, and splintered by brooding suspicions between the races. Though a number of solutions seemed possible, they knew of none with greater promise than music. "Music," counseled the Atlanta Music Club's motto, "is the essence of order, and leads to all that is good, just and beautiful." For evidence they had only to follow the concerts given at the state penitentiary, as hardened criminals "went back to their ordered places . . . with a happier smile than they had worn before, and with a deeper look of patience and contentment with their lot."[136] That anyone even cared to bring the luxury of Mozart and Beethoven to such reckless and dangerous members of society proved that music fostered bonds of humanity in ways matched only by Christianity. Carroll, for example, relied on religious turns of phrase, casting herself and her colleagues as missionaries of the "the gospel of beauty" and lashing out at those who kept this brand of the gospel to themselves. When in 1909 a group of Methodist ministers had warned that a proposed series of public concerts on the Sabbath pointed "the wrong way" and that they were "fraught with evil to the cause of religion and good morals,"[137] women like Bertha Harwood bristled. "Instead of wishing to desecrate the Lord's day," she fired back, she "wished to lead people to a higher life through the realm of tone, that could not be reached by word."[138] The recitals the club women sponsored and the lectures they planned had a greater purpose, therefore, than entertainment. By promoting recitals designed to have mass appeal, by offering public lectures to prepare audiences for what they were to hear, and by reducing ticket prices to encourage all classes to attend, they refused to confine themselves to a narrow domestic ministry. In short, Atlanta Music Club members believed that they had the power and the responsibility to "utilize the vast forces for law and order and beauty inherent in the feminine sex" to improve not only their own lives, but also the general welfare of their New South.[139]

"Four-Thousand Husbands Would Come a-Runnin' Out!"

The feminine seizure of the concert hall sent Atlanta's men backpedaling furiously. Aware of classical music's "feminization" both at home and in the nation more broadly, any man who cherished his masculinity embraced music with caution. Although Emory University's E. K. Turner counseled that because "the great composers of the world have practically all been men," attending concerts would be "of great benefit to our men as well as our women," such reassurances generally fell on plugged ears.[140] Year after year the papers printed stories and anecdotes about men dragged to the opera by zealous women, prompting one waggish colonel to declare on behalf of all men, "It is glorious to attend grand opera, but more glorious to survive it."[141] Men were expected to find opera boring, to loathe the "sentimental indulgence of temperamental femininity" that it often fostered, and to find the mysterious conventions of dress and behavior vexing in the extreme.[142] On the surface, men conceded the concert hall as a feminine space, affirming their masculinity by displaying their confusion and discomfort within this realm.

Newspaper advertisements betray the intense anxiety men felt (or were expected to feel) at the mere mention of opera. Stores catering to women simply advertised their wares with the assumption that, like the jewelry at Davis and Freeman, "Atlanta women know well how to wear them."[143] Men's clothiers, on the other hand, preyed upon fears of a social gaffe. There would be "thousands of strangers within our gates," cautioned Muse's Department Store, and Atlantans would be "the cynosure of all eyes." Everyone must "do his part to place everything above criticism." Fortunately, Muse's could assist the customer navigating the treacherous shoals of evening wear by offering sound advice "upon the question of what to wear."[144] In 1915 Muse's again warned men that "a distinguished jury will 'sit upon' the case of your good taste." Fear not, the ad continued, for the "Muse Full Dress has passed the censorship of social approval," boasting "all the recognized regulations" and relieving the wearer from any "uncertainty about modes."[145] Not to be outdone by Muse's, Parks-Chambers-Hardwick Company responded with a headline—"OPERA WEEK!"—that crashed boldly through a forest of newsprint. "Custom has made it imperative for you to be correctly dressed, according to the demands of Polite Society." A dapper gentleman in evening dress staring out from the ad radiated confidence: "Atlanta Men . . . are expected to take cognizance of these Requisites—and bear in mind the standard of Correctness and Quality accompanying each and every article."[146] Cloud-Stanford Company on Peachtree Street, which claimed Enrico Caruso as a customer and catered to men who could "discriminate between the commonplace and the superb,"[147] observed as a cautionary reminder that "Men Will Appear at the Opera in Full Evening Dress." If a frantic perusal of the closet yielded nothing encouraging, the Atlanta man could rest easy knowing that he could purchase over the telephone any requisite article he lacked, and Cloud-Stanford would guarantee its arrival by special messenger that evening before the curtain rose.[148] In short, a profound ignorance of even the proper attire, though certain to cause anxiety, nevertheless affirmed a masculinity that had no patience with opera's fussy customs.

The clothing hurdle crossed, the opera awaited. Clutching the steering wheel or the streetcar strap as they hurtled toward the auditorium, such individuals might meditate on the cast. Like their counterparts elsewhere in America, Atlanta's tough-nosed, scrappy men of business considered the famed artistic "temperament" more than a little queer. Luckily, the city enjoyed visits from some of the sporty, regular-fellow musicians then coming into vogue. "It used to be the fashion for a violinist to wear long tangles of shadowy hair," the *Atlanta Journal* noted in 1909 prior to the first Great Southern Music Festival, but the featured soloist Albert Spalding "wears his hair like that of any business man." And though it was natural to assume that any great musician "must be melancholy and something of a freak," Spalding dressed "without the slightest effort to appear different from other people." What is more, "he laughs and talks with his friends like any other sane, normal, well-poised human being."[149] When the perennially feted baritone Antonio Scotti came to town the *Journal* commented that here again was a man who was "'real folks,' with a hearty handshake and a smile," and who had "nothing 'temperamental'" about him.[150] Almost a decade later the Chamber of Commerce's official magazine, the *City Builder*, tried to persuade readers that with men like Spalding and Scotti in the lead, the "artistic temperament" was a thing of the past. George Lindner, the head of the Atlanta Conservatory, attempted to dispel the common assumption that musicians were "wholly irresponsible and incurably absent-minded, often overlooking meal times and subject to frequent brainstorms and breaking up the furniture." World War I had decisively shown that "the best fighters were not among the day laborers but were found among the musicians and artists." Their work, just like that of the businessman, was "so standardized" that there was "no opportunity for the supposed 'artistic temperament' to hold sway. Only through the strictest discipline is he able to be always in form." No less than the businessman who subscribed to *City Builder*, musicians were fully capable of "being just plain folks" and listening to them required no compromise of masculinity.[151]

Attired correctly and assured that they would not have to endure the antics of long-haired sissies, men were expected to take their seats in the concert hall with an almost prideful ignorance of the evening's entertainment. "I do not like [music]" one gentleman gallantly declared to his friends before a performance; another was overheard confessing, "I never go to the opera if I can help it."[152] But they could not help it, of course, because their masculine duty as husbands and fathers insisted on it. To assure themselves that the opera had merely dealt their masculinity a glancing blow, they neglected to acquire even a skeletal knowledge of the operas or to indulge in what the Atlanta Music Club was pleased to call "music appreciation." Though the club launched a fleet of lectures and training exercises to make men more aware of the plot summaries, proper behavior, and fine points of each star's vocal technique, one woman found it "rather discouraging" that "in many cases there was more curiosity about the theme of the opera and popular arias than in the more constructive technical parts."[153] She cited one example of an ignoramus who blurted out during a preparatory lecture: "Why have all this talk about it? Would it not be easier just to have a good victrola and let us hear the music and become familiar with the tune?" Heavy sighs of strained patience no doubt filled the room while a "loving spouse" reproved her husband and "forced" him "to hear the instructive side."[154] He acknowledged his error and promised to be more attentive, but few men so quickly surrendered their ignorance.

Every year the papers announced as if by fiat that women had made significant progress in their educational efforts, asserting that the number of men "who managed to forego business for music" had increased noticeably.[155] In 1909 the *Constitution* sensed that though "men frequently pose as not caring for the more classical or artistic music, suggesting that it is that over which women rhapsodize," the evening presented compelling evidence that "the call after call following the artistic masterpieces, was expressed in applause too vigorous and strong not to have been the enthusiasm and appreciation of the sterner sex."[156] Seven years later a journalist wrote that "not even the masculine poseurs who in their fear of being 'high brows' or their desire to be funny, complained about the opera as they so often do."[157] By 1917 baritone Pasquale Amato could tell a gathering of distinguished businessmen that they had "now gotten to the point where they can rave over an opera which hasn't a single tune in it."[158]

The 1919 season, however, seemed to prove otherwise. Even after a decade of dutiful instruction, numerous businessmen were "tickled over the absence of 'highbrow' operas, and the inclusion of so much pure Italian melody." They rushed the box office before the Met decided to "spring some of the German heavies again."[159] Earlier that year the *City Builder* reminded men, "as you have already heard from the ladies at home," that the time had come to think about purchasing season tickets. Though in previous years a week of indigestible operas might have proven unappetizing, this season promised much lighter fare. "No heavy opera—no German works to bore you—no 'high brow' novelties to puzzle you. Just the pure, limpid music of the Italian and French schools, tuneful and charming, and interesting from the rise of the curtain to the final curtain call." In other words, the article continued frankly, "after you finally get the dress clothes adjusted and the tie on straight, your worries are over. There is nothing to take the joy out of life."[160] The performance of *Martha* did not disappoint, and the paper reported "a remarkably large attendance of men at yesterday's matinee," explaining this oddity by asserting that its smashing plot and tuneful arias "delights the male element of music lovers."[161]

As was true across the nation, then, opera dress, opera musicians, and opera music threatened to further erode a brand of masculinity already seen as endangered. Consequently, women made up the majority of Atlanta's opera audience, often flooding the matinees because their "husbands are not artistic" and refused to "go to evening performances."[162] Men, anxious lest attending the performances betray the onset of feminization, advertised their boredom and ignorance. Not surprisingly, one of the more popular jokes described the mayor arriving late for a performance only to discover that the doorman would not let him in. "If I was to open them big doors right now," he told the mayor, "four-thousand husbands would come a-runnin' out!"[163] By constantly affirming their aversion to opera and to the feminizing entanglements it necessarily entailed, Atlanta's men of business found in opera a way to demonstrate that they had kept alive some vital aspect of their masculinity. They could glance sympathetically at one another in the auditorium as hour after unremitting hour ticked on, knowing that beneath their ironed shirtfronts lay the hearts of men unmoved by the pretty fancies that entranced the softer sex.

"The Presence of MEN*"*

Yet Atlanta's men did not hate opera. In fact, they adored it. Businessmen, lawyers, and bankers—precisely the kind of men the mayor could expect to trample him when the auditorium doors sprung open—monopolized the Atlanta Music Festival Association's board and never asked a woman to join them. Every year they flooded the auditorium's boxes, balconies, and promenades, exchanging satisfied nods with their colleagues and business partners. Like their fellows elsewhere in the nation, men never claimed that their love of opera arose from music's power to reform social inequities or to awaken religious brotherhood, nor did they claim to follow music for a love of the art. Those were the reasons that women liked music. Those were the aspects of music that made men consider opera, as one Atlanta paper put it, a "domestic duty."[164]

Men arrived at their own reasons for so enthusiastically embracing an event they otherwise publicly loathed. Opera, one editorial explained, allowed men to "lay aside worries and dull care, and to get a fresh and more vigorous start in the perpetual battle."[165] Rejuvenated by the encounter, they could once again call upon what the *Constitution* called their "restless and resistless genius, that recognizes no obstacle."[166] Rather than effeminizing them, opera could awaken a slumbering virility. In 1915, for instance, when war raged in Europe and cotton prices sagged at home, Atlanta's businessmen bragged that they still had the necessary capital to host an opera season "in the old invincible way."[167] Women never described the opera season as "invincible," nor did members of the Atlanta Music Club get credit for a "restless and resistless genius." As was true nationally, Atlanta's men embraced music as "a monument to the courage and the enterprise of the business men" whose "daring in financiering" made it all possible.[168] They attended opera because it promoted themselves, their city, and their region as superb specimens of wide-awake masculinity. "Eliminating entirely the artistic side," noted an editorial in the *Constitution*, "the publicity has increased the international prestige of the city."[169] By overlooking the "artistic side" of opera week, men sought to claim their own share of the concert hall's power and prestige.

For men, the crowning glory of opera week was money, not music. In dramatic and compelling fashion, opera night "bespoke universal prosperity."[170] Flashing jewels, costly fabrics, and bewitching perfumes invaded the senses, reflecting credit on those men who financed the parade of affluence. Before one performance, ticket holders disembarked from their cars at the auditorium while the city's humbler citizens crowded the opposite sidewalk. The scene reminded one reporter of "a crowd abroad drawn up in rank and file to note the passage of royalty." Gawkers were not disappointed, for "royalty they saw, the royalty which wealth and beauty gives."[171] The newspapers avidly colluded with the members of the city's aristocracy, lavishing attention on their expensive attire, generously praising their sophisticated manners, and fawning over their "royal entertaining."[172]

Despite genuine attempts by the festival board to keep ticket prices reasonable, the opera belied democratic impulses. Though opera drew together "people of every class," the *Constitution* conceded that only "the most notable and beautiful" attended "in force."[173] It was the nobility, not the masses, whose participation during opera week received admiring scrutiny. For the "most prominent people" and for the "social leaders of the southern states," opera week afforded "a magnificent social occasion."[174] The papers frequently reported that the glittering audience rivaled the opera as one of the evening's most "inspiring features."[175] Virtually every year the papers announced that "it was not an audience which went for the purpose of seeing or being seen,"[176] or that the proportion of those attending "because they wish to be seen" had diminished, but with so much ink devoted to their exploits no one could deny that opera night paid tribute to wealth and its possessors.[177]

Because box seats were "specially adapted" to "give an effective mounting to the flash and sparkle of fashion,"[178] they became the object of intense interest. Every year renewed the scramble to land tickets and distinguished guests whose presence lent distinction to the occupants. Those fortunate enough to secure box seats found their name printed in the paper and could look forward to the annual social joust where they vied with neighbors "in point of beauty and wealth of color and costly stones."[179] Having one of the Met's stars join the box party during a performance added immeasurably to the social luster. Not only would "hundreds of strollers between the acts" surge by "to get a close glimpse of the stars in real life,"[180] they could also acknowledge those notable personalities who imparted "that social importance to opera which has been a great factor in its success."[181] At intermission the entire auditorium became a churning mass of humanity, as virtually everyone bolted from their seats and strolled about "exchanging friendly nods and glances of recognition and silent appreciation."[182] Whatever the opera's artistic merits, it was always "society's night,"[183] and the single-minded focus on what the papers called "the social aspect" helped the city's wealthy citizens display and justify their power.[184]

Regardless of an undeniable satisfaction in lording their riches over others, the New South men in the audience expressed far more interest in how the Metropolitan Opera contributed to "the business growth and the general prosperity of the city" than in thumbing their noses at the poor.[185] Though often conceding that "one cannot listen to a magnificent opera without being filled with the inspiration that money is not all—that there are other things that count," such pronouncements put an agreeable veneer on an opera season most men considered as an investment in local business and regional publicity. "Money is the crudest measure of the beautiful," the *Journal* granted in 1910; nevertheless, it was worth noting that "there is a breadth of definite meaning in the fact that during the season now ending the Metropolitan company has expended more than two million dollars on its performances."[186] Five days later, the *Journal* wrote again that "money is the crudest measure of our grand opera success" but then gleefully rubbed its hands contemplating how "the financial success of this week opens a sure and ample way for future undertakings."[187]

Indeed, the "crude measure" of money proved irresistible. "Anyone who gives the matter of Metropolitan opera in Atlanta careful thought," wrote one enthusiastic supporter, "cannot refrain from admitting that our opera season is a good business investment to our merchants, real estate owners, railroads, etc."[188] Almost no man could discuss the opera without mentioning money. In *Opera Magazine*, an Atlanta-based correspondent noted that "there has always been a profit at the end of a season" and that the upcoming season "promises receipts of nearly $100,000."[189] The newspapers played their part by keeping the reading public up-to-date on ticket sales, listing the amount each major contributor placed in the guarantee fund and tallying up how much the whole venture raked in at week's end. They frequently reminded local merchants that opera brought thousands of visitors, many of whom "combined their opera treat with shopping expeditions," and therefore represented a rich source of "purchasing power."[190] One entrepreneur pointed out that the railroads cut fares for all passengers bound for Atlanta, thereby enabling large numbers to visit the city "at a reduced rate, whether interested in music or not." These tourists often did "all their spring and summer shopping," while those attending the opera indulged in purchasing additional "small items such as gloves, hosiery, etc" so necessary to rounding out a proper outfit.[191] Opera week's financial rewards not only reflected "credit upon the aggressive civic spirit of this city," they also gave Atlanta's men a reason to invest their money and their reputations in an endeavor that might otherwise cast their masculinity into question.[192]

Opera thus made tangible the power and genius of those New South men whose money had made the event possible. The "well dressed, prosperous people" ambling about the floor redounded credit to the tycoon "who stands at the top of his profession and who bears a name known and honored on two continents."[193] Atlanta's men used opera and its expensive rituals to distinguish themselves as supremely capable men, whose savvy had guided their city out of the primitive early grasping stages of urban development into a new era of "metropolitan eminence." One patriot explained that "the present proud position of Atlanta" was attributable to "the presence of MEN, real, live, red-blooded, active, ambitious, honorable men."[194] Moreover, by focusing on opera as primarily a financial investment, men distinguished their patronage from those clubwomen who insisted that music was a means toward moral improvement and social welfare. Men, of course, conceded that morality and civic virtue were essential to their New South, but the gritty work of city building left them no time to chase after such niceties. The civic work that club ladies found so engaging merely added decorative touches to the great metropolises men had hewn. Opera was not, therefore, solely the province of women. In emphasizing the season's business prospects, and in advertising their distance from feminine conventions and virtues, Atlanta's New South men aimed to create a brand of urban masculinity impervious to opera's more dangerous charms.

"This Artistic Union of the North and South"

More than simply confirming the masculinity of its wealthy backers, opera and the jingling coins it poured into Atlanta banks sounded a sweet duet in the ears of men determined to renew their South. Beginning with Henry Grady's messianic rhetoric in the 1870s, white Atlantans had appointed themselves the leaders of a movement to build a New South of industrial might and agricultural abundance. By the time the Metropolitan Opera came to town, Atlantans had already hosted two widely praised expositions to make the point. Yet city leaders wanted something more compelling than statistics of guano production to prove the region's resurgence. They wanted the city's name to evoke the same mystical awe that attached to places like Chicago, Boston, and New York, or even Berlin, Paris, and London. Moreover, opera week was designed to crush any southern rival that might seek to claim for itself the distinction of leading the New South. "You are," one Metropolitan Opera official told a gathering of Atlanta businessmen, "proving your qualifications and your title to leadership amongst the cities of America."[195]

The decision to initiate the Great Southern Music Festival in 1909 and to invite the Metropolitan Opera the following year reflected an insatiable craving among white Atlantans to demonstrate "a commanding position over all the cities which might otherwise wish to rival us."[196] In fact, the festival had its genesis not among the city's self-styled "music lovers," but in the editorial office of the *Atlanta Journal*.[197] The paper's editor sought to enlist financial support by emphasizing the distinction and prestige such events conferred upon their host cities. He called the festival "one of the most notable strides towards metropolitan eminence ever taken by this progressive city."[198] Another enthusiastic supporter reasoned that even if "we don't make a cent on the festival," he still supported the event because it represented "a splendid investment simply for the advertisement the festival would bring the city, and hence every-thing connected with the city."[199] Year after year the papers congratu-lated local residents on the role they took in "uphold[ing] Atlanta's pres-tige" and the admiration they won from envious competitors.[200] "I have talked with business men returning from journeys to the Far West and into Canada, and always they say that at least one person in every city has remarked: 'From Atlanta? That's where you have the Metropolitan Opera Company every year, isn't it? Tell me, how do you do it'?"[201] The opera added an imperishable luster of cultural sophistication to a city already noted for its manufacturing and banking prowess.

Year in and year out, the press loudly proclaimed that the opera's significance lay in recognizing Atlanta's leading role in the South. "It is a great credit" to Atlanta, said one visitor, that it had given "the south such an institution as grand opera."[202] As the self-described "center of a large musical constituency," the city occupied "a most influential posi-tion in the musical life of the South."[203] Atlanta had competitors, of course. Following Charlotte, North Carolina's own spring music festi-val in 1919, residents of the Queen City declared that their fair me-tropolis had become "the musical mecca of the entire South."[204] But if Atlanta had rivals, none could claim boosters of greater stamina. Year after year, a tsunami of opera week hyperbole crashed upon the pub-lic, and the papers poured forth an ocean of civic puffery and self-congratulation. Following the 1914 opera season one editorial declared that "the paramount significance of the week just past" lay in the knowl-edge that "Atlanta's unique pre-eminence over the entire south is again asserted."[205] Five years later the *Constitution* proudly asserted, "Metro-politan opera in Atlanta is not an Atlanta institution at all, but belongs to the entire south."[206] Thus, the opera merely confirmed the belief that Atlanta, led by its businessmen, stood at the forefront of the resurgent South.

In addition to building their esteem and asserting their superiority over regional rivals, Gate City residents hoped an annual season of opera would aid in demolishing popular perceptions that Atlanta and the South remained, as one hostile critic wrote, "stagnant and compla-cent, having progressed culturally scarcely beyond the early Victorian era."[207] In recent memory Americans across the country had chuckled over a humorous sketch, entitled "A Georgian at the Opera," that ap-peared in *Harper's New Monthly Magazine.* In appropriately uncouth dia-lect, the story told of a visitor from "Georgy" attending an "Opery" in

"Isn't It a Dainty Dish to Set before a Queen?" Atlanta serves up the Met's stars to an admiring and grateful South. Atlanta Journal, *April 23, 1911. Courtesy of the Atlanta History Center.*

New York City. Predictably the Georgian, who endeavored "not to look green" as he was determined to "be a honor to [his] State," completely misconstrued the "lung tearin', ear bustin' blowouts" and wondered if perhaps he had not "got into a lunatic asylum."[208] Such accounts did little to persuade the rest of the nation that opera, not "opery," dominated the entertainments of southern audiences.

Fiction was bad enough, but numerous gaffes and crudities of southern audiences surely made Dixie's defenders cringe. In 1913, following the "mad scene" in Donizetti's *Lucia di Lammermoor*, a Dallas, Texas, audience whooped and hollered until the singer obliged by going "mad" again, then regained sufficient sanity to encore with "Dixie."[209] A few years earlier an Atlanta audience had pulled a similar trick, boisterously demanding an immediate reprise of Marguerite's strenuous death in *Faust*.[210] The Russian Symphony Orchestra drove a Florence, Alabama, audience into a piercing chorus of rebel yells when the Russians began a spirited rendition of "Dixie."[211]

Atlanta's annual opera season seemed a propitious time to educate southern audiences in a more orderly appreciation of the music so their behavior would reflect credit upon the city and the region. Year after year, however, Atlanta failed the test. In her regular column on the city's musical life, Annie May Carroll complained that during the performances people insisted on keeping up "a running fire of comment or gossip or scandal or some private grievance of which it was absolutely necessary to relieve the mind instantly." She mingled her frustration with resigned disappointment, writing that such ill conduct "came from persons of evident respectability and some show of culture."[212] Loose-lipped members of the audience caused widespread consternation, such as the man who wondered loudly, "Why don't they pick out good-looking women for these weepy parts." No less aggravating was the woman who whispered to her neighbor, "Why does Mrs. Blank insist on wearing that deadly shade of green so near her face?" or the man who mistook the chubby chorus member for Caruso and said to the person next to him, "Why I thought somebody said he was thinner than he used to be." Looks of withering disapproval only resulted in "an attack of giggles from the offender."[213]

Ill-timed commentary only topped a long list of grievances. The *Constitution*'s social editor wrote that she and others found it "irritating" that many applauded the arias without waiting for the orchestral accompaniment to finish. "Can't something be done to keep them from applauding at the wrong time," she wondered. She concluded that "this is always going to happen in communities . . . where all people are not prepared ahead or educated up to what constitutes complete opera."[214] If some applauded too early, others applauded too much. After Caruso mesmerized the house with an aria from *Il Pagliacci*, "the wildly enthusiastic" cheering "simply wouldn't stop" until members of the audience were "brought to their senses by a little hissing."[215] Others arrived late and left early. In 1917 the "sound of closing seats from those in a hurry to get away" obscured the final notes of Moussorgsky's coolly received *Boris Godunov*. Repeated volleys of ineffective hissing chastised these tactless auditors.[216] In 1911 the festival's officers addressed another persistent problem, lecturing attendees who arrived late that they would be locked out of the performance's first act. Furthermore, the harangue continued, "the striking of matches during any of the dark scenes of the operas is positively prohibited."[217] Still others found themselves unable to refrain from nervously rattling, bending, and folding their programs. Louise Dooly sarcastically suggested that "some people ought not to be allowed to have programs until they first stand an examination on the proper handling of them."[218] All told, close students of the opera feared that Atlanta audiences demonstrated an inability to "appreciate" opera because they simply did "not care to understand" the composer's intent or the work's larger significance.[219] Instead, they smoked, talked, laughed, snored, squirmed, and generally made themselves, not opera, the center of their evening's entertainment.[220]

Incidents like these confirmed suspicions that across the South audiences possessed a backwoods appreciation for even the highest-class musical entertainment. Statistics collected by the U.S. Census Bureau added weight to dreary anecdotal evidence. Of the nineteen states with the fewest number of musicians and music teachers per capita, fourteen were in the South. The numbers took on an even grimmer cast when considering that the only other places with a musical outlook as bleak were such thinly populated states as Alaska, the Dakotas, and Wyoming.[221]

Southern partisans led a vigorous counterattack against sniggering Yankees. Birmingham, Charleston, Knoxville, Louisville, Savannah, and Memphis sparred with northeastern cities to book prominent performers; soon smaller locales like Augusta, Raleigh, Richmond, Columbia, and even Monteagle, Tennessee, began hosting their own music festivals.[222] Some Southerners wrote lengthy pieces extolling the region's musical past and chastising New England snobs whose cultural vision did not extend beyond the length of their upturned noses. "The story of Southern music has been somewhat unduly neglected," began a testy article entitled "The Music of Our South." "Concerts were given in the Southern colonies which were at least as pleasing to the ear as the psalms of the pilgrim fathers," the author continued; taking a similar tone throughout, she assailed every time-honored stereotype that prevented

Dixie from getting its due.[223] Another huffy partisan observed: "It has always struck me as strange, if not indeed amazing, that some effort is not made to provide operatic fare for the most prosperous of American peoples — and I ought to add the most musical."[224] A touchy essay in the *Constitution* noted that "it has been said that the south has played the part of the laggard in its appreciation of the greatest in operatic art." "If that indictment be true," the author snapped, "it is not the fault of the south." The region had labored under a dual burden of digging out from the Civil War's financial crush and of forming the bedrock for the North's postwar fortunes. Consequently, the South lacked many opportunities of coming "face to face with the operatic art in the highest stage of its development." With the Met in Atlanta, however, the day was not distant when "the pivot of the musical center" would "swing southward, where it properly belongs."[225] Nevertheless, for all their valiant patriotism, southerners raged against a torrent of popular images running in the opposite direction.

As self-proclaimed leaders of a New South, Atlantans brushed off these discomfiting setbacks and put on a brave face. They rented New York's opera company and then marveled at how the two great metropolises had so much in common. After all, Georgians had taken to calling their home the "Empire State of the South," a self-conscious bow to New York, whose claim to the title "Empire State" required no regional modifier. A 1915 Atlanta *Constitution* editorial set the tone, stating, "*New York and Atlanta, side by side are the only two cities on the continent that are this year to enjoy a season of grand opera.* The nation will not lose the significance of this coincidence."[226] Apparently the nation risked making precisely this error, since the papers deemed it necessary to remind readers every year. Opera program booklets added their voices to the chorus of booster propaganda, smugly announcing that "little if any difference exists between the musical tastes of the Northern Metropolis and that of the patrons of Atlanta's Operatic Festivals."[227] After the 1911 season one booster wrote that "citizens of Atlanta and our friends from every southern state had the privilege of seeing here exactly what they see in New York, which fact they appreciated fully."[228] Four years later the program noted significantly that "while other cities have found it impracticable, New York and Atlanta alone in the United States have been able to maintain their customary operatic seasons."[229] New Yorkers themselves were not above marveling "that a city the size of Atlanta should have succeeded where other cities 10 and 20 times the size have failed," calling it "nothing short of miraculous."[230] The flattery immensely pleased countless Atlantans for whom the comparison proved that theirs was indeed a New South.

Nevertheless, beneath their pride lurked a deep insecurity, betrayed by the eagerness with which the papers printed even the feeblest compliments that the Met's stars sprinkled about. Even as mundane a matter as traffic became a source of civic pride when one Met official declared that, though he had managed pre-opera congestion in many cities, he had "never seen a situation handled as admirably as this."[231] Others offered more wide-ranging praise, such as the Met official who said, "in effect, that Atlanta is the most marvelous city in the world of which he has any knowledge."[232] When asked her impressions of the region and its residents, singer Frances Alda stopped just short of tears, telling reporters: "O, it is wonderful! This is a wonderful section!" She had, the paper reported with satisfaction, fallen "in love with the South and its people."[233] Some years later Alda was at it again. This time, returning from a motoring expedition in the surrounding countryside loaded down with "native Georgia 'wild honeysuckers,'" she proclaimed them "a fairer flower than New York's rarest orchid."[234] Not restricting themselves to the region's botanical wonders, other visitors were perfectly charmed by the food. At their 1911 reception William and Lucy Peel delighted guests with cornbread pones and Virginia ham. Many of them "had never seen corn bread in the pone and they looked upon it as the daintiest morsel."[235] Other visitors found themselves utterly distracted by the mint julep. "I never tasted anything so delicious," one performer burbled. "My, what good things you southern people do have."[236] Whether traffic management or corn pones, Atlantans were anxious for New Yorkers to confirm the Gate City's exalted opinion of itself.

Gratifying though the similarities with Gotham were, the press wondered whether stopping there sold Atlanta short. Looking at it objectively, after all, the Music Festival was clearly "more brilliant than any the south every dreamed of, [and] more alluring in its variety than any the north or east ever dared undertake."[237] After enjoying less than fourteen days of opera over a two-year period, one patriotic citizen felt moved to declare that the Gate City now possessed "a musical prestige beyond that of any other city in the United States."[238] Surveying even wider vistas, Atlantans spied no competitors. Contemplating one year's program, the Music Festival Association's officers mused that it "had never been equaled in a week's time in any city in America"; the discernment of the audiences far excelled what the singers had grown accustomed to "in Milan, Berlin, Paris, or New York."[239] In a particularly breathtaking example of hyperbolic excess, one resident proclaimed that the "size of the audience, brilliance of the scene, receipts, splendor of the production and the voices—everything considering last night's 'Aida' was the greatest operatic event the world has ever seen."[240] All of this added up to an inescapable conclusion: that, as the *Constitution* wrote without a blush, Atlanta could lay "just claim to the title 'music center of the world.'"[241] The only disturbing ripple in such pronouncements came in topping them the next year.

Wild-eyed civic boosterism was, of course, an expected part of any enterprise that New South Atlantans undertook. Yet the praise of New York's cultural elite and artists of European sophistication lent credibility to what skeptics might otherwise have dismissed as bluster. Banner headlines like "Baltimore Financier Thinks Atlanta Audiences More Brilliant Than Those of New York" linked opera with a larger crusade to refashion the South's image as a region of cosmopolitan delights and financial power.[242] Opera made Atlanta's official seal—a phoenix rising from a bed of flames, surrounded by the word "Resurgens"—more than simply a clever rhetorical device. It conclusively demonstrated the New South's eagerness to break free from the isolation and poverty that had hog-tied it in postwar years. As equals and partners who shared a common understanding of all that opera meant to a city, Atlantans reached out to Yankees for a sectional reconciliation that swept away the humiliation of Confederate defeat and postwar economic colonization. "Long may this artistic union of the north and south continue," toasted the Met's business manager in 1914.[243] He and his opera company promised sectional reconciliation on the basis of mutual respect and on terms that the South could finally embrace.

"I Am a Nice White Man, Not Black"

The willingness of their northern guests to agree that white southerners understood and knew best how to solve "the race problem" proved one of the most satisfying concessions in this new reconciliation.[244] No member of the Met's entourage publicly criticized Atlanta's rigid racial caste system. On the contrary, they endorsed it in word and deed, thereby lending Jim Crow independent credibility and removing from segregation the stench of local bigotry. While possibly harboring a deep dismay with racism, segregation, lynching, and rioting, the Met's performers no less than their hosts believed in the power of their white skins. More subtly but no less forcefully than legal and extralegal methods of racial intimidation, opera gave form and substance to abstract concepts of white supremacy.

In his famous "Atlanta Compromise" speech of 1895, Booker T. Washington told a crowd that "the opportunity to earn a dollar in a factory just now is worth infinitely more than the opportunity to spend a dollar in an opera house."[245] White Atlantans took him at his word, and when the opera came to town in later years, blacks never even had the chance to buy tickets. Logistics played no part in this decision, since the auditorium's balcony often served black patrons. In part, it reflected an almost innate racial reflex among whites, who assumed that opera would not interest blacks. Ben Davis, editor of the city's black newspaper, approached the festival's managers about obtaining tickets for the black community, but after some consternation the board told him that "tickets had been sold promiscuously without taking into consideration the Negro." Davis fully endorsed the "social separation of the races" as a policy "so sound, sane and godly, there is no question of its wisdom." So why, he asked, was it not simply "an easy matter . . . to have set aside a section of this great auditorium for black folk"? The shaky excuses offered by the festival's board only confirmed that the decision was "purely a question of meanness and race hatred."[246] Whereas the festival board might plausibly plead ignorance in its first year, arguing that it had not foreseen any interest in opera within the black community, Davis's prodding produced no results in subsequent years. Tickets never went on sale for black patrons. The closest they could get was hiring themselves out to whites who had neither the time nor the patience to stand in long lines at the ticket office.[247]

Evidence abounded that blacks thirsted to hear the music so jealously guarded by whites. In 1910, for instance, when concert promoters consented to open up segregated seating for an organ recital at the auditorium, the *Constitution* noted with surprise that "between 400 and 500 colored people were present."[248] Yet opera always remained out of reach. Ushering at the performances, listening at the auditorium's open windows, or having the good fortune to hear an impromptu recital remained the only way blacks could hear the era's greatest opera singers.[249] In 1919 members of the black community got a rare opportunity to hear Enrico Caruso when he visited Morris Brown University. After the school's choir sang him "a number of the haunting negro melodies," the audience demanded that Caruso sing. "Fair swap ain't no stealin'," cried one. Caruso agreed, and those present reveled in arias and songs "with as close attention and as deep appreciation as any white audience ever displayed." The *Constitution* noted that the black audience listened as though it had "suddenly found the gates to paradise swung open."[250] Blacks' keen appreciation, however, granted them only fleeting glimpses into that forbidden realm. Opera remained a privilege of whiteness.

Though whites never allowed blacks to attend the performances, they wanted blacks on hand throughout opera week. Like cornpone and mint juleps, fifty thousand black residents proved useful in giving the visiting artists a regional spice unavailable in New York, Paris, or Berlin. In 1909 guests at the Capital City Club's reception found their seats at tables set with "attractively designed place card[s], depicting the familiar pickaninny's face grinning from the heart of a watermelon."[251] The seating cards set a lighthearted, regional mood, and dusky pickaninnies slurping watermelon provided a chuckling contrast to the evening's distinguished guests. Blacks also became a must on the tourist's agenda. Locals gleefully escorted their visitors down to Decatur Street, a place famous for its "squalid negro hovels that teem with vice and vermin."[252] It was a necessary stop, the *Constitution* noted, because it provided Atlantans "the satisfaction of unrolling before the eyes of the uninitiated the eighth wonder of the world."[253] In short, blacks were a tourist attraction, the likes of which artists of such erudition would never meet elsewhere in all their exotic travels.

More importantly, the stroll down Decatur Street and the grinning pickaninny place cards both exposed the degradation of the city's blacks and illuminated the sophistication of the white community. The comparison fascinated the press. Newspapers continually reported on interactions between opera stars and local blacks, always finding in the incidents further telling evidence of black inferiority. In 1909 the *Constitution* reported that a trio of opera singers sashayed along Decatur Street but were never "once recognized by any as the most prominent figures of this wonderful street."[254] In 1913 the same paper could not help snickering when it reported that several "world-famed opera stars" had been treated to an impromptu recital starring "two genuine cornfield negroes in their native melodies."[255] Those blacks whose artistic horizons stretched into classical music received a puzzled, lukewarm response. In 1910 a university student sang for some of the Met's performers, prompting them to concede that she had "a very good natural voice" and that "with a little advanced training" it could be "developed still further."[256] No one suggested that eventually her talents might win her a place on the Met's roster. The results of developing her voice "still further" were left intentionally ambiguous.

Newspapers and visiting singers were far more comfortable when interactions with black folks followed a more predictable minstrel show pattern. In 1917, for instance, one singer solemnly vowed that he had been born with a monocle, causing consternation among the hotel's bellboy fraternity. While one was "willing to bet on it with the second bellboy," another dryly remarked, "Go on, man, you know dey ain't no babies bawn wid eyeglasses."[257] Tittering readers, sharing the joke around the club or table before an evening's opera, found the story a comforting measure of their distance from blacks. Such stories reassured whites that blacks simply lacked the mental agility to understand the highest reaches of white culture. Of course, some whites in the opera audience betrayed unmistakable signs of ignorance themselves, but their white skins entitled them to patient instruction. It was a simple matter, whites argued, of two races in different stages of development. Through opera week, whites determined to establish racial hierarchies as a verifiable fact rather than as merely conventional wisdom.

The whiteness of opera week received its most compelling assertion in the widespread rhetorical conflation of Music, Woman, and Christianity. A flurry of religious metaphors imbued the entertainment with holy significance. In 1914 the *Journal* observed that Atlanta had become a "shrine to which hundreds of happy pilgrims are journeying."[258] Another reporter described opera as a "sacred" event; "each new concert brings together the same group of worshipers at the shrine of beauty."[259] Music possessed such spiritual power that it alone could rescue a ribald plot: Puccini's "divine music," for example, redeemed *Tosca* from its "wicked" theme.[260] Librettos alone did not constitute the extent of music's moral suasion. Sunday concerts for the disadvantaged and other experiments that mixed music with social reform seemed to transform social dislocation and moral evil into human brotherhood and upright behavior. Music, one teacher informed the *Journal*, reached "the immortal part of laboring, burdened humanity" and inspired people "to nobler and diviner lives."[261] A prison recital, in which soprano Geraldine Farrar serenaded a motley assortment of rapists, murderers, and thieves prompted the *Constitution* to wonder: "Who knows but what the prima donna's songs have sown within the hearts of some the seed of aspiration that in later years will bear the fruit of upright honesty and straightforward integrity of life."[262] Music, then, paralleled religion in its ability to reclaim lost souls and to access something beyond the grubby details of everyday life. From opera, an editorial in the *Constitution* opined, "flows inspiration to nobler thought, [and] higher citizenship."[263]

The conduit for music's sacred power was, of course, white womanhood. This was precisely the logic women's music clubs had insisted on for years. After Farrar's prison recital the *Constitution*'s music critic noted that her "distinctly feminine" voice was "soft as a woman's ought to be and yet carrying as far as a woman's influence."[264] Indeed, reporters alternated between describing opera week as a religious rite and as a homage to women. Headlines such as "Queen Music Rules Atlanta for Three Days,"[265] and efforts at poesy like "music had her triumph last night, and thousands of the vanquished followed in brilliant pageant her victorious car, waving before her the incense of their pleasure, strewing in her path the flowers of their applause,"[266] reinforced the already well-established link between women and music. The papers generally ignored the men in the audience, lavishing their attention instead on the women. As the advertisement for a florist shop noted, during each performance "there will be beautifully gowned women, vying with the artists and the productions themselves in the all-absorbing interest of Atlanta and her guests."[267] Their every gesture, bauble, and frill received admiring attention, and their serene faces graced the social pages for days. In 1919 a reporter gushed that "beautiful women turned the ground floor of the big building into a nodding garden of human flowers," and that "in the midst of the crowd, every moment, the face of some woman which almost dazes by the perfection of its beauty, flashes out."[268] Year after year women became part of the performance, making their loveliness, their grace, and their charm an inescapable rival to the evening's musical entertainment. "Beauty Carnival Will Rival the Music," a typical headline enthused.[269] The complicated interweaving of Music, Woman, and Christianity made the opera, in part, a devotional exercise designed to worship one of the white South's most holy icons: white womanhood.

Given the powerful assumptions about race, religion, and gender that swirled around the opera, whites considered it sheer folly to provide blacks with tickets. Black editor Ben Davis complained that the festival's official policy proved "the disposition of the white man to force the 'color line' in every phase of our community or national life."[270] Yet officers of the Atlanta Music Festival Association had no intention of permitting black men an unobstructed view of the "bare shoulders of beautiful women," even from segregated seats.[271] As one influential author reminded readers in his 1916 jeremiad *The Passing of the Great Race*, women "of fair skin have always been the objects of keen envy by those of the sex whose skins are black, yellow, or red."[272] Atlanta's white women, therefore, depended on the association's men to fasten tight the entrance to the holy inner recesses of whiteness and to protect them from the ravenous beasts clawing at the gates. There, safe from the leering stare and the gross insult, white women found safe harbor. There, relaxed from their unceasing vigilance, white men enjoyed the fruits of patriarchy. There, for a few hours black people disappeared and all was whiteness.

The assumptions about race and gender that swirled around opera week rarely surfaced more compellingly than in 1911, when the Met produced Verdi's *Otello*. Both the *Journal* and the *Constitution* laughingly related how the evening's lead, Leo Slezak, quaked at playing "a black Moor" who dallies with a white woman. As the Met's train descended into the Deep South, the papers reported, Slezak's colleagues passed the journey by sketching "interesting little word pictures of how southerners would hang him up to the nearest tree and puncture his splendid physique with bullet holes." The Czech tenor called upon white racial solidarity to literally and figuratively save his skin. "Will you plees to tell the people that I am a nice white man," he pleaded in broken English after arriving at the Atlanta train station. "Say I am a nice white man, not black." "He is really nervous," the *Journal* giggled, and the *Constitution* chuckled over the "comical" gag pulled over by the Met's crew. The joke rested on the absurdity of accidentally lynching a white man. It embraced all whites in its humor, assuring them that though they were engaged in the same sexual acts that condemned black men to torturous executions, the bonds of whiteness protected them from the lynch mob's fury.[273] It winked at racial violence and dismissed flayed black corpses as a whimsical regional custom. Though humorously depicting the darkest aspects of white supremacy, the story so lovingly concocted by the Met's entourage and so gleefully reported in the Atlanta papers gave flesh and sinew to assumptions about race and gender normally lurking below the surface.

Women and men in early-twentieth-century America expected to experience music in ways significantly shaped by their gender. Of course, the differences between the sexes were supposed to be comple-

Leo Slezak in the title role of Verdi's Otello. *The opera
star considered himself "a nice white man, not black."
Courtesy of the New York Metropolitan Opera Archives.*

mentary, not inimical. "Man and woman were made to live together, and to contribute their respective qualities to a common fund," wrote an author in the *Atlantic Monthly*. "Where one predominates, the result will be one-sided, imperfect culture."[274] The concert hall was one place where men and women tried to put rhetoric into practice, forging that unified, balanced culture. But the process grew exceedingly complex because it required discerning just which "respective qualities" were masculine and which were feminine.

The growing number of women involved in music as both amateurs and professionals generated intense anxieties among men *and* women, because the confusion that resulted seemed to further muddle gender roles in the new century. Countless women, torn between an interest in civic concerns and a duty to the home, found a compromise in music. By fusing music and religion, women justified their growing social, cultural, and economic power by declaring that their work merely extended their traditional moral and domestic interest into a larger arena. Music teachers, musicians, and clubwomen, therefore, conceived of themselves as social missionaries working to mitigate the unintended consequences of capitalistic expansion. They cast their work as the spiritual complement of city building and an aspect of urban development that men building fortunes and egos often neglected. Music reminded men of the larger purpose of the profits they earned, the buildings they erected, and the musical events they financed. In short, they believed that music did not invade the male sphere, it simply advanced the female sphere into its logical public role. Yet few failed to recognize that within such rhetoric lay an important shift in the scope of female activity.

The assurance that "the time has gone by when men need fear that they will have to do the sewing if their wives devote themselves to higher pursuits" carried little weight with men in early-twentieth-century America.[275] More frequently they concurred in the warning broadcast by the editor of *Century Magazine* who told an audience that "feminism does mean the usurpation by women of the place and the power of men."[276] Having lost their overwhelming dominance on the concert stage and having yielded the audience to great swaths of organza and tulle, men sought new ways to claim their own place in American classical music. Portraying themselves the equal of the era's sports and business heroes, male musicians and composers struggled to enhance the virility of their professional image. Using the rhetoric of finance and boosterism, men who patronized musical institutions did so to rescue their cities from feminization and themselves from civic obsolescence.

The anxieties about gender that so interested the popular north-eastern periodicals resonated deeply with white New South Atlantans. Though themselves self-proclaimed agents of modernization, upper-class white Atlantans felt more than a little queasy by the rapid pace of change they worked so hard to foster. While almost desperate for signs of their parity with the great northeastern cities, of which opera represented an important symbol, they nevertheless remained ambivalent about the changes that inevitably trailed in modernization's wake. Not least among them were the changes in the definitions of masculinity and femininity.

Just like women in clubs elsewhere, members of the Atlanta Music Club threw themselves into the "cultural upbuilding of Atlanta" in a way commensurate with its financial growth.[277] Through their attempts to create permanent, professional symphonies that were civic institutions rather than private hobbies, women tried to mark their presence in a city that otherwise advertised itself through monuments to masculine endeavor. Men countered with an annual opera season, which they used to wrest back control over music's civic purpose and to reinforce the supremacy of men in the public arena. While granting the special regard women had for music, they refused to allow that appreciation to mean anything more than the indulgence of the feminine temperament. The manner in which the opera engaged deeply held anxieties about gender, then, differed little from the anxieties harbored in the Northeast.

Yet the alleged presence of black rapists lurking at every Atlanta street corner made gender roles an exceedingly sensitive topic in the New South's capital. "With the Anglo-Saxon," wrote the editor of the *Atlanta Constitution* in 1906, "all things begin—all things end—with the chastity, the inviolability of the women of the race." Protecting that purity was "the duty manhood lays upon us."[278] Though widely feared throughout the country, feminization took on special meaning when all that separated black beasts from white angels were New South boosters in somber business suits. Any ambiguity in gender roles and any crack in the masculine façade, therefore, had possibly catastrophic consequences.

Opera patrolled whiteness without resorting to the kinds of physical intimidation that ensured northern censure and southern defensiveness. The Met's entourage colluded with its hosts to demonstrate how opera rooted white supremacy in something more noble and more profound than fists, ropes, and laws. Of course, the city's racial and sexual politics were too intricate to crystallize entirely around a single week of opera. Nevertheless, opera supplied the tune for a complex and sometimes macabre minuet between gender and race that only intensified after the Metropolitan Opera returned to New York.

The Colored Music Festival

Despite claims of its musical preeminence, opera week swiftly confronted a rival in its own house. "It looks as if the Auditorium will be taxed to capacity," a city paper reported breathlessly in the summer of 1910. "The greatest musical entertainment in the history of the South is to be witnessed." Customers besieged the Gate City Drug Store in a scramble for tickets, and inbound trains groaned under the crush of excited passengers bound for musical glory. As in the case of opera week, the entertainment promised stars so luminous as to dazzle the senses. "Every artist on the program is a star and could fill a whole evening," the paper proclaimed.[1] For some Atlantans it was obvious that opera week's reign as the social calendar's crowning event had come to an abrupt end. Yet even this unexpected development failed to ruffle the implacable men who organized the opera season. After all, they reasoned, any entertainment that boasted African Americans performing classical music as the main attraction was merely a novelty. Consequently, they gave the new undertaking their heartiest endorsement.

Opera week festivities had reminded the black community, especially those in its middle class, of the numerous checks on their civic participation. Although only a year earlier the *Atlanta Journal* had declared that "there is no bond so deep and wide among all mankind as the

love of music," whites made it clear that whatever sense of brotherhood music awakened would slumber unperturbed when opera came
to town.[2] Members of the freshly minted Atlanta Colored Music Festival
Association, however, demanded that whites live up to their rhetoric.
Recognizing that no amount of protest would open either literal or figu-
rative doors to the opera season, Reverend Henry Hugh Proctor spear-
headed an effort in 1910 to put on a Colored Music Festival that would
celebrate the musical, financial, and social accomplishments of blacks,
just as the opera celebrated whites. The city's black newspaper, the *Independent,* claimed that "in point of quality and superbness the Atlanta
May Festival of the whites does not out distance Dr. Proctor's entertainment."[3] Of the featured soloist Harry Burleigh, the paper observed that
he had "sung before all the crowned heads of Europe, and those who
have heard him say he is as good as Caruso, before whom he sung."[4]
Organizers kept tickets prices exceptionally reasonable to make the festival financially accessible and invited artists who were "the best the race
affords."[5] The Colored Music Festival was, in short, no minstrel show or
vaudeville routine. Proctor and his colleagues were determined to put
on an event in which sophisticated black artists starred and in which
sophisticated black music held center stage.

It is hard to overestimate the enormous race pride the festival generated. Opening night would have stunned the parents of these sons
and daughters of freedom. Gone were the ill-fitting shifts, clumsy bro-
gans, and callused hands of slavery. The female performers were resplen-
dent in their gowns and shimmering jewels. "Never in the history of
our city," one observer wrote with immense gratification, would "the
women of the race be shown to better advantage."[6] Gone, too, were the
decaying cabin and the hog and hominy of bondage. Families threw
parties in homes of the highest fashion, and gentlemen of refinement
presided over tables laden with delicacies of culinary artistry. Gone were
the plunking banjo and the scraping fiddle of rural hoedowns. The festival's program featured black performers from around the nation who
thrilled the audience with their training and artistic breadth. Gone was
the hushed secrecy of the brush-arbor meeting. Black composers, determined to honor the music of their enslaved ancestors, arranged the
spirituals for the concert stage, transforming them into some of the most
exciting and innovative works in American classical music. For blacks
hounded on every side by laws and customs designed to deflate their
self-worth, the annual Colored Music Festival was a heady event.[7]

TAKE THIS HOME WITH YOU

Souvenir Program

THIRD ANNUAL MUSIC FESTIVAL

Under Auspices		Branch of The
Atlanta Colored Music Festival Association		**Institutional Department of First Congregational Church**

REV. H. H. PROCTOR, D.D., Pastor

Auditorium-Armory
ATLANTA, GEORGIA

Thursday and Friday Evenings, Eight o'Clock
August 15 and 16, 1912

Program for the 1912 Colored Music Festival. Courtesy of the Amistad Research Center at Tulane University, New Orleans, Louisiana.

In addition to swelling race pride for its black audience, the festival obliquely challenged a color line growing frightfully taut. For centuries whites had conceded the innate superiority of African American musicians, an acknowledgment blacks throughout Jim Crow America determined to exploit. Given an opening wedge into white sympathies, blacks hoped to demonstrate that the spiritual's transformation from vernacular hymnody to art song paralleled the race's swift rise from slavery and demonstrated its limitless potential. The implications were clear. As F. G. Rathbun, the director of music at Hampton University put it, "If these people in their former degradation could and did produce such beautiful melodies, what may they not do?"[8] Atlanta's blacks, therefore, used the festival to nurture their own New South within the confines of a Jim Crow hothouse.

Gate City whites, however, made themselves virtually deaf to the Colored Music Festival's implicit and explicit denunciation of reigning racial hierarchies. Instead, they heard far more palatable harmonies that reminded them of happy days on the old plantation. Rather than racial progress, they heard racial stasis; rather than rebellion, they heard contentment. These were enormously comforting sounds to a generation of white southerners whose lamentations for the passing of the Old South's "aunties" and "uncles" reached nearly deafening proportions. Despite the older generation's efforts to "pass on to the youth of their race the wholesome lessons learned under the strict tho' kindly discipline of Slavery," one South Carolinian wailed, the New Negroes seemed to peevishly defy instruction.[9] Such rhetorical hand-wringing betrayed a certain degree of nostalgia, to be sure, but New South boosters rarely entombed themselves in morbid lamentations for the past.[10] Their dirges for the Old South and its faithful darkies reflected their deep concern about the New South and its quarrelsome Negroes. As one journalist wrote of whites in Atlanta, "They want the New South, but the old Negro."[11]

Whites believed that perhaps nothing more powerfully symbolized the black population's postwar descent than its indifference to the "soul-stirring songs" of the "trustworthy old retainers."[12] A detailed search through the antebellum spirituals, one southern professor noted, revealed neither a "vindictive spirit" nor a "prayer for vengeance," but the Negro's modern-day output suggested a "bitter and vindictive tone" that did not bode well for the region's peace.[13] More troubling still, because of their reputedly instinctual drive to imitate white culture and because of their powerful influence on American popular music, blacks threatened to short-circuit segregation through cultural miscegenation. But the Colored Music Festival relieved whites of their anxiety. Whites viewed the festival as an opportunity to nurture within the black community a "separate but equal" culture that would complement the "separate but equal" dictum sanctioned by the U.S. Supreme Court. In both word and deed, whites attending the festival strove to convince African Americans that segregation liberated black culture from certain annihilation.[14] Gate City whites thus found themselves enthralled by the slave spiritual not because they longed to resurrect the plantation South amid their industrial, urban empire. Instead, the spiritual provided them the means to insist on the fundamental differences between the races, as well as the necessity and magnanimity of a New South designed to preserve those differences.

During the 1912 Colored Music Festival the *Atlanta Georgian* observed that the evening's program "had a two-fold appeal because of its racial significance and artistic excellence."[15] Atlantans of both races would have agreed heartily. Without question the festival provided a delightful diversion for its audience, but the interest it generated rested on its power to address some of the era's most pressing concerns. Everyone recognized that the sophistication with which black artists and composers handled the spirituals on the program made clearer than ever the radical transformation in black life and culture since the Civil War. If it was a New South for whites, it was so, too, for blacks. The implications for this acknowledgment were, however, far from settled or clear. Having sustained countless Old South slaves during moments of trial and doubt, the spiritual experienced a New South revival, but in what guise and to what purpose remained open to intense debate.[16]

"Keeping Alive the Spirituals among the Negro Race"

As early as the eighteenth century, whites expressed fascination with the skill of black musicians. In 1781, for instance, Thomas Jefferson wrote of Virginia's African American population that "in music they are more generally gifted than the whites with accurate ears for tune and time."[17] Such convictions lasted long after slavery's demise, even receiving purportedly scientific validation in the early twentieth century. One prominent Harvard professor observed in 1904 that blacks had a "striking aesthetic capacity" for music and that their voices were "on the average much better than that of any other well known race."[18] Yet whites in the New South could not ignore that blacks appeared startlingly disinterested in continuing to cultivate their racial gift. It seemed that an eerie silence had descended on the region. "The Negroes were always singing" one white southerner puzzled; "nothing is a greater contrast to that time than the quietness of the Negroes now."[19] An Atlanta resident similarly confided to journalist Ray Stannard Baker that blacks "don't sing as they used to."[20]

The real difference was in fact not silence, but that blacks did not sound like they had during slavery. The field hollers, work songs, and spirituals that had enchanted whites in a bygone era appeared to have been discarded with the chains and whips of bondage. Indeed, the alacrity with which blacks abandoned the Old South tunes mystified and even angered many whites. A 1910 editorial in *Musical America* snapped that blacks had lately assumed "a vapid intellectual snobbery" by letting the old spirituals fall into disuse.[21] The underlying assumptions that motivated such chastisement was that the extinction of slavery's tunes portended the gradual convergence of white and black culture at precisely the moment that whites made increasingly determined attempts to separate white and black bodies.[22] Whites accused New South Negroes of indulging in their supposedly innate racial desire to mimic the manners, clothing, and speech of the superior race. It was surely true, fretted one South Carolinian, "that certain ineradicable racial traits persist, even in Negroes who have risen to distinction in business, in literature, or in the arts," but it was equally true that those traits remained "hidden in the cultured Negro's heart."[23] By refusing to sing the old songs of slavery and by refusing to sing their "own" music, blacks made it harder to draw the cultural color line.

In response, many whites turned to folklore. The American scholars and interested amateurs who comprised folklore's most ardent followers in the early twentieth century had slaked their academic thirst from the discipline's European headwaters, which stressed that customs, beliefs, and songs of "the folk" were the uninhibited outpouring of innate racial consciousness.[24] As one writer explained, "A folk song gives with a few symbolist strokes all the essential elements of a racial psychology."[25] Consequently, studious attention to black folklore and folk song would peel back "the veneer of civilization" caused by centuries of living with whites and confirm that "the African is under it all."[26] Folklorists provided segregation's advocates with ammunition to contest critics who saw the new Jim Crow laws and entrenched racial etiquette as merely evidence of irrational racial phobias. Instead, folklore seemed to prove in dispassionately scientific ways that each race's natural genius risked contamination unless its essential racial folk heritage was kept inviolate. Thus, segregation became a duty whites owed to themselves, but, equally important, it was a paternalistic responsibility to blacks who otherwise stood on the precipice of racial suicide.

It was this sense of obligation that led countless white folklorists to ignore the innumerable sites of interracial contact that had always made southern vernacular culture so vibrant and to focus instead on disentangling and preserving distinct "African" and "Anglo-Saxon" strands. That it was a task of Herculean proportions "so vast and perplexing as to baffle the most ardent student" did not deter them or lead them to question its logic.[27] It merely confirmed their pessimism and added urgency to the task. They descended on the Georgia and South Carolina Sea Islands and the Deep South Black Belt with a particularly ravenous interest, because in these locations they located the vivid remnants of Africa within America that they so eagerly sought. Here were the populations of black people who had escaped the corroding effects of interracial propinquity, and who confirmed the fundamental and irrevocable distinctions that forever separated whites and blacks. "Geographic isolation," the principal of St. Helena Island's Penn School explained, had permitted the inhabitants "to retain their native racial characteristics."[28] The area's residents were deemed more authentically black than their counterparts in other regions. They were, as one school administrator put it, "the real negroes of our country."[29]

Yet, of course, the Sea Islands and the Black Belt were miniscule islands of racial purity amid a swampy morass of cultural interracialism. One looked in vain across wide stretches of Dixie's soil for more "real negroes." The dearth of authentic black people and authentic black culture proved a disturbing prospect for whites whose paternalistic leanings made them fear for the future of any race so eager to discard its own identity. The white superintendent of Atlanta's black elementary schools urged teachers to reacquaint their students with "the beauty and cultural value of the old spirituals, work songs, and plantation melodies."[30] Her attempt to revive the slave spiritual found ample support from whites across the South. Determined to resuscitate the Old South "darkey" and his phantasmagoria of songs and sayings, a number of white performers staged a new generation of minstrel shows that in-

Polk Miller's Old South Quartette, four "genuine negroes." Courtesy of the Southern Folklife Collection, Wilson Library, University of North Carolina at Chapel Hill.

corporated dialect, superstitions, music, and tales. These New South minstrels, however, distanced themselves from the disdainful effects of burned cork, stoved-in top hats, and wild tomfoolery. They emphasized the folkloric authenticity of their performance, often claiming that their shows were based on intimate childhood acquaintance with real planta-tion Negroes. The performers undertook their task with a keen obliga-tion, as one put it, "to posterity to see that the genuine African music be handed down in all its purity."[31] With postemancipation advances in black education, political power, and economic success, whites felt it imperative to remind blacks that they were still Africans first. Efforts to preserve African American folklore qualified the claims blacks could make on America since their identity, and thus their true home, lay in Africa.

One of the first and most widely hailed Old Negro impersonators was a Virginian named Polk Miller. Born in 1844 on a large plantation, Miller served as a private in a Confederate artillery regiment during the Civil War and opened a drugstore in Richmond after the surrender. Beginning in the mid-1890s, he utilized his plantation upbringing to craft a series of enormously successful "dialect recitals" that aimed to perpetuate the songs, stories, and superstitions of the Old Negro. No less an authority than Mark Twain praised Miller, and popular writer of Old South tales Thomas Nelson Page testified that Miller could "tell a negro story, and give the true negro dialect better than any man living."[32] Though Miller played in Carnegie Hall and entertained Boston clubs, he found his most enthusiastic audiences at the Confederate reunions he loyally attended throughout the South. Described as "a typical Virginia gentleman," Miller so accurately rendered his subject that veterans of the war rubbed their eyes to assure themselves "that the veritable Sambo [was] not there in person."[33]

At the turn of the century, Miller added four "genuine negroes" who "look, act, and sing like the 'old times'" to his act.[34] Taking a swipe at black college choirs specializing in classically arranged spirituals, Miller advertised that his Old South Quartette did not "dress in pigeon-tailed coats, patent leather shoes, [and] white shirt fronts," nor would it "try to let you see how nearly a Negro can act *the White Man* while parading in a dark skin." Instead, he promised that his Negroes dressed, acted, and sang "like the real *Southern Darkey*."[35] Another advertisement labeled the quartette as simply "the REAL THING!"[36] Like Sea Island blacks on whom "the yoke of civilization rests but lightly," Miller and his Old South Quartette purported to transport African Americans to authentic, pristine blackness, and to thereby ensure that blacks would stay in the Old South rather than crowd the New.[37]

Miller disbanded the act shortly before his death in 1913, but a startling number of other white performers shared his zeal for preserving "the real *Southern Darkey*." In 1898 Kentucky's Jeannette Robinson Murphy won fame for her "unique rendering of negro slave songs" and reportedly enjoyed "a marked success in New York's most exclusive society."[38] In the 1920s soprano Edna Thomas began performing the songs she had "learned from her 'mammy.'" Carrying a parasol and wearing a dress reminiscent of an Old South plantation mistress, Thomas used her performance to keep alive "the soul-history of the Negro."[39] Such shows, as had blackface minstrelsy in an earlier era, enjoyed transatlantic appeal. In 1912 an American contralto in the Darmstadt Royal Opera "enchanted" the Grand Duke of Hesse by singing "some genuine negro melodies. . . . Dressed in the costume of a negro 'mammy,'" the singer made "the greatest success of the evening" at the "big Künstlerfest in

Darmstadt."[40] When introduced to Kitty Cheatham, yet another American keeping alive her mammy's songs, Princess Victoria of Schleswig-Holstein was utterly charmed by "these out-of-the-way melodies and thoughts of the child race of the world."[41] Like her counterparts, Cheatham fretted that "the negro seems to be ashamed of his old melodies," and she made rescuing African American lore and music her particular mission.[42]

Perhaps few whites expressed more enthusiasm for the old spirituals than a group of wealthy Charleston, South Carolina, socialites who, in 1922, organized themselves into the Society for the Preservation of Spirituals. The elite group limited its membership to those who had grown up on plantations. The organization, a Savannah paper marveled, "was born and is existing for the sole purpose of preserving these spirituals and keeping them from being forgotten after the darkies who sing them now are educated out of them."[43] Its members sought out the oldest plantation blacks they could find, pumping them for tunes that the society added to its repertoire after assiduously perfecting the dialect and rhythmic clapping. Though not originally created for public performances, the society within a year of organizing gave concerts in Charleston and Savannah and began negotiating the possible release of a recording with both Victor and Columbia. Their performances, the *Charleston News and Courier* bubbled, presented accurate renditions of spirituals "such as have been sung for generations by old time darkies in their country churches far from the civilizing effect of city life."[44] In their public performances society members dressed in the plantation clothes of white masters and mistresses, and stood amid an ethereal cloud of Spanish moss, azaleas, and palms.[45]

Whenever the society performed, or whenever Polk Miller tuned up his banjo, whites in the audience expressed astonishment at the mimicry. Yet they also conceded that the shows merely shadowed reality. Whites could never really become black, any more than blacks could become white. "At best," a Savannah reporter wrote about a Society for the Preservation of Spirituals concert, "these reproductions by the whites are only copies[,] though they are admirable copies and are always lacking somewhat in their realities. No human of the white skin can translate himself into this temperamental Gullah human with the black skin."[46] Of course, the reverse was true as well. Neither race had within it the tools necessary to alter its supposedly fundamental racial predispositions, and it was folly and tragedy to attempt it. Polk Miller, Edna

Thomas, and Kitty Cheatham did not delude themselves into thinking that, at least for those moments on stage, they actually were black. Instead, they took as their task providing the supposedly imitative Negroes an attractive path to follow back to their own separate racial identity. Through "judicious praise of their 'spirituals,'" according to one writer, whites could "do much to prolong their life." But the only way to "effectually preserve the old slave music" would be "for the negroes themselves . . . to awaken to the real value of this wonderful music."[47] In a similar vein, a 1922 concert by black children in Charleston was "well patronized" by whites because, the reporter explained, they wanted "to show their interest in keeping alive the spirituals among the Negro race."[48]

Nostalgia certainly accounts for much of the enthusiasm for genteel minstrelsy. The shows, full of funny sayings, silly superstitions, and rousing melodies, temporarily immersed the audience in a confectionary world of black loyalty, humor, and harmlessness. It contrasted starkly with the reportedly rising tide of New Negro rapists, murderers, and thieves who lunged through the daily newspapers. As one astute African American professor noted, the loudest laments for the passing of the old songs were "felt more keenly and expressed more fully by the Southern white man who was a part of the system of slavery" than by any one else, because "these old songs link the Southern white man to a romantic past."[49] Nevertheless, the genteel minstrels also crafted their imitations at precisely the moment when efforts at legally sanctifying racial segregation reached a fever pitch. Jim Crow's most pressing task was marking the public spaces and rituals to quarantine the races. While the logical and practical difficulties became immediately apparent, they seemed ephemeral when compared to untangling a culture that had been biracial for centuries. The genteel minstrels offered a promising start. By emphasizing the African folkloric inheritance bequeathed to even the cultured "darkey" as a birthright, they reaffirmed their audiences's belief that black people were so fundamentally different from whites that the two races must forever remain on separate paths. Thus, like Old South planters who defended the "peculiar institution" as "a positive good," New South minstrels implicitly endorsed segregation as a boon to the inferior race; it prevented black people from abandoning all their endearing traits in vain attempts to become white. The obvious advice the performers offered the black community was to lay aside its economic, political, and social ambitions and return to its noble, if primitive, African roots.[50] There would be no New South for Africa's emigrants.

"An Entirely New Phase of Race Consciousness"

As whites scoured black folklore from rural byways and fading memories, African Americans were not idle. In fact, they shared a fear that, as one black educator wrote, "the so-called educated Negro, under the shadow of this overpowering Anglo-Saxon civilization, may become ashamed of his own distinctive features."[51] Such anxiety was not altogether misplaced, particularly given the increasingly stiff resistance that black churches and schools put up against the spiritual. Writing in the 1922 *Journal of American Folklore*, one folklorist stated that "the elite churches of the race" had "almost entirely discarded" the spirituals because the music seemed to have "no striking meaning for the spirit and life of the forward and intelligent groups of Negroes to-day."[52] The *Colored American Magazine* concurred, noting that many "despise the Negro folk-songs as a vestige of slavery" and see them "as something of which we should be ashamed."[53]

Numerous examples confirmed these speculative statements. One black Florida choir director did not program "the old plantation melodies" because he wished to "educate my people to something higher!"[54] Robert Moton, later president of Tuskegee Institute, Alabama, recalled that as a college freshman he had been disappointed to find the slave spirituals such an integral part of Hampton University's curriculum. Although familiar with the music since childhood, he had expected "to hear regular church music such as would be sung by white people." After all, he wrote in his autobiography, "I had come to school to learn to do things differently; to sing, to speak, and to use the language, and of course, the music, not of coloured people but of white people." Moreover, he "objected to exhibiting the religious and emotional side of our people to white folks" who viewed this intimate expression of black religiosity as a source of delicious amusement.[55] Moton later reconsidered his early opinions. Many others did not.

At various times in the first two decades of the twentieth century students at Fisk, Howard, and Hampton Universities revolted against continuing the familiar practice of singing spirituals for white visitors.[56] One Hampton graduate proudly told how the spirituals "are now rarely heard on the lips of the Virginia negro."[57] Students at Wilberforce College refused to sing spirituals at all.[58] Some argued that the spirituals were "dragging" students "back into slavery."[59] In 1909 a professor at Howard informed Booker T. Washington that students did not feel "that it is becoming this Institution devoted to the higher aims and ideals of the race to emphasize these melodies."[60] Others complained about what they perceived as the servile attitude these songs implied to white listeners. "I wondered why these philanthropists were not equally eager to find students who were brilliant mathematicians," one Morehouse College student recalled. Singing the old spirituals, he believed, "was a subtle way of telling the Negro that no matter what he learned and how well he learned it, he was still a singer of religious spirituals at the bidding of the master."[61] Though black college choirs played a crucial role in generating and spreading interest in slave spirituals, they nevertheless remained divided about the value of their work. As long as the spirituals stood as a monument to rural isolation, ignorance, poverty, and above all slavery, many African Americans would find little endearing in the melodies of bondage.

Despite the significant numbers of students and congregations who treated the spiritual with suspicion, some leading black intellectuals were determined to overcome the disfavor. They insisted that the songs both rejected Old South nostalgia and New South degradation. They argued forcefully that—far from keeping them in "their place"—folklore and folk song could provide historical grounding for the race's advancement. Poet James Weldon Johnson, for example, gloried that the "reawakening of the Negro to the value and beauty of the Spirituals" marked "an entirely new phase of race consciousness."[62] The work of folklorists who collected African elements in folk tales, songs, beliefs, and dialect resonated with a wider search for African roots, whether in Marcus Garvey's back-to-Africa movement or in the fascination with African art and history among Harlem Renaissance intellectuals.[63] African folklore in America proved that blacks had a long history, stretching back to a period before slavery and Jim Crow. Folklore and folk song, then, were not simply a crude reminder of slavery, but a proud testament of a resilient black culture. "When the Negro landed here, a slave, the only weapon that he brought with him was his songs," wrote a New York City music teacher.[64] Many were determined that such a weapon should not lose its edge in freedom.

The first cut was to sever the link between the spirituals and arguments about black inferiority. As James Weldon Johnson astutely observed, many whites proved unwilling to concede "the creation of so much pure beauty to a people they wish to feel is absolutely inferior" because "once that power is conceded, the idea of absolute inferiority cannot hold."[65] But so many whites openly confessed their admiration for the spirituals that blacks found themselves with a powerful means of presenting "the cause of [their] people before the bar of humanity."[66] Fully aware that the spirituals cultivated white sympathies, black colleges used spirituals to charm money from philanthropists's bank accounts. From this beginning, whites might reexamine their other assumptions about the limits of black capabilities. If unlettered slaves could create such inspired music under the most adverse and hostile conditions, what might the free men and women accomplish without the strictures of blind prejudice? In his 1903 work, *The Souls of Black Folk*, W. E. B. Du Bois suggested that whites would find it increasingly difficult to deny "freedom of opportunity to those who brought the Sorrow Songs to the Seats of the Mighty."[67] The spirituals thus promised to effectively combat racial hostility by demonstrating the aesthetic and moral capacities of black people.

In their attempt to wrest control of the spirituals' meaning from paternalistic whites and to elevate the music to a proper artistic appreciation, African American musicians and intellectuals received an unexpected ally in Bohemian composer Antonín Dvořák. His 1893 symphony, *From the New World*, showcased the possibilities of a uniquely American style of composition based on the nation's folk music inheritance. He laid particular emphasis on the spirituals, noting that "in the negro melodies of America I discover all that is needed for a great and noble school of music."[68] It was a startling pronouncement and one met with hostility among some whites. For them, it was impossible to imagine that any music claiming the title "American" could have as its source such degraded members of society. Nor was it possible to concede American identity to anyone who was not white. If folk music was the bedrock of a national style, as composers like Dvořák, Smetana, Bartók, Glinka, Mussorgsky, and Grieg insisted, America had a problem. "We find," wrote critic John Tasker Howard, "that the greater part of our folk-tunes really belong to only certain portions of our population with whom we never wish to be joined by ties of blood."[69] Making a similar assertion, one musician acidly observing that if Dvořák's logic were to be followed to its inescapable conclusion, "the Negro and the white must become one race, which thing is absurd."[70] Though ostensibly an artistic experiment, the "New World Symphony" offered a significant ideological challenge to an American identity rooted in white people.

Blacks, however, were quick to exploit Dvořák's imprimatur. Composers savored the delicious irony that "the cry of the slave in America should stand forth as America's sole music."[71] A new generation of musicians, led by Harry T. Burleigh, Robert Nathaniel Dett, and Afro-British composer Samuel Coleridge-Taylor, began shaping the spirituals into a concert repertoire to rival the great choral works of Handel and Bach. They kept college and church choirs amply supplied with arrangements, as well as responding to the demand among singers to rewrite spirituals in the art-song tradition of Schubert and Schumann.[72] Permutations of Dvořák's reasoning found its way into the mouths of hundreds, from Booker T. Washington, who wrote that black folk music represented the nation's "only distinctively American music,"[73] to a speaker at the National Association of Colored Women who declared that "America has no real American music save that furnished by Negroes."[74] It was a unique moment in which blacks could claim a central role in what it meant to be "American," and to explore for themselves the music's full complexity and richness without the interference of Polk Miller, the Society for the Preservation of Spirituals, and other white performers.

In a number of striking ways, then, the spirituals were at the heart of a sustained debate about the future of black people in Jim Crow America and about their place in society. Both whites and blacks struggled to control the public meaning of these songs because they believed that in so doing they could control black people themselves. Listening to tobacco graders singing while they worked led one folklorist to ponder, "Is it not in the Song of the Negro that we glimpse the spirit of the race reaching forward toward development and eventual unfolding?"[75] This rhetorical question sparked virulent disputes, but almost no one doubted that in music they could find the answer.

"The Negro upon Whom Ruin Waits"

In 1909 white Atlantans listened with interest to the "primal sentiments" offered by Dvořák's most famous symphony and found themselves drawn to its "complexities of progress and awakening life and desires."[76] But it did not incline them toward optimism when it came to the progress of black folks. Their own eyes seemed to indicate something far more ominous, and they expressed dismay at the apparent

sharp divide between the "darkeys" of the Old South and the Negroes of
the New South. The genteel minstrel Polk Miller offered further proof of
this divide when he brought his banjo, fiddle, and tales of "the amusing
traits of the old Southern darkey" to town in 1894. During his presentation, Miller recalled that the old southern plantation "was a garden
of Eden to both the white man and the black," and that the strains of
war had brought the races into an even more perfect union of sympathy
and trust. For evidence, Miller reminded his audience of the "loyalty"
with which blacks "adhered to the cause of their masters and continued
to live with them after the war." [77] On dozens of other occasions at the
turn of the century whites indulged in similarly sentimental reveries for
the dwindling numbers of "old time darkeys," convinced that their in-
evitable demise would lead to racial conflict on an unprecedented scale.
In 1895, not far from the podium where Booker T. Washington urged
racial peace, viewers of the Atlanta Exposition could wander among the
"young bucks and thickliped [*sic*] African maidens, 'happy as a big sun-
flower'" exhibited at the exposition's "Old Plantation." [78] In 1910 a minister named Lincoln McConnell reportedly delivered a hilarious lecture
"on the subject of 'Colored Folks.'" His talk was not, the *Journal* assured
readers, "a discussion of the race question, but an evening of imperson-
ations of the old time darkey as well as the modern negro." [79]

Writing in 1912 under the title "The Negro upon Whom Ruin Waits,"
the *Constitution*'s editor summed up what "every unbiased observer of
conditions in the south has long known." He bemoaned the dwindling
number of "survivors of the ante-bellum regime" who had been "trained
under the watchful eye and the sympathetic but firm hand of the master
or mistress of the 'old plantation.'" The new generation, lacking guidance "under the patriarchal system," was nothing less than a "discouraging, hopeless conglomeration of inefficiency, complicated here and
there by tendencies toward crime and disease." Aside from a few "ex-
ceptional" cases, the editor concluded, "the twentieth century negro . . .
is a square peg in the round hole of the south's twentieth century civilization." [80] Where these New Negroes might take a New South remained
a popular subject of parlor divination and editorial speculation, but the
answers seldom reassured the anxious.

The 1906 race riot, of course, had contributed to a deep pessimism
about the future of the city's race relations. Efforts at reconciliation
masked a profound sense of gloom that the two races could ever coexist
peacefully. [81] Yet far less spectacular events of a daily nature may have

proved more alarming in the long run than a temporary violent carnival. On February 6, 1914, to take but one day, the *Constitution* reported that Patrolman W. E. Englett was stabbed and slashed by "a drug crazed negro whom he had put under arrest" for drunk and disorderly conduct. Fighting Englett and his partner "like a caged animal," the "stalwart young negro" soon found aid in the presence of "hundreds of negro men and women" who "gathered at the scene, muttering threats and promising disturbance." The timely arrival of police reinforcements from headquarters "beat back the muttering crowd of blacks" and quelled an "incipient riot."[82] Earlier in the day, according to the same paper, Mr. and Mrs. J. Harrison encountered an unnamed "burly negro" on a trolley car who refused to remove his hand, which rested "several inches" into the area where the Harrisons sat. When the enraged Mr. Harrison determined to rebuke such insolence with his fists, the offending passenger responded in similar fashion, missing his target and cracking Mrs. Harrison in the jaw. Mr. Harrison pulled out his revolver, and though initially encumbered by the conductor and "a number of male passengers," managed to wound the fleeing passenger, who was immediately taken into police custody. The outraged white couple were "permitted to continue the trip."[83]

These two incidents, both occurring on the same day, illustrate the daily level of anxiety experienced on both sides of the color line. Frustrated that not even a hand could cross the barrier between white and black, and that city police targeted blacks for arrest, members of the black community struck back in ways that endangered their very lives. After his arrival in the Gate City in 1921, educator Benjamin E. Mays found himself constantly assaulted by reminders that "every Negro should be consistently subjected to humiliating injustices and insults calculated to destroy his self-respect, his pride, and his sense of manhood." Segregated elevators, trolley cars, restaurants, rest rooms, theaters, churches, building entrances, taxis, waiting rooms, tax return forms, bank teller windows, city parks, schools, ambulances, hospitals, courthouses—"*anything*," Mays concluded, "to be offensive."[84] For their part, whites like W. E. Englett and J. Harrison felt strapped astride a bellowing beast that threatened to tear them to pieces unless they struck first. As one leading white citizen noted after the 1906 race riot, "indiscriminate violence" could teach "a needed lesson" to "the child race among us."[85] More conciliatory efforts at racial healing, such as the work of the liberal Commission on Interracial Cooperation, sought to relieve this pressure, not by abolishing segregation and the logic that supported it, but by improving "conditions between the races *within the segregated system.*"[86] Blacks and whites eyed each other nervously in the Gate City, alternating violence and cautious reconciliation.

"Better Class of Negroes"

Events in the summer of 1910 did little to calm agitated nerves. On July 4 virtually every resident in the city found his or her attention riveted on a boxing match in Reno, Nevada. Normally a bout over two thousand miles away would not have generated much interest on the nation's birthday, when Atlantans could hear patriotic speeches, watch fireworks, attend a band concert, or watch a baseball game. The Reno contest, however, was more than just another fight. It pitted African American heavyweight boxer Jack Johnson against his white opponent Jim Jeffries in a battle that had quickly become billed as a test for white superiority.

In the days leading up to the event, the *Constitution* covered virtually every conceivable angle and boasted that it would have a telegrapher within inches of ringside, relaying each blow, each feint, and each shuffle. On the day of the fight the *Constitution* reported Johnson's rather startling proclamation: "I Am Jeffries' Master." The White Hope responded reassuringly that those of the "white race" who had been "looking to me to defend its athletic superiority" could "feel assured that I am fit to do my best."[87] Shortly before the opening bell, large crowds in Atlanta braved occasional downpours to gather outside the *Constitution*'s office and at scattered locations throughout the city to hear the results come in.

Johnson whipped Jeffries.

Across the country race riots and scuffles erupted as enraged whites clashed with jubilant blacks. In Atlanta, several thousand whites began milling around in the Five Points area soon after the fight result became widely known. It was a scene that vividly recalled the white mob that had congregated at the same spot four years earlier before launching a racial massacre. This time whites attempted to snatch a black bystander before mounted police intervened and dispersed the crowd. All day long, rumors of riot snaked their way to anxious white and black ears. By nightfall, however, it was clear that Atlanta had escaped another open racial conflagration.[88]

The day after the bout, the mayor and the chairman of the police commission introduced a resolution to the city council banning any theater from showing films of the fight. The council acted swiftly and decisively. "Some of us live on the outskirts of the city and we don't want these pictures to be shown in Atlanta," explained Councilman Ragsdale. "When we have riots, the police are called from our own neighborhoods to the center of the city to prevent these disturbances, consequently we are left without protection." The Atlanta Chamber of Commerce praised the city council's action, viewing "with alarm the further excitement of racial feeling on a large scale by the degrading exhibition of the fight in moving pictures."[89] By 1910 repression had become an almost instinctual response when whites confronted fissures in the city's racial hierarchies.

Yet more than control, whites wanted cooperation. "Let the supreme race—the race that ALWAYS WILL BE SUPREME—remember its accompanying moral obligations, and the state's portentous motto: WISDOM, JUSTICE, MODERATION!"[90] Though they were fully prepared to do so, whites did not want to kill and maim to sustain their power. They wanted a New South in which each race recognized its relative position and mutual obligations. "The negro is a child race," reasoned a member of the Chamber of Commerce. "We are a strong race, their guardians." The Negro "only knows how to do those things we teach him to do; it is our Christian duty to protect him."[91] Jack Johnson's victory had upset the paternalistic hierarchy, and whites scrambled to find evidence that black euphoria represented a temporary delirium rather than a deeply rooted hostility. Not surprisingly, the old slave spiritual was one of the first places they looked to reassure themselves.

Only weeks after blacks cheered Johnson's conquest, the white papers distracted the public from the fight's more ominous implications by running a series of excited articles about the inaugural Colored Music Festival to be held at the Auditorium-Armory on August 4. Sponsored by a number of the city's leading black businessmen and ministers, organizers designed the festival to mirror the opera season held for whites earlier in the year. The program bristled with talent, ranging from the Fisk Jubilee Singers to baritone and composer Harry T. Burleigh. Frederick Douglass's grandson Joseph, a widely respected violinist, was an object of particularly intense interest. The festival's proceeds would benefit the outreach work of Reverend Henry Hugh Proctor's First Congregational Church, one of the city's most widely respected black churches. Proctor and other festival officials sent invitations to the governor, members of the state legislature, local clergy, and the mayor, and they set aside general seating for white patrons "separate from the others and in no way in contact with the main body of the Auditorium."[92] One of the city's largest music stores promised to sell tickets so that white patrons would not have to tramp through Atlanta's black neighborhoods to secure them.[93]

Proctor drew white support for his festival by cleverly touching the raw nerve Johnson's victory had irritated. In a veiled reference to the nationwide jubilation in black communities over Johnson's recent triumph, Reverend Proctor explained that "the always imitative negro too often attains notoriety by following whatever bad examples may be set for him." Whites who attended the festival would see that "there is another class that is eager to follow the good and not [the] bad in striving for the better things of life."[94] The *Constitution* took the bait eagerly, contrasting the festival's "better class of negroes" with "the prize fight element represented by Johnson at Reno."[95] The editor considered the festival's organizers "constructive and redeeming," embodying "the hope of the entire race." Compare them, he asked readers, with Johnson's partisans, who were "of the jungle, malignant, brutal" and possessed "such seeds of discord as quench hope and development in their germinal stages." The conclusion was obvious and reassuring. "There would no longer be any race problem, nor further cause for antagonism and racial animosity if the whole race were inspired by the standard so well represented by its better element."[96] The editor, along with countless whites who flocked to the auditorium, found in the Colored Music Festival a hopeful sign that no Jack Johnsons strutted down Atlanta's avenues or sat in Proctor's pews. If music indeed soothed the savage breast, whites could think of no more propitious time to employ its mystical power.

"A Great Solvent of Racial Antipathies"

The praise and attention of the city's "leading white men and women" no doubt pleased the festival's organizers.[97] For once, so it seemed, the press covered black achievement with the same avidity it normally reserved for chronicling the latest "outrage." Yet for all their efforts to calm Atlanta's white citizens, the Colored Music Festival's organizers did not overlook the black community it served. After an anxious July of racial antagonism and even embarrassment, upper- and middle-

Clarence Cameron White, one of the most accomplished violinists of the early twentieth century, performed at the 1913 Colored Music Festival. Courtesy of the Clarence Cameron White Photograph Collection, Photographs and Prints Division, Schomburg Center for Research in Black Culture, The New York Public Library, Astor, Lenox and Tilden Foundations.

class black Atlantans could look forward to an event that demonstrated the "culture, beauty and refinement of the race."[98] Reminiscent of opera week hyperbole, the city's African American paper declared unequivocally that the festival would be "the greatest musical entertainment in the history of the South."[99] And, just as when opera came to town, visitors steamed into the train depot from all over the state, seated next to South Carolinians, Alabamians, Mississippians, Floridians, and Tennesseans equally eager to attend the festival. Even the indignity of the station's "colored" waiting room through which they passed could hardly dampen their excitement as they and their hosts made a beeline for the black-owned shops on Auburn Avenue, choosing clothes, hats, shoes, and jewelry appropriate to the upcoming occasion. Parties lent a festive atmosphere and provided the stately leisure necessary to properly display the accoutrements of respectability. The auditorium glittered with fashion and crackled with excitement. The program included a full slate of talented artists who offered works by black composers who were intent on injecting an African American sensibility into their work and who were on the cutting edge of American musical creativity. Altogether, the Colored Music Festival was an immensely satisfying display of race pride and achievement.

Try though they might, however, members of the audience could not ignore Jim Crow's glowering presence. The festival's organizers and the event's mainly black spectators keenly understood that the performers were not the only ones whites in the balcony had come to watch. Consequently, the festival took on enormous symbolic importance, and blacks used the event to strike back at their crumbling political, social, and economic power. The organizers challenged white theories that blacks swung precariously between childhood innocence and jungle savagery, they challenged the notion that blacks had contributed nothing to the nation's cultural life, and they challenged whites to rise to the level of interracial civility that the festival modeled. Finally, and perhaps most significantly, blacks used the festival to make whites live out the logical implication of segregation. If the New South were to be "separate but equal," blacks must control their own lives and their own destiny.

The Colored Music Festival never attacked Jim Crow head on with fiery rhetoric. Instead, its board took a conciliatory approach, believing, as the treasurer wrote, that by "promoting good feeling between the races," the event would be "a great solvent of racial antipathies."[100] None of the organizers or performers openly stated that they staged the concert in large part because whites prohibited them from attending the annual opera week. Rather than returning the snub, upper-class blacks magnanimously requested whites to attend the festival. Nor did they force those whites who accepted the invitation to sit in integrated sections. The festival's board made it clear that the one thousand seats reserved for whites were, as the *Journal* delicately noted, "on the Gilmer street side, so that entrance and exit may be convenient."[101] In fact, the board reserved the auditorium's entire balcony so that whites did not even have to sit on the same floor as blacks. From the outset, the festival tempered blacks' frustration with the city's rigid racial hierarchies by embracing the limits of dissent.

Though the Colored Music Festival seemed to endorse segregation's most revered pieties, it nevertheless sought to undermine the racist logic that gave Jim Crow its legal and cultural justification. From the outset, the festival forced whites to acknowledge that a significant portion of the city's black population was responsible, refined, and capable. In so doing they challenged whites to recognize what the editor of the black newspaper called "our pride and racial integrity."[102] In addition, black intellectuals, artists, social workers, and educators insisted that whites recognize them as equal partners in any solution to the "race problem." They made it clear that the New South's future, a topic that intoxicated the city's boosters, depended on respect and cooperation, rather than condescension and violence.

No one worked harder to make the festival an instrument of constructive racial politics than the event's treasurer, Reverend Henry Hugh Proctor. Though he held only a nominal post on the festival's board, both races regarded him as its moving spirit and prime spokesman. In 1911, for instance, the city's black paper called the event "Dr. Proctor's entertainment," and in the following year the *Constitution* labeled him "a leading spirit in the festival."[103] A popular advocate for black uplift, a friend and admirer of Booker T. Washington and W. E. B. Du Bois, and a man keenly attuned to what he called the South's "baffling racial atmosphere,"[104] Proctor had secured his reputation among whites as a trustworthy "race leader" through his efforts to calm the city following the 1906 riot.[105] Born in Tennessee in 1868, Proctor attended Fisk University and then Yale, from which he received a bachelor of divinity degree. At age twenty-six he arrived in Atlanta to shepherd the First Congregational Church. Before long, he had fashioned the church into one of the South's most prominent social service congregations. Visited by two presidents, the First Congregational Church was a showcase for the city's wealthiest black families and their efforts to "uplift the race" with missions and a regimen of physical, mental, cultural, and religious programs.[106] The festival, which benefited the church's institutional outreach, was yet another of Proctor's attempts to appeal to moderate whites and to give blacks breathing room in the constricting atmosphere of Jim Crow Atlanta.

Music had long interested Proctor. At Yale, his senior thesis examined the theology of the spirituals. Like others working in the field of black folk music, he argued that these "religious songs are indicative of [the Negro's] real character." In them he found "a tenacious grasp of the fundamental and central truths of Christianity," which he considered one of the unmistakably original qualities "of mind and heart of the Negro people." He admired "the entire absence of the spirit of revenge in these songs," declaring that "there cannot be found in them a single trace of ill will!" Yet the spirituals were not simply a tool to discern the religious sentiments of a bygone people. They could serve as a moral compass to a freed population facing bitter hostility. "Coming generations will read

Reverend Henry Hugh Proctor. Photo by T. E. Askew Photography. Courtesy of the Amistad Research Center at Tulane University, New Orleans, Louisiana.

with admiring wonder of this oppressed people," he predicted, "who so forcibly remind one of Him who was oppressed, yet humbled himself and opened not his mouth."[107] Without gall and without vengeance, the New Negroes moved forward from slavery asking only fair treatment and equal opportunity. Their ultimate hope lay within themselves. If all blacks did not share Proctor's admiration of steadfast calm in the face of racial horror, he clearly saw in it a viable strategy for survival in a Jim Crow age. Proctor believed that by demonstrating their own qualities of leadership in a conciliatory manner, blacks could force whites to recognize the nobility of blacks who had unjustly suffered through slavery and postemancipation degradation. The spirituals were ample testimony. Thus, for Proctor as for many other blacks and whites, music was an allegory of the race.

Proctor put the allegory on stage in a 1912 pageant entitled "Up to Freedom," which he wrote specifically for the Colored Music Festival. Inspired by a pageant he had seen the previous year at London's Crystal Palace, as well as by the growing rage for historical pageantry in America, he determined that the race's past and future was best told through its music.[108] Designed, as the *Constitution* put it, to display the history of blacks "upward from cannibalism through slavery to freedom and education," the pageant was three acts long and divided into nine scenes.[109] The first act, "Paganism," depicted an African village, slaves huddled on the African coast awaiting transport, and a "Dutch slave ship on the seas." The second act portrayed a slave market, a "plantation with cabins," and a battle scene from the Civil War. The final act, "Freedom," took place in a home, a school, and a church.[110] Each scene had music "appropriate to the circumstance."[111] In the section on slavery, for instance, the performers sang camp meeting songs, while during the scenes at school the stage rang with college songs. Through music Proctor believed that he could gain an audience for an interpretation of history that made black people figures of animation. The pageant showed blacks moving through space and time, dynamically pursuing their own destiny. Though aided by whites at critical points, blacks had in the past and must continue to guide the destiny of their race themselves, using their own native genius. Each race must bear its own burdens and "work out its own salvation," Proctor wrote in his 1925 autobiography. "The colored people must work out their own problem, under the guidance of their own leaders, and in cooperation with the better elements of the white American." No race, he concluded, "has ever solved the problem of another."[112] Thus, the Colored Music Festival challenged whites to recognize the balance required in "separate but equal" by granting blacks the space to pursue their own unique destiny. If modestly put, it was nevertheless a startling demand.

"The Commendation of the White People Present"

To a large degree Proctor hit his mark. On numerous occasions whites expressed astonishment that "the most interesting thing of all was the neat and orderly appearance of the audience" or that "the audience itself was a revelation."[113] The *Georgian* marveled in 1911 that "the entire program was surprisingly excellent."[114] In an age of racial massacre and reflexive bigotry, such concessions seemed to signal a breach in racial thinking through which Proctor hoped to advance. Moreover, by pursuing the city's white residents he forced them to acknowledge their own responsibilities in ensuring racial harmony. "The association is particularly anxious to have the white people attend this Festival," Proctor informed the *Journal* in 1912. "It is a source of great encouragement to the colored people that the Southern white people take pride in the progress they are making." Atlanta's "leading whites" could hardly ignore such a blatant call for assistance, and they eagerly cast their lot with what the *Journal* labeled the "enlightened and progressive members of the colored race."[115] As the *Constitution* observed, whites had a moral obligation to encourage "what is best and soundest in the colored people," and so it joined the other city papers in urging whites to buy tickets for their servants and even for themselves.[116] In 1910 the *Constitution* explained that the Colored Music Festival was "well worthy of the encouragement and patronage, not only of the race in whose behalf and by which it is given, but also of all those white people who are interested in encouraging good citizenship among all classes, white and black."[117] Calling upon the paternalism that whites used to deflect Jim Crow's critics, Proctor reminded whites to temper repression with sympathy.

Prodded by such calls to conscience, "leading whites" praised and attended the Colored Music Festival with enthusiasm. In 1910 the mayor, members of the city council, and nearly one thousand other white citizens attended the inaugural festival, and they applauded energetically.[118] "Program Was Well Chosen, and Pleased White People as Well as Negroes," read the next day's headline in the *Constitution*. The article reported that "some of the most enthusiastic applause was from the white

people."[119] In 1911 the *Constitution* tried to drum up support by reminding readers that at last year's festival whites had been "loud in their
praise of the merit of the music rendered and of the fine decorum
manifested throughout."[120] That year soprano Anita Patti Brown set off
a round of vocal pyrotechnics that was met with a barrage of hand-
clapping "as vociferous in the balcony set apart for white persons as
from the body of the Auditorium."[121] In 1912 the *Constitution* noted
Harry Burleigh's name on the program and confirmed that he "was
rated high by the white musical critics of this city."[122] By constantly adding their approval, encouraging feelings of race pride, acknowledging
the talent of black performers, and applauding the audience and the
music with equal vigor, whites believed that they were fulfilling their
racial obligations. Proctor convinced them that their presence and support gave the event an added significance and pointed the way toward
racial reconciliation based on mutual interest rather than mutual fear.

At the same time Proctor demanded that whites recognize the ability
of blacks to improve themselves without the threat of white violence and
humiliation. Again, he succeeded. The papers were impressed by what
one called "a most gratifying expression . . . of the better element of
the negro race" and the optimistic signs "of a self-development on the
part of the leading element of colored citizenship."[123] In 1911 the *Constitution* commended the program for its "morally uplifting effect upon
the colored race as a whole." By "turn[ing] their minds away from that
which is low to that which is high," the festival benefited not only the
black working class but also "the entire city," because it would "prove an
antidote to the wave of crime that has been sweeping over the colored
people in this city."[124] Two years later the same paper argued that "there
are so many places in this city that tend to drag down the colored servant
that any occasion of this type that is elevating in its nature proves a benefit to the whole city life, which is so much affected by the character of its
servants."[125] In short, aside from admitting their own responsibilities in
the city's "race problem," whites acknowledged that blacks themselves
had the vision, the leadership, and the intellect required to help make
a New South.

Evidence for the skeptic could be found not only in the festival itself,
but also in the charity into whose coffers its proceeds poured: Proctor's First Congregational Church. Located on prestigious Auburn Avenue, the church counted members, according to one paper, who were
"known as quiet, property-owning, home-loving people," among whom

The First Congregational Church received a number of distinguished white visitors who were impressed and relieved by Proctor's commitment to "uplifting the race." Here church dignitaries welcome William Howard Taft. Photo by T. E. Askew Photography. Courtesy of the Amistad Research Center at Tulane University, New Orleans, Louisiana.

it was "the rarest thing that an arrest is made." Moreover, its "quiet and orderly" weekly services did not differ "from the ordinary church among any people." Members expressed no "excess of emotionalism" and insisted on "a high standard of living" and "a rigid form of discipline." This fact alone inspired confidence, but the commitment of Reverend Proctor and his congregants to the "uplift" of lower-class blacks inspired universal acclaim. Missions on the rough-and-tumble of Decatur Street, cooking classes, a library, a kindergarten, sewing instruction, and similar services demonstrated that "this type of church life among the colored people makes for the peace and prosperity of both races."[126] Proctor and his colleagues thus promoted their festival as more than simply an annual indulgence for the rich. They used it to encourage sympathy among whites and "thrift, love of law and greater efficiency among the negroes of this community."[127] With these aims it is not surprising that whites greeted the event enthusiastically. In 1910 the *Constitution* asserted that "the festival was one in which the negroes may well take pride and which received the commendation of the white people present."[128]

"Plantation Melodies Will Be Big Feature"

The ideological concessions Proctor and his colleagues wrung from the festival's white audience were not negligible, but ultimately they failed to improve the city's racial climate for African Americans. The festival lured white audiences by relying on music, a universally acclaimed aspect of black culture, but also the most encrusted with stereotypes. Proctor, like so many others, argued that the spirituals looked forward, not backward, and that they laid the foundation for racial uplift. Whites, however, heard the same tunes as evidence of a shared nostalgia for "the faithful black 'mammy'" and all of her "darkey" associates.[129] Rather than significantly challenging Jim Crow, the festival reassured whites that blacks endorsed segregation as a reasonable solution to the New South's frayed racial atmosphere. Genuinely afraid despite the extent of their own power, whites clung to the spirituals as the "balm in Gilead" that would make their wounded spirits whole.

Whites in the audience took almost no note of the festival's artists unless they sang spirituals. Indeed, most whites attended solely to hear the spirituals sung by blacks. "Negro Music Festival Will Be Gala Event; Plantation Melodies Will Be Big Feature," one headline promised; another announced, "Melodies of Old South Are Heard at Negro Festival."[130] Every year the Fisk Jubilee Singers, renowned for their interpretations of old plantation songs, received a tumultuous greeting. After the inaugural festival in 1910 the *Georgian* noted cursorily that other artists on the program had performed "a few renditions of classical music, strikingly well done and holding deserved attention," but that the Fisk Jubilee Singers were the "triumph of the evening. . . . They might have sung the harmonies of the immortal composers with credit, but what they did sing were the good old cornfield melodies that the South loves so well."[131] Their appeal proved so alluring that the next year an entire evening was devoted to their renditions, and one paper reported that "repeated calls" had "forced them to sing again and again."[132] Following the concert the *Constitution* cooed that the Fisk Jubilee Singers "displayed the utmost good sense and artistic taste in choosing . . . characteristic negro melodies."[133] To whites it mattered little that black composers and artists had radically transformed the spirituals into modern

Negro Music Festival Will Be Gala Event;
Plantation Melodies Will Be Big Feature

*Headline demonstrating that although the Colored Music Festival showcased musicians
of great artistic breadth, whites were most interested in hearing "plantation melodies."
From left to right: J. W. Work, director of the chorus; Anita Patti Brown, soprano;
R. W. Hayes, tenor; and Henry Hugh Proctor. From* Atlanta Constitution, *
June 29, 1913. Courtesy of the Atlanta History Center.*

works of art. By programming the spirituals, the Fisk Jubilee Singers delighted white patrons by seemingly indicating a mutual enthusiasm for
the world that gave the spirituals their birth.

Whites, of course, could not ignore that significant portions of the
festival's program were given over to works in the classical repertoire.
The papers proved tolerant but discomfited. The *Constitution* considered
that although blacks might perform classical music with some skill, the
"peculiar quality in the negro voice" found "its best and truest expression in the folksongs of the race."[134] It was best, therefore, if blacks performed their "own" music. When Harry Burleigh sang an aria from *Il
Pagliacci*, a journalist conceded that the rendition was fine, but that he
"could not help regretting that simpler songs had not been chosen."[135]
Two years later Anita Patti Brown sang several opera arias, "but in her
encores she tastefully chose some of the older and simpler songs, and
'Suwannee River' in dialect, captured her hearers."[136] The *Journal* applauded several other performers who were "perhaps as well-trained as
the average grand opera singer," but who sensibly "did not select any
classic pieces, but sang the simple, plaintive melodies in which the negro
voice excels."[137] Yet each year the musicians insisted on mingling renowned German composers with anonymous Old South slaves. White
patrons fully grasped the radical implication for racial hierarchies. If

"Gretchen am Spinnrade" and "Wade in the Water" differed little in their artistic magnitude, and if Harry Burleigh's baritone matched in quality Enrico Caruso's tenor, then the logic of white superiority began to teeter in discomforting ways. By removing the spirituals from this political context, whites salvaged their commitment to racial hierarchies and saved themselves the chore of fundamentally rethinking their racialist assumptions.

In a similar fashion, whites deliberately blinded themselves to the more provocative implications of Proctor's pageant "Up to Freedom." Swept away by "costumes of barbaric glory" and the sentimental beauty of "Way Down on the Suwanee River" sung by a soloist "in costume on the auction block," whites drowned their introspection and self-doubt with rivers of delight.[138] The pageant seemed to celebrate the advances blacks had made, not in the face of white bigotry and repression, but in the face of their own ignorance and paganism. After all, the pageant's title, "Up to Freedom," implied initial degradation and a gradual evolution in which whites could take a measure of credit and relief. The pageant reassured white southerners that, far from repressive as critics charged, slavery and its modern Jim Crow equivalent had aided blacks by providing them guidance and support at critical points. During slavery, opined one writer in the *Journal*, "southern negroes learned to imitate the manners and customs of their white masters" and "forgot practically all of their barbaric customs."[139] Whites thus used the festival to celebrate the black middle and upper classes for their commitment to racial uplift and harmony, while simultaneously crediting themselves with every admirable trait that blacks might aspire to. The festival was undoubtedly a promising start, but whites insisted that blacks had far to go before they could participate in the making of a New South.

Rather than a decisive strike for racial liberation, as Proctor, his colleagues, and the performers intended, the Colored Music Festival merely reaffirmed the white commitment to maintaining rigid racial hierarchies. Dislodging that commitment would have required far greater moral and physical power than even as forceful a man as Proctor could have mustered. Yet, ironically, his success and his failure were intertwined. For whites to recognize and to act upon Jim Crow's logical inconsistencies that the festival illuminated might severely dent the whole segregationist enterprise. Whites, aware of this, retreated into a misty-eyed condescension toward what the *Constitution* called "this even yet half-child race."[140] In every performer and in every performance whites looked for blacks to endorse their own marginalization. Their scrutiny seemed rewarded at the 1912 festival when, during a performance of "Suwannee River," "an old negro, bent with years of toil, only a bit of gray hair in the 'place where the wool ought to grow,' leaning on a hickory cane cut direct from the forest, rose to hobble out. He was met by one of the ushers, a well-dressed youth, who directed him to the nearest exit, and then took his arm to assist him. To the strains of a true southern song, the new south, as the white people chose to view it, gave attention to the old."[141]

The festival's "appreciated incident" deftly underscored the degree to which Atlanta's middle- and upper-class whites felt hostage to the transformations they supposedly directed. With a black population largely beyond their control, whites could only encourage those like the "well-dressed youth" who paid homage to the generation still wearing slavery's psychological shackles. At the same time, the incident demonstrated the impossible task Proctor set for himself, his festival, and the spirituals of his ancestors. Uncertain how best to negotiate the increasingly hostile waters in which they found themselves, blacks like Proctor sought safe harbor in a culture that appealed to both races. Here whites encouraged blacks to drop anchor and to bob forever on the tranquil waters of their past, while blacks rolled out charts and scanned the horizon for alternative routes. Whites and blacks agreed that the spirituals meant something important for the future of both races and for the making of a New South, but their precise meaning remained open to vigorous debate.

Within a few short years after its inauguration in 1910, the festival's popularity dwindled. American entry into a world war forced the event's cancellation in 1918, and when in the following year Proctor left Atlanta for a church in Brooklyn, the festival died. In part, Proctor's organizational skills and his support within the white community were necessary to making the festival a success, and his departure left a hole in the festival board's structure.[142] Yet the event had begun to atrophy even before Proctor left. In part, he lost the support of the city's black paper, whose editor rebuked the entertainment as an excuse for the minister to aggrandize himself and to enrich the church's coffers.[143] The upshot was that the *Independent* completely ignored the Colored Music Festival from 1913 on, refusing to carry any advertisements, announcements, or stories that mentioned it. Moreover, the festival competed with an ever-widening array of entertainments in black Atlanta. The city's emergence as a major center for blues, as well as the availability of excellent recitals and guest appearances at the black universities, provided blacks of all classes a variety of musical offerings from which to choose.[144] For their part, whites contented themselves with opera week and the dozens of Music Club recitals and Atlanta Symphony Orchestra concerts. Those anxious to taste black music and life were far more likely to join the "slumming craze," finding refuge in nightclub shows featuring black jazz bands.[145] In the 1920s the renowned 81 Theater began hosting "Midnight Frolics" in which whites could attend on Friday nights assured that they would encounter no blacks except those on stage.[146] In short, competing diversions offered as much if not more excitement than what seemed like a black version of opera week.

Yet the festival's decline also rested within a broader Jim Crow context. As it became increasingly clear that the event would have little influence in modifying the color line's growing severity, Proctor's approach, both in Atlanta and more widely, lost much of its credibility within the black community.[147] Proctor's claim that "the black man and the white man" were "complementary opposites, not irreconcilable opponents" seemed insupportable when measured against the weight of lynched bodies, local segregation statutes, and daily insults.[148] The condescending attitude of the white papers must have grated on many black concertgoers and made it clear that their efforts to use music as a cudgel against prejudice was doomed. No matter how carefully blacks phrased their objections to Jim Crow, whites seemed determined to misconstrue them as endorsement.

Concessions from the white community, while permitting some room for black maneuver, allowed whites to turn back assaults on racial hierarchies. They gladly granted the connections between African American culture and its historical antecedents in Africa. Yet rather than challenging the segregationist rationale, these observations seemed to confirm it, because they provided room for building "separate but equal" cultures.[149] A white Kentuckian summarized this argument with remarkable clarity. "Side by side with the too highly civilized white race," she wrote in 1923,

> the negro must in time have eliminated from him all his God-given best instincts and so fail utterly. For are they not already ashamed in our large cities of their old African music? They should be taught that slavery, with its occasional abuses, was simply a valuable training

in their evolution from savagery, and not look upon their bondage with shame. For during that period these songs could develop *because* the negro was kept in such perfect segregation, and his instincts and talents had full play.[150]

Whites believed that the patterns of racial control they established in the making of their New South were magnanimous gestures extended to preserve the integrity of a weaker race. When the alternative was bloody coercion, Proctor understood that his Colored Music Festival could only push so far.

The Georgia Old-Time
Fiddling Contest

In February 1914 thousands of city residents crammed into the civic Auditorium-Armory to enjoy what was quickly becoming one of Atlanta's most celebrated musical events: the Georgia Old-Time Fiddlers' Convention. The first convention, held during three days in April just the year before, had been so wildly successful that the fiddlers had formed themselves into the Georgia Fiddlers' Association and vowed to have another convention the following year "as soon as spring plowing is done."[1] They found themselves back in Atlanta before the end of February, determined to crown anew the best fiddler in the state. For days leading up to the event, the city's white working class had flooded Shepard's Cigar Store on the corner of North Pryor Street and Edgewood Avenue to snag tickets. The heavy scent of tobacco mingled with light-hearted banter as friends chided one another about their hometown fiddling heroes. Many of those anticipating the fiddling contest had only recently moved to Atlanta from any one of the numberless surrounding poverty-stricken rural counties and now worked in one of three big cotton mills.

When the fiddlers rosined their bows for the first show on Wednesday night, the audience numbered close to three thousand. In just over two months the auditorium's stage would be outfitted with a golden curtain to suit the needs of the New York Metropolitan Opera, but tonight the contrast could not be more striking. On the stage sat fifty fiddlers, some smoking corncob pipes, others with beards worthy of the patriarchs. When at last the master of ceremonies, old Deacon Ludwig from up Cobb County way, called on the first fiddler to commence, the audience went wild. Things never really simmered down after that. People jigged in the aisles and others in the audience cheered, hollered, and guffawed as the fiddlers played "Devil's Dream," "Soap Suds over the Fence," and "Billy in the Low Ground."

Though mill villagers made up the bulk of the raucous crowd, they had no small competition from a large cross section of Atlanta's most prominent bankers, lawyers, judges, entrepreneurs, newspaper editors, and politicians whose presence alone caused comment and whose behavior caused outright astonishment. For those unable to trust their eyes, the papers confirmed on the following day that Colonel William Lawson Peel—the "father of opera in Atlanta" and "one of the South's leading bankers"—had grown so excited under the spell of "Devil in the Wheat Patch" and "Wild Hog in the Cane Brake" that he had jubilantly cried out "Swing your corners! Ladies change!" What's more, his friend Judge Russell responded with "forward and back and down the center!" Numerous other wealthy businessmen had been observed laughing uproariously. Only Mayor Woodward seemed to have retained a semblance of dignity, but the next day it was reported that when he got to work he was still smiling and patting his feet.[2]

Beginning in 1913 and continuing until the Great Depression, the annual old-time fiddling contest beguiled a broad cross section of white Atlantans "from Peachtree to Tinker's alley."[3] Every year the fiddlers could expect to look out on a sea of faces numbering in the thousands. People went because the Georgia Old-Time Fiddlers' Convention was fun—a lot of fun. "It is not exactly like a wampus chorus, neither does it resemble a shebang," one newswriter kidded. "It's more like a cross between a thing-a-ma-jig and a doo-lollie."[4] In the days leading up to the contest, the city's three daily newspapers ran infectious stories about the "fiddlin' fools" streaming into the city toting ancient instruments, freshly ground cornmeal, and an ample supply of moonshine. To make their stories even more colorful, journalists ignored the range of Georgia cities, towns, and farms the contestants called home, writing instead as if every fiddler in the state had just stumbled into Atlanta by way of some Appalachian mountain pass. The press was clear: if you were not

Oldtime Fiddlers Go Hog Wild and Saw The Catgut Until it Screams for Aid

One of the colorful headlines that contributed to the fiddling contest's hilarity. From left to right: *Millard Fillmore Hall; "Moonshiner" Bob Young; Florence Hall, age eleven; "Shorty" Harper; and "Red-Necked" Jim Lawson. From* Atlanta Journal, *February 19, 1914. Courtesy of the Atlanta History Center.*

from the mountains, you were not a fiddler. The old-timey habits, queer speech, and faithful hound dogs of these rustics left readers chuckling, and colorful headlines added to the hilarity: "Big Crowd at Auditorium Rocks with Mirth as Tantalizin' Tunes Move Staid Atlantans,"[5] "Just Couldn't Make Their Feet Behave Last Night When the Fiddlers Got to Playing at the Auditorium,"[6] "Oldtime Fiddlers Go Hog Wild and Saw the Catgut until It Screams for Aid."[7] Not only was the contest fun, but also tickets were inexpensive. William Peel shelled out over $40.00 for his opera box, but when the fiddlers came to town the same seats cost him just $1.40. Civil War veterans got in for free.

Cheap tickets and good times by themselves, however, cannot explain why old-time fiddling attracted Atlantans who otherwise spent much of their lives frantically demonstrating their urbane respectability. William Peel adored Caruso, but no one had ever seen this New South titan dance a hornpipe during an aria or holler with jubilation when Caruso stepped onto the stage. Indeed, even crinkling the program at an inopportune moment, let alone jigging in the aisles, would have devastated the image he cultivated with such care. Nor is nostalgia for a vanishing rural world sufficient to account for the sudden interest in mountain life and music. Appalachian men and women had streamed into Atlanta since Reconstruction, but until the early twentieth century their lives, their habits, and their music had never attracted much attention among the city's wealthy residents. In fact, for most nineteenth-century Americans the mountain people evinced shock and disgust. "One can hardly believe," stammered an 1885 *New York Times* editorial, "that any part of the United States is cursed with people so lawless and degraded."[8] Bewitching melodies, colorful characters, cornball humor, and wistful nostalgia were not alone sufficient to dismantle such entrenched and widely shared prejudice.

The fiddling contest emerged at a time when white Atlantans, and white Americans generally, began reconsidering their low opinion of Appalachian people. Numerous missionaries, educators, folklorists, and sociologists wrote articles and books for popular consumption that downplayed, discounted, and overturned the backward characteristics that had offended earlier observers.[9] "The tales of awful degradation in the mountains may be true," one educator counseled, "but such tales are not to be taken as representative."[10] Though the new wave of writings necessarily stressed many different angles, virtually every account agreed that because the region's inhabitants still lived in conditions reminiscent of the nation's pioneer era, "Appalachian America may be useful as furnishing a fixed point which enables us to measure the progress of the moving world!"[11] The region's partisans revealed, however, that the "the moving world" captivated them more than the "fixed point." Hence, the reassessment of Appalachia took place largely because urban white Americans at the turn of the twentieth century wished to evaluate the dramatic changes they had witnessed and had wrought.

New South Atlantans were certainly not immune to Appalachia's charms. No less than grand opera and Old South spirituals, Appalachian fiddle tunes helped codify a number of anxieties swirling around the heads and hearts of those white men making a New South. They were particularly enchanted by assurances from the region's experts that the mountaineers preserved the genes, culture, and values of the nation's Anglo-Saxon pioneers. Writers repeatedly stressed that Appalachia's peaks had sheltered the region's inhabitants from the mongrel hordes of immigrants and blacks purportedly bent on America's moral and genetic destruction. Naturally, claims to Anglo-Saxon racial purity resonated in a city moving rapidly from Civil War ruin to Jim Crow metropolis. In fact, it was only two months after the inaugural fiddlers' contest in 1913 that the city council passed its first major residential segregation law.[12] The fiddlers helped demonstrate how to extend such Jim Crow restrictions far beyond merely separating white and black bodies. They showed what "separate but equal" *cultures* might look like. For upper-class white Atlantans so utterly immersed in a biracial society, the fiddlers provided guidance on how to craft the white half of this "separate but equal" culture.

Of course, New South Atlantans knew very well that the challenge to Anglo-Saxon superiority did not merely stem from African Americans. Pushing their city and their region to industrialize, they understood that the emergence of a white working underclass presented the prospect of devastating intraracial conflict. If not properly attended to, such fissures might cause white supremacy to self-destruct and send the New South into a tailspin of class animosities and racial warfare. New South Atlantans did not have to look far to find disconcerting confirmation of their dark portents. Though opera week might astound northern financiers, the event clearly did little to impress Atlanta's poor. The fiddling contest quickly revealed just how little working-class whites admired the swells and grandees who made opera their habit. In addition, the city's cotton mill workers who called Appalachia home began showing distinct signs of unrest. When workers at the Fulton Bag Mills went on strike in 1915, few failed to note that one of the fiddling contest's most popular participants joined the walkout. The Georgia Old-Time Fiddling Contest, therefore, offered wealthy New South men an opportunity to repair fences. They added their voices to the national chorus praising Appalachia, and they repeatedly and publicly paid obeisance to the simple virtues of backwoods fiddlers.

Wealthy Atlantans found much to praise, but the men credited with the making of a New South were especially impressed with the serenity of mountain home life. Again, Appalachia's partisans set the tone by writing admiringly of scrappy mountain men whose lives revolved around feuding, drinking, and solitary wanderings amid the ferocious bounties of untamed nature. Mountain wives, readers were told, admired such conduct, nay, even encouraged it. For their own part, they wasted no time on literary clubs, music soirees, or suffragists meetings, but instead devoted themselves to maintaining house and kin. Compared to the gender confusion reigning in a city that relied on women to work and that steadily stole masculine virility, the mountains seemed a perfect idyll. The fiddlers helped reassert male prerogatives and to counteract the effects of too much luxury and too much opera.

The Gate City's New South visionaries who so avidly followed the fiddling contests and so liberally supported Georgia's mountain educators found in Appalachia a solution to the demons of racial degeneracy, class warfare, and "feminization." Appalachia's champions understood and ably tapped into these fears because they shared them. Consequently, they situated Appalachia—or, more accurately, their *idea* of Appalachia—at the headwaters of a powerful stream of cultural anxieties. Their Appalachia remained blissfully unmoved by the forces rushing their America toward the very precipice of ruin. No blacks cast lecherous glances at their highland lasses, no workers muttered grim socialist rantings, and no women shouted shrewish condemnations at their highlanders. Such portraits of the region required myopic vision, but because desire marked their Appalachia, Atlantans ignored such incongruities.[13] Their intense longing to present the region as an alternative to modern, polyglot, urban America led them to piece together scraps of selective evidence, and to argue that the mountaineers preserved the genes, culture, and values of the nation's early white settlers. For the self-appointed architects of a New South, the mountains offered a tantalizing supply of physical and ideological raw materials. Though admittedly a little rough around the edges, Georgia's old-time fiddlers and their annual contest nevertheless displayed the power of these raw materials in action.

"The Inextinguishable Excellence of the Anglo-Saxon Race"

Few people did more to rescue the mountaineer from public opprobrium than the president of Berea College, William Goodell Frost.[14] From his base in the Kentucky foothills he poured forth a torrent of speeches and essays that turned popular prejudices on their head. Frost met Appalachia's critics head-on, demonstrating that the vices outsiders found so offensive were the logical outcome of physical isolation. "Their condition has come about through natural causes," he cautioned, "so that we cannot blame the people as negligent nor despise them as inferior."[15] Frost explained that the English and Scottish settlers who had surged into the mountains following Daniel Boone's lead soon found themselves imprisoned in their new arcadia. Inadequate roads and forbidding terrain severed contact between the mountain pioneers and the rest of America, so that at the dawn of the twentieth century they lived "in the conditions of the colonial times."[16] This geographic fact accounted for the social conditions that repulsed so many genteel Americans.

Frost urged "a little sympathy and patience." He reminded readers that the mountain people were not some alien race, but, rather, a "creditable" mixture of Scottish and English blood. Indeed, making largely correct assumptions about his audience, he declared the mountain people "our contemporary ancestors."[17] The clever turn of phrase relied on the unstated assumption that the collective "our" he addressed was white. For those who missed the subtlety, Frost made the point boldly. Of the "interesting facts regarding this region," he wrote in 1912, "first, it is inhabited by white people." In fact, of all the arrows in his rhetorical quiver, none hit the mark with greater force than his contention that mountain people and mountain culture preserved a uniquely pure strain of whiteness. He portrayed the region as so void of racial and ethnic variety that he resented even using the common term "mountain whites." After all, he asked, did anyone ever say "Boston whites"? He dismissed both phrases as redundant. Moreover, he feared that it might cause outsiders to confuse "mountain whites" with "poor whites," a comparison Frost thought slandered the highlanders. Slavery, he explained, had "deterred" the South's poor whites "from honest exertion," and they had consequently built up "a false pride" that ill-served them.[18] Brought into a racially destructive partnership with black southerners, they barely registered on the scales of whiteness. The Appalachian mountaineer, on the other hand, had never fallen prey to the peculiar institution's allure and had therefore escaped its corrosive effects. The more recent plague of immigrants who now flooded the nation had likewise found themselves unwelcome in Appalachia's coves and hollers. With "no foreign immigration," Frost beamed, the mountains contained "a larger proportion of 'Sons' and 'Daughters' of the Revolution than any other part of our country."[19] In one mountain county he had counted a mere "46 Negroes" and "not one single inhabitant who is 'foreign born'!"[20] In short, to wrest sympathy from a skeptical public, William Frost worked the one advantage he could exploit. Understanding the widespread fear among native white Americans for their very survival, he constructed an Appalachia in which white people not only dominated, they did so without contest. Put simply, he bet Appalachia's redemption on race. Under the title "Race Conservation," an article in Berea College's newsletter noted that Frost and his colleagues at the school saw it as their mission to "conserve the fine racial traits surviving in our southern mountains."[21]

William Frost was hardly the voice of one crying in the wilderness. Rather, he led a swelling chorus of missionaries, writers, and educators who shared his messianic zeal and matched his journalistic output. Deftly tapping into nativist fears gaining momentum throughout the nation, they predicated an appreciation for mountain people on the uniquely pure white racial stock of the residents.[22] "There is no other ethnic group in America," one writer observed, "so unmixed as these mountaineers and so segregated from all others."[23] Echoing the strain, another influential and widely read study claimed that the rugged terrain had prevented "all intermixture," sparing the region "the tide of foreign immigrants" lately storming the country. Moreover, the mountains were "as free from [Negroes] as northern Vermont." As a result they harbored "the purest Anglo-Saxon stock in all the United States."[24] Their racial isolation was so complete, another observer marveled, "that they have no race consciousness at all."[25] Though Appalachia's champions could never quite settle on an appropriate ethnographic label to describe these alabaster mountaineers, they nevertheless shared a mutual admiration for a fairy-tale world where whites so dominated that they were no longer conscious of being white at all.[26]

Folklorists brought their own covered dish to the love feast, arguing that the Appalachian peoples' claim to whiteness did not rest solely on dusty genealogies and pioneer migration patterns.[27] Folklore—the habits, beliefs, and practices of mountain people—proved an even more reliable indication of racial purity. "Blood tells," assured one Presbyterian missionary. "Were all the southern highlanders to deny their ancestry, thousands of voices would yet cry out of their physical, intellectual, and religious characteristics."[28] A Berea College professor concurred, stating that "wherever they go and whatever they do, the fundamental traits of the Mountain People crop out, as do those of Scots, Jews, or any other race."[29] Thus, even if the precise mixture of Saxon, Anglo, and Celtic blood could not be accurately measured, the continued survival of songs, sayings, and customs firmly linked the mountaineers to those western Europeans credited as the acme of white civilization.

Although admittedly crude by modern standards, the region's folklore had the virtue of linking whites to their racial roots. A ruthless environment had, of course, kept Appalachian people in a primitive state, but the tribulations of mountain life had tested and proved the white race's mettle. Whereas mountain life might have sunk other races into barbarism, the southern highlanders had merely idled. Even the crudest of them had "social codes and moral standards which are most strictly observed." "Herein," William Frost explained, "the 'mountain white' shows his genus."[30] Popular Kentucky novelist John Fox Jr. whole-heartedly agreed, writing, "to my mind there is but one strain of blood that could have stood that ordeal quite so well, and that comes from the sturdy Scotch-Irish."[31] The genetic and folkloric evidence stacked up to an inescapable conclusion: "the inextinguishable excellence of the Anglo-Saxon race."[32] When taken as a whole, then, Appalachia became a living museum honoring white people. The exhibits of racial purity preserved in the highlands allayed fears that immigration and race friction would in the near future pulverize native Anglo-Saxons into obscurity and irrelevance.

"The Folk-Songs and Folk-Ballads of the Race"

Appalachia's music—especially its ballad tradition—became an object of admiring scrutiny because, as one writer glowed, it was "a 'proof patent' of good British descent."[33] With almost no effort, folk song prospectors unearthed literally hundreds of ballads whose origins lay in the misty backwaters of British history. On the one hand, it was a stunning discovery. Singers kept alive ballads that were centuries old, and the strange dramas of magic, murder, ghosts, and castles lent an overwhelming romanticism to mountain life. On the other hand, the ballads surprised no one. Determined as they were to see mountain people as idling versions of early white settlers, ballad collectors merely reaffirmed their already set conviction in the region's racial purity.

Despite an early smattering of enthusiasm for ballad scholarship in America, it took a Harvard philologist's five-volume study, entitled *English and Scottish Popular Ballads*, to jump-start widespread national interest. Published between 1882 and 1898, Francis James Child's monumental collection brought together 305 ballad texts, as well as their countless variants, that he had gathered from ancient manuscripts and old books. As a literary scholar, Child's main interest lay in how these fifteenth- to nineteenth-century texts traced the development of English literature and language.[34] Yet when missionaries and educators in the early twentieth century reported that southern mountaineers still sang many of these ancient ballads, the discovery lit a fire in the nation's imagination and sent folk song enthusiasts scurrying to the mountains, pencil and paper in hand. Suddenly, wrote one folk song collector in *Harper's*, "the romance of a primitive people . . . became heightened and enhanced with a new and richer note."[35] Between 1905 and 1915 ballad collectors systematized their work by founding seven statewide folklore societies that held regular meetings and published occasional pamphlets.[36] Scholars in those states with claims to the Appalachian region worked with special vigor, publishing their findings in the *Journal of American Folklore* as well as in more popular journals and eventually in an impressive set of book-length studies.[37]

Far from challenging reigning assumptions about mountain Anglo-Saxons, their work gave these opinions even greater weight. The almost exclusive emphasis on collecting what became known as the "Child ballads" led folk song scholars to downplay, ignore, or dismiss vital aspects of mountain music. They completely avoided Appalachian blacks, and even among whites most collectors viewed religious songs and hymns, railroad songs, topical ballads, instrumental music (aside from "Elizabethan" dulcimers), or anything that smacked of post–Elizabethan England as so much chaff they had to sift through before getting what they were really after. In 1913 the U.S. Department of Education joined with a University of Virginia English professor in sending out a nationwide circular asking teachers and professors to gather Child ballads from students and neighbors but did not encourage collecting anything else.[38] Following a ballad hunt through the Kentucky hills, William Aspenwall Bradley declared that the folk songs that mountaineers created about their own lives and histories were of "the crudest and coarsest texture" and did not "possess any particular poetic quality or appeal."[39] Another enthusiast, Josephine McGill, agreed. She tossed aside contemporary ballads, complaining that "the narratives are usually tedious, the metres cheap and the tunes tawdry."[40] Yet her admiration knew no bounds when singers produced a "Barbara Allen" or a "Fair Margaret and Sweet William." The mountain people commanded attention with their music only so long as the tunes confirmed their links to the Anglo-Saxon past.[41]

Assumptions about balladry and race purity received an endorsement from one of Europe's most respected folk song scholars. Cecil Sharp had spent years collecting folk songs in England's rural hamlets

One of the many folklorists who scoured the mountains to collect and preserve old ballads, at left, records a fiddler. From the Annabel Morris Buchanan Papers, Southern Historical Collection, Wilson Library, University of North Carolina at Chapel Hill.

and villages, but his work made him increasingly pessimistic about the future of the ancient ballads that he loved. It was not simply the death of a noble repertoire that troubled him. The disappearance of "Lord Randall," "The Twa Sisters," "Bonnie James Campbell," and their musical kin marked the dissolution of British identity and race pride. He asserted that the "national type is always to be found in its purest, as well as in its most stable and permanent form, in the folk-arts of a nation," but if there were no folk arts, there could be no "national type."[42] Sharp blamed immigration and modernization for destroying Anglo-Saxon folk traditions, and he recommended that public schools teach "the folk-songs and folk-ballads of the race" so that children could "as quickly as possible enter into their racial inheritance."[43] The songs would, he explained, "arouse that love of country and pride of race, the absence of which we now deplore."[44] In Sharp's mind, racial identity and folk music were inseparable, and his commitment to the ballads was both personal and patriotic.

News that the British ballads still hung on the lips of Appalachian mountaineers thrilled the despondent Englishman. Between 1916 and 1918 Sharp spent forty-six weeks collecting ballads in the West Virginia, Tennessee, Kentucky, Virginia, and North Carolina mountains, publishing his findings in 1917 under the title *English Folk Songs from the Southern Appalachians*.[45] Despite new vistas and new acquaintances, his grand Appalachian adventure did nothing to modify his earlier opinions. Like his American predecessors, he possessed a single-minded determination to find only ballads and he attributed their remarkable survival to racial purity. Sharp admired what he called the mountaineers's "racial heritage," evident in the "language, wisdom, manners, and the many graces of life that are theirs." These "racial attributes" had been "gradually acquired and accumulated in past centuries and handed down generation by generation," kept alive because no outside influences disturbed the racial tranquility.[46] It was a precious heritage, indeed. Without this reservoir of racial purity, whites on either side of the Atlantic might drift from their racial moorings and float aimlessly to their destruction.

A number of other Appalachian folk song enthusiasts shared Sharp's racial theories, and their work reinforced his conclusions. Olive Dame Campbell, whose initial spadework in North Carolina and Georgia had attracted Sharp's attention, observed that ballads served as "an unconscious record of the character, temper and development of our race."[47] A professor at Berea College argued that the old ballads could survive only where there was "homogeneousness . . . in racial or tribal feeling"— a sentiment echoed by South Carolina folk song scholar Reed Smith, who said that a prime reason medieval ballads survived in the mountains was because of Appalachia's "racial purity and integrity."[48] Though hardly the first to conflate folk culture and race, Sharp's impeccable scholarly credentials lent authority to claims of Anglo-Saxon purity and inspired others to emulate his work. Countless scholars battled fatigue and brambles to find a singer whose ancient ballads could reaffirm the survival of whiteness.

As Sharp and his collaborators make clear, the ballads possessed a significance far beyond the thrill of their discovery. They were, one folklorist commented, "more than the mountaineers's own legacy."[49] They belonged to the Anglo-Saxon race, and their remarkable survival gave hope that Anglo-Saxons would not, after all, be overwhelmed by the racial foes arrayed against them. Severe privations had tested the ballads and their singers, but the resulting blemishes and crudities could not mask the underlying strength of Anglo-Saxon culture. The ballads renewed confidence in the capacity of the Anglo-Saxon race to defend its innate superiority and reassured self-proclaimed members of the Anglo-Saxon tribe that their race deserved and could defend its privileged place in America.

"The Man's Prerogative to Order and Be Obeyed"

The ballad collectors joined a number of both southern and northern whites who found in Appalachia a salve for their fears that immigrants and blacks threatened to overwhelm "real simon-pure Americans."[50] Yet they tempered their excitement with anxiety, worrying that a generation of Anglo-Saxons gone racially flabby amid their urban comforts did not retain sufficient vigor to implement the lessons mountain people taught. Of particular concern was the state of white masculinity. Without question, the cities that men built and the fineries that adorned them reflected credit on their power and manhood. Yet perhaps they had made a Faustian bargain, exchanging virility for comfort. As Theodore Roosevelt cautioned in 1896, "it is an admirable thing to possess refinement and cultivation, but the price is too dear if they must be paid for at the cost of the rugged fighting qualities which make a man able to do a man's work in the world."[51] Surly immigrants, abrasive suffragists, and impudent blacks all pointed to the failure of America's Anglo-Saxon men to live up to the standards set by their "contemporary ancestors."[52]

Roosevelt, Owen Wister, Frederic Remington, and many lesser lights formed a cavalcade of men in the late nineteenth century who ventured into the "wild" West to resuscitate their racial birthright before returning East to take their place at the head of society. Their early-twentieth-century counterparts, however, could not follow their dusty trail. The buffalo were gone, the Indians were safely corralled, and the empty acreage was fenced. The frontier, they were told, was closed. Yet the problems that propelled their forebears to western ranges remained. Where, then, could the neurasthenic patient encounter the "strenuous life" so essential to those who held society's reigns? Appalachia.

For those restless about the state of modern masculinity, the contrast between highland and urban men could hardly have been more telling. City men lay waste their powers in a daily round of getting and spending. Their luxurious surroundings sapped them of their independence, resourcefulness, and virility. The mountain man, on the other hand, inhabited "the land of do without."[53] Unlike his citified cousins, William Frost explained, the mountaineer could not "step to the telephone and by a supernatural fiat 'order' whatever may be desired." Instead, he had to travel "into the forest and find or fashion some rude substitute."[54] Should nature and ingenuity fail him, he simply went without. Whatever the outcome, the constant struggle for existence against a "remorseless environment" ensured that the mountain man had "nerves in this day of neurasthenia."[55] Rather than rearing back in horror at feuds, scraps, and brawls, Frost suggested that his readers should "take pride in the memory of the fighting ancestry that lies back of us." He noted pointedly that it was "seldom possible to supply virility where it is lacking."[56] For certain, another writer granted, the mountain man was a little crude, but that judgment used "a feminized modern standard" and neglected the "sterling qualities of manliness" that "our nation can ill afford to waste."[57] Emulating the "mixture of savagery and civility" that highland men kept alive would help them reclaim "the man's prerogative to order and be obeyed."[58]

Few saw greater redemptive possibilities in mountain virility than a forty-two-year-old St. Louis librarian, who, following a nervous collapse in 1904, scrambled to escape "the devil of business and everything that suggest[ed] it."[59] Like so many of his contemporaries, Horace Kephart longed for somewhere "back of beyond" to escape from the stultifying life of the modern city, which he considered "an abrupt and violent change from what the race has been bred to these many thousands of years."[60] Anxious to reclaim his racial fortitude, he forsook an allegedly happy marriage and a respectable career and disappeared into the North Carolina mountains. "Aye it was good to be alive, and to be far, far way from the broken bottles and old tin cans of civilization," he exclaimed.[61] He described and prescribed his experiences in two major books, *Our Southern Highlanders* (1913; revised 1922) and *Camping and Woodcraft* (1906; revised 1921), both of which established his reputation as a leading expert on Appalachia and backwoods life in general. Kephart used his writings to entice other men to follow his example and retreat, if only temporarily, from the modern world. "The best vacation an over-civilized man can have," he advised, "is to go where he can hunt, capture, and cook his own meat, erect his own shelter, [and] do his own chores."[62] The lessons learned in the mountains would make even more palpable the contrast between the "teeming millions" of modern city folks, "who can exist only in a state of mutual dependence and cultivation," and the highlanders, whose "warlike arts" had "subdued the beasts and savages, felled the forests and made our land habitable."[63] Only by testing themselves against such towering figures of masculinity could urban men claim to stand "man to man on a footing of equal manliness" with their contemporary ancestors.[64] Bringing those virtues to bear on the particular ills confronting urban men would enable them to revitalize the masculine, Anglo-Saxon virtues that city life worked daily to extinguish.

For all the admiring attention devoted to the region's "vigorous native manhood," its "charmingly simple womanhood" did not go unnoticed.[65] Just as city men differed from their highland kin, so did the modern woman diverge from her mountain sisters. While talk of a "New Woman" filled the popular press, detailing her fashions, attitudes, and amusements, the mountain woman longed for none of these changes.[66] William Frost's wife noted that "wherever one goes in the world at large, the restless woman is prominent." She conceded that from the "public woman, active in promoting 'causes,'" and from the "social climber" certainly "some good will come out." But she could not help contrasting their restless activity with the peaceful mothering, cooking, and mending that occupied Appalachian women. "She has found her task," she reported. "She is patiently doing it and taking with resignation the hardships involved."[67] If anything, then, the New Woman was a cultural indictment of urban men, symptomatic of their declining patriarchal authority. The harsh circumstances of mountain life and the irreproachable masculinity of mountain men had never given women the time or inclination to complain about their lives.

Horace Kephart, whose admiration of mountain masculinity knew no bounds, marveled at the efficiency and tranquility of mountain home life. A wife in the highlands "would scarce respect her husband if he did not lord it over her and cast upon her the menial tasks." This did not make a woman powerless by any means. Indeed, within the home's confines she was queen of her "kingdom," and "her man seldom meddles with its administration." As was natural to all women, Kephart observed, now and then she got "fussy over trifles," but men quietly chalked it up as "natural to the weaker vessel." Yet any woman crossing the line into shrewishness received "a curt 'Shet up!'" Though such lordly conduct might earn a city man a lifetime of vicious enmity, a mountain wife

"She Knows No Other Lot." This photo of a quiescent Appalachian mother appeared in Horace Kephart's Our Southern Highlanders. *Courtesy of Western Carolina University.*

took it neither as "discourtesy" nor as "disregard for her finer nature." After all, Kephart asserted, "it is 'manners' for a woman to drudge and obey." Unlike her agitated city cousins, the mountain woman wanted it no other way. She "seldom complains of her lot."[68]

Her "lot" included far more than uncomplaining obedience to patriarchal authority, of course. Writers also pointed out the "blessings of copious motherhood" that so many highland women enjoyed.[69] Indeed, the frequent praise for the "mountain Madonna" was intended as no slander to the highlanders' fierce Protestantism, but, rather, as a tribute to the maternal ambitions every woman had harbored since girlhood.[70] Never before did the survival of that motherly instinct portend greater dividends than during the turn of the century, when the popular press began expounding on the dangers of "race suicide." In days crowded with club work, political organizing, and social obligations, it appeared that city women left no time to spare for motherhood. Consequently, one scholar lamented, the "birth rate among the most valuable classes" had decreased disastrously while "the birth rate of the lower classes" remained "unaffected."[71] People who considered themselves the racial heart and soul of the nation suddenly confronted a squalling pack of immigrant children with the promise of plenty more to come. Their own precious darlings were too few to reply. Mountain women, however, gladly gave their wombs to the cause, churning out children at a pleasingly rapid and prolific pace. Noting the large size of Appalachian families, one native-turned-scholar beamed, "race suicide is not a question for the sociologist to struggle with in the mountains of Kentucky."[72]

Summarizing the role women played in mountain society, a Berea College professor wrote that "she works a sixteen-hour day, scarcely gets one baby weaned before the next arrives, and for wages gets a home, the blessings of copious motherhood, and the privilege of wearing her husband's name on her tombstone."[73] The implication of this and similar tributes was always that whereas women of this caliber were as common as pokeweed in Appalachia, their equals were rare as rubies outside the region. Rather than bickering endlessly over the extent of their rights, frittering away days in idle social engagements, and rejecting the honors of motherhood, a highland lass contented herself with weaving, spinning, suckling babes, and singing "songs of old sorrows and dire dooms."[74] Accepting her "lot" with quietude, she offered an example of womanhood no less endearing than the rough-and-tumble masculinity of her husband. Perhaps, the region's defenders concluded, it would be wise to inquire whether the highlanders "may have something to contribute to our own brand-new civilization—something which of old we cherished but now perhaps have forgotten."[75] Racial purity and old-fashioned gender roles, they repeatedly suggested, were highland virtues that promised to remedy countless urban cares and confusions.

"They Are Our Own Race and Blood"

William Goodell Frost and his contemporaries painted a portrait of Appalachia that deftly enchanted their audience. They peopled an achingly beautiful canvas with quaint, noble souls whose lives offered precious glimpses into a simpler America now fast receding into time's misty shroud. Yet the quaint habits and queer speech they described should not confine the mountain folk to simply "an antiquarian inter-

est." Though Frost considered "the possible value of such a population
. . . sufficiently evident," he did not let the reader ponder unaided precisely what he envisioned. He called the region "one of God's grand
divisions," a force of enormous power held in reserve by nature. "When
once enlightened" with the knowledge accumulated since the Revolution, the mountain people could take their place in the front ranks of
a nation battling the "nervous prostration" of modern life.[76] With ban-
ners flying and drums pounding, these "patriotic, capable people, with
unjaded nerves and red blood" stood poised to "reenforce the vigor of
the nation."[77] What a "priceless possession," thrilled one of Frost's colleagues, this "unspoiled heritage of the American people."[78] Sending
money to educate mountain youths at Berea College, then, did not just
reward the donor's conscience. The philanthropist invested in a mighty
host of truly "native born" Americans whose strength of character and
purity of blood could turn back the clock on a nation fracturing along
every conceivable line. Appalachia's appeal lay only partly in yearning
for a simpler past. Even more compelling than nostalgia was the certainty that mountain people and mountain culture had a critical role
to play in the nation's future. God had "stored away in this great mountain reservoir of humanity five millions of sturdy race," wrote missionary
Samuel Tyndale Wilson, "to be a source of refreshment and strength
to the nation in trying days to come." In uplifting Appalachia, donors
invested in the future of the Anglo-Saxon race.[79]

Beginning in the early twentieth century the mountains bristled with
schools designed to meet the peculiar needs of the Appalachian people.
Cicero and Aristotle had no part in the curriculum of a Georgia school
where awestruck students "looked on with admiration and respect" as
several Atlanta women demonstrated making fudge and divinity candy.[80]
Other youths devoted themselves with equal fervor to learning Morris
dances, Child ballads, and whittling techniques to please school admin-
istrators bent on reviving such temporarily "forgotten" bits of Anglo-
Saxon mountain heritage. Just as Booker T. Washington emphasized
industrial education as fit training for ambitious blacks, so, too, did
mountain school workers emphasize agricultural labor and "folk crafts"
as the proper ken of the mountain people.[81]

Educational missionaries canvassing for mountain schools had one
enormous advantage over Booker T. Washington, however; their students were white.[82] "Let us not forget," Horace Kephart intoned, "that
these highlanders are blood of our blood and bone of our bone."[83] A

number of Appalachia's partisans impatiently pushed other educational charities aside, insisting that egregious philanthropic imbalances had for too long denied needy whites their proper due. John Fox Jr. railed that the mountain people "surely deserve as much consideration from the nation as the negroes" and the "heathen." After all, the highlanders were "easy to uplift" and their values were an "important offset to the Old World outcasts" who flooded America's shores and to "the negroes, for whom we have done, and are doing so much."[84] In perhaps the most strident call to action, mountain educator Martha Sawyer Gielow sounded the "call of the race." Americans had shamefully ignored the last remains of "an unadulterated Anglo-Saxon race," allowing the "very 'seed corn' of American patriotism" to lay fallow. "This is the twentieth century," she thundered, "they are our own race and blood."[85] Whites had shouldered the burden of uplifting every downtrodden and indigent race the world over. In the name of humanity, one writer observed with disgust, well-meaning patrons had contributed to the proliferation of "moral perverts, mental defectives and hereditary cripples."[86] It was high time that needy whites received their due, and there was no more promising place to start than in Appalachia.

"The Sturdiest Element in Georgia"

White Atlantans were not deaf to such stirring appeals. City residents took a personal interest in what the *Journal* called "the purest strain of sturdy colonists who sought freedom on this side of the ocean" and what the *Constitution* labeled "the sturdiest element in Georgia— the pure, original Anglo-Saxon stock."[87] An early chronicler of the city's history claimed that it was precisely these rugged individualists, not aristocratic slaveowners, who first settled and "laid the foundation of Atlanta's prosperity."[88] The Baptist Home Mission Board, which looked after those who remained in the mountains, made Atlanta its headquarters, and within the span of seven years "noble Georgians" helped found three schools for the state's mountain children: Martha Berry's school in Rome (1902), Rabun Gap Industrial School (1908), and Tallulah Falls Industrial School (1909).[89]

In canvassing the Gate City for funds, these schools and missions recycled the same persuasive rhetoric that Frost, Kephart, Sharp, and dozens of other writers employed. They placed a heavy emphasis on the region's Anglo-Saxon purity. Andrew Ritchie, the director of the

Rabun Gap Industrial School, told an Atlanta audience that the time had come to "face the fact that the negro problem is not the only race problem with which the south has to deal." Echoing Martha Sawyer Gielow's "call of the race," Ritchie explained that Appalachia still possessed "the greatest national reserve of original American stock on the continent." Money wisely spent on educating mountain children was a patriotic investment, he explained. As a "natural reservoir" of genetic purity, the mountain's "virile stock" stood ready to "reinforce the best elements of American civilization."[90] Four years later an article in the *Constitution* lauded the mountain work done by the Baptist Home Mission Board. The paper described the objects of Baptist philanthropy as "the purest blooded Anglo-Saxon descent of any people now to be found in America." In fact, it continued by way of illustration, "there are whole counties in this district in which not a single foreigner or negro can be found." The article detailed the "primitive" pioneer conditions in which the mountaineers lived and how consequently they had "retained their pristine simplicity and quaintness." Like it or not, however, times were changing, and each Atlantan must decide for himself or herself whether "these mountain people become flotsam on the surging waves of our material progress" or would "be equipped to go into the great stream for its own purification and the public welfare."[91] Once again, the plea touched a sensitive nerve.

Few jolted their audience with greater efficacy than Mrs. S. B. C. Morgan, who headed the State Association for the Education of Georgia Mountaineers. In 1911 she pointedly reminded an Atlanta audience that in the last forty-one years white Georgians had spent almost ten million dollars on the "education of the negro," and that equally vast sums had been deducted from Gate City bank accounts to "educate and Christianize alien peoples." While scribbling checks for schools in Alabama and for missions in China, however, Atlantans had robbed the highlanders "of their birthright of education." She pleaded with the city's women to forgo "a dessert from your table, a theater ticket, a plume for your hat" and forward the savings to the southern hills. She audaciously scolded the men of the city. "The north has done more to force upon the south the equality of the negro than the south has done by educational or industrial [training] to maintain the supremacy of the white race." What were Atlanta's businessmen going to do about it? she asked. "It is the call of the blood," she cried out. "We are our brothers' keeper."[92] Morgan's call did not land on deaf ears. Like their counterparts across the nation, white Atlantans found in highland education assurances that white values, white institutions, and white blood would not disappear under the hurricane of social change unleashed by their New South.

"Like a Magazine Story Moonshiner"

A large number of white Atlantans responded to Morgan's "drastic appeal" not merely by emptying their wallets, but by flocking to the Georgia Old-Time Fiddlers' Convention.[93] Begun in 1913 at a high tide of interest in Appalachia, the annual contest tapped into an already keen nationwide fascination with the region's inhabitants and culture. The stereotypes William Frost, Horace Kephart, and other writers so lovingly crafted proved invaluable for Atlanta journalists as they described the fiddlers and their music. A fiddler had only to bring bow and string together to evoke dozens of ready-made images. Newspaper articles frequently referred to the region's "pure and persistent Anglo-Saxon lineage" and to reservoirs "of the purest Anglo-Saxon stock on the continent," directly borrowing from the rhetoric more seasoned observers of mountain life had already developed.[94] Some journalists dusted off log cabins and moonshine stills to make their portraits all the more compelling. In listening to "Shorty" Harper, for instance, one reporter heard "raindrops dripping from the eaves of some lone cabin on the hill"; other fiddlers called forth the "the little old cabin . . . and the sour mash still bubbling out its distilled sunshine just over the brow of the hill, where the revenoors haven't looked yet."[95] Fiddling instantaneously evoked a rich palette of Appalachian imagery already provided by the region's most prominent interpreters.

While the music brought to life powerful images of cabins and moonshine, the fiddlers themselves fairly disappeared into a thicket of familiar and comforting generalizations. "If ever a man looked like a magazine story moonshiner, Mr. Young is that individual,"[96] reported the *Constitution* in 1913; the *Journal* praised him for bringing "his fiddle in a flour sack, just as a fiddle should be carried."[97] Fiddlin' John Carson became a convention favorite through the years for conforming so closely to what his Atlanta audience had come to expect of the highlander. In 1914 the *Constitution* reported that Carson, accompanied by "the sorriest looking hound that every bayed the moon," had just arrived in Atlanta "with many pauses to view the sights of the city."[98] Journalists ignored or did not care that Carson had been working at an Atlanta cotton mill for fourteen years; his middle- and upper-class

Participants in the fiddling contest outside the Atlanta Auditorium. Courtesy of the John Edwards Memorial Foundation, Southern Folklife Collection, Wilson Library, University of North Carolina at Chapel Hill.

audience wanted to believe that he lived in Fannin County, one of the state's remotest mountain areas.[99] While listeners imagined that Carson's "backwoods tunes" were "echoing against the mountains," in fact it was the newspaper articles that reverberated with recycled images crafted by the region's experts.[100]

The fiddlers themselves helped perpetuate the stereotypes. Though many of them did have rural roots, and some even hailed from the mountains, to increase gate receipts they conformed to public expectations about what fiddlers should do and say. In 1919, for instance, the organizers bedecked the stage with "an old-time log cabin, a picket fence and several live chickens which roosted high and refused to be awakened even when several of the fiddlers broke into an impromptu clog dance."[101] At another convention fiddlers refreshed themselves from a "water bucket" complete with a "crook-handled gourd." To prevent contestants from monopolizing the stage, the master of ceremonies "yanked on the rope of a big farm bell" to stop them.[102] In 1916 the convention's master of ceremonies, who dubbed himself Alec Smart, wrote a letter from his home in "Damascus, RFD No. 1, Ga." to the "Gentlemen of the fiddlers Convention Committee," which naturally turned up at the *Constitution*'s office as well. Full of whimsical grammatical and spelling errors and rustic wit, Smart's letter explained that at the current mo-

Gid Tanner, one of the contest audience's perennial favorites. Courtesy of the Southern Folklife Collection, Wilson Library, University of North Carolina at Chapel Hill.

ment he and his family "were all very buisy killing hogs and making our sausage meet," but that he was delighted to receive an "invertation" to host this year's contest. "My neace Marthy-Ann Dugglas and Deacon Hadocks Middle Gal Sally-Lou aire sure both comeing and so will Squire Bradler if the rumitiz don't get his Fiddlin arm," Smart continued.[103] By doing little to upset popular expectations and by skillfully using newspaper publicity, the contest's organizers brought in substantial revenues and kept the event going for years.

In reality, however, some fiddlers chafed at how they had to present themselves and their music. Clayton McMichen, for instance, was hardly the country rube or backwoods hilltopper of magazine story legend. His father ran a sawmill in Atlanta and was known for fiddling Viennese waltzes at society balls in his hometown of Dallas, Georgia. From him, McMichen learned to appreciate a wide array of styles, and he picked up techniques from radio, records, jazz combos, acquaintances, and chance encounters with members of the Metropolitan Opera Orchestra, as well as by listening to the Atlanta Symphony. In later years he expressed irritation with the stock mountain character he was forced to play, complaining that he was "serious about fiddling" and that he had no interest in "foolishness."[104] Playing a fiddle did not require "getting bent over, get[ting] your hair all mussed up, and losing your shoes, and all that stuff," but he recognized that without the buffoonery members of the audience would "sit on their hands." He expressed similar exasperation with the antics of Alec Smart. McMichen recalled that Smart was "supposed to be funny, but I didn't think he was very funny." The audience was, he concluded, "just like a bunch of children. They're the easiest people on earth to fool."[105] He went along with the act because it brought in more money. "When they quit talking about you, either good or bad, is when you're hurting."[106] By 1921 McMichen joined a growing contingent of fiddlers who lost patience with how often relatively mediocre but immensely popular fiddlers like Gid Tanner and John Carson beat their more talented competition, and they worked to organize a rival fiddling contest.[107] Apparently nothing came of their efforts. The press presented this fissure as a predictable example of mountain feuding, and they ignored the serious internal conflict within the organization about the proper direction and presentation of old-time fiddle music. In short, perceptions of the music and contestants at the annual Georgia Old-Time Fiddlers' Contest rested on a solid foundation of Appalachian writing and opinion.

"One of These Here Violinists"

In 1906 one sociologist observed that "in Atlanta the 'cracker' has come into his own."[108] Not least among these "crackers" were the highlanders, who enjoyed an exalted reputation among upper-crust white Atlantans for the same reasons that they found a sympathetic audience elsewhere in the nation. Yet Appalachian people and culture had a special appeal to the city's New South visionaries. The mountain people were, after all, "our *Southern* highlanders."[109] Although the Appalachian mountain range stretches into the Northeast, writers consistently ignored anyone who lived north of West Virginia.[110] Atlantans, then, inflated regional pride by claiming for the South all the accolades bestowed on their highland cousins, and by claiming that southerners were the last true Americans. "The South has the purest American white population of any section of the country," beamed one Atlanta businessman, "and the Southern white man is the real American of today."[111] The mountaineer proved an excellent ambassador, easing white Atlanta into the nation's cultural mainstream without sacrificing a distinctive southern identity.[112]

In the South, the highlander offered a different hope. The specter of populism, which in the 1890s temporarily brought together the mutual economic grievances of black and white farmers, still haunted New South boosters. Though populism died a certain death in the 1890s, and though its aging patriarch vehemently repudiated his earlier interracial apostasy, upper-class Atlantans still eyed the specter of cross-racial politics with alarm. Disfranchisement, segregation, and fiery rhetoric helped unite whites on one side of the color line, and to these effective means of racial unity the mountaineer made his own contribution. The "Southern Problem" was not blacks, wrote Methodist missionary Samuel H. Thompson, but whites.[113] In his 1910 study *The Highlanders of the South*, Thompson chastised upper-class whites for turning their backs on the needy of their race. "It may seem strange," he wrote,

> but certainly in no part of the world are there people of a common ancestry who are at such extremes of poverty and wealth, of ignorance and learning, of uncouthness and culture, as you find in the Southern States. The tragedy of the whole thing is that the man of wealth, learning, and culture has so little sympathy with his brother of poverty, ignorance, and uncouthness. . . . It is perhaps not too much to say that in many instances he would sooner help the negro than a poor white man.

If America wished to remain "a white man's country . . . for untold generations," he explained, its white citizens needed to pull together on the same side of the rope.[114]

White Atlantans had a unique opportunity to test Thompson's theory,

Fiddlin' John Carson and his dog about to be evicted from their mill housing during the Fulton Bag and Cotton Mills strike, 1914. Courtesy of the Tracy W. O'Neal Photographic Collection, Special Collections Department, Pullen Library, Georgia State University.

but the results were not promising. When racial violence pitted white and black citizens against one another in the 1906 riot, the *Constitution* observed with distress that the "mob-spirit" was "BECOMING CARELESS OF RACE AND COLOR." In fact, a "white mob" had begun "FIRING INTO A GROUP OF WHITE MILITIAMEN AND WHITE CITIZENS." Such incidents, the paper concluded, "cannot but strike apprehension into the mind of the conservative thinker."[115] These apprehensions seemed further confirmed in October 1913, six months after the first Georgia Old-Time Fiddlers' Convention, when labor troubles erupted at the Fulton Bag and Cotton Mills. Workers launched a full-scale strike the following spring. Fiddlin' John Carson, like many of his fellow strikers, found himself on the street when management evicted him from his mill housing.

Like comparable southern mills, Fulton Bag was stocked with its complement of white Appalachian refugees who had, it was widely assumed, "cheerfully left the mountain farm and distillery to take places in cotton mills or other factories." Once there, the newly relocated highlanders supposedly discovered that there was "no difference in blood or heritage between them and the mill managers and mill owners" and hence no cause for ugly disputes between capital and labor.[116] Reporting on conditions in the North Carolina mountains, one journalist assured readers that, in a nation "overrun with a mob of strikers born in other lands," the highlanders could be counted on to resist the blandishments of labor organizers.[117] The Fulton Bag strike and the threat of more widespread union activity in the Gate City quickly exposed the fallacy of these rosy pronouncements. As the strike lurched on, Atlanta boosters alternately wrung their hands over the influx of labor agitators and chastised the mill's owner Jacob Elsas for destroying what his critics insisted had always been the city's cordial relations between labor and management.[118] If the "Atlanta Spirit" meant "*co-operation*" among white citizens, such class fissures needed attention.[119]

The fiddling contest, however, spelled yet more trouble. In their "annual 'rural grand opera,'"[120] the fiddlers and their homespun skits burlesqued the pomposity of Atlanta's leading citizens, centering their humor on the city's infatuation with highbrow classical music. Acts like the Simp Phony Orchestry, the Hoe Cake Orchestra, and the Lick Skillet Orchestra took aim at the traveling orchestras and civic symphonies that serenaded the city's elite and did little to indicate that opera week had inspired awe among white working-class Atlantans. In 1914 three idle contestants took their campaign to the very heart of the enemy. Tramping down to the Kimball House hotel, they found the house orchestra entertaining guests with a variety of light classical selections. Rosining their bows and tuning their instruments, the fiddlers launched a salvo of "Billy in the Lowground," sending their stuffy competitors into ignominious retreat.[121] It was perhaps some of these same deflated orchestra members who were scornfully turned away from the 1919 fiddling competition when it was reported that "two or three Atlanta fiddlers — regular professional violinists who play by note and took lessons, and all that kind of thing" had applied to participate. Musical exclusiveness, the fiddlers insisted, could work both ways. Justifying the decision to bar "fancy fiddlers" from the competition, Fiddlin' John Carson explained that he and his compatriots had no interest listening to folks who "played a half-hour at a time and never struck a tune." He conceded that "they may go all right in grand opery, but they don't belong in a fiddling contest for the championship of Georgia."[122] No sir. The fiddlers did not seem disposed toward the social and cultural deference that classical music was designed to promote. Indeed, they resented it. Seeking to articulate the difference between a fiddler and "one of these here violinists," a contestant drawled that he reckoned "a violinist draws down about a thousand a night, or week or month, or whatever it is," while a fiddler "is lucky to get the neck of the chicken and what's left in the bottle after it's done been round the room."[123] In Atlanta, as in fiddling, all was not harmonious.

The city's newspapers seemed eager to pile on, flinging their own rhetorical grenades at Gate City sophisticates. At one contest the *Journal* promised that the fiddlers stood prepared to give the city "a thrill not surpassed by grand operas, virtuosos or temperamental artists of international repute."[124] The *Constitution* heartily agreed, telling readers that "grand opera coloratura sopranos . . . and all the rest of the 'high' stuff can't compare with a bunch of genuine Georgia fiddlers,"[125] while a writer for the *Georgian* snickered that the cow bell used to signal when the fiddler's time was up "would help in some other concerts."[126] Tired of the pomposity and pretension that always hung about the classical artist, journalists cooed their admiration for the rough-hewn fiddler and lashed out at snobs who scoffed at the state's backwoods musicians. Prominent classical violinists like Fritz Kreisler and Jan Kubelik came up short when measured against Georgia luminaries who brought with them fiddles "such as Kreisler never saw and Kubelik never dreamed of touching."[127] Gid Tanner was variously described as "a brawlie, homespun Kreisler" and as possessing "a vocal range which Caruso might envy."[128] That the fiddlers did not grasp the intricacies of musical theory or perform delectable morsels of aesthetic contemplation was to their credit and advantage. "Unhampered by technique" and scorning "all tricks of 'temperament' save those of homespun vigor and wistfulness" allowed them to cut through the thicket of affectation and "sense and express the spirit that is in all worth while music."[129] And though "no famous Italian name is to be found scrawled inside the brown belly of a Georgia fiddle," thus denying it an impeccable artistic lineage, the mountain fiddle claimed a naive simplicity that no violin could taint.[130]

During opera week the city's elite used music to insist on the superiority of rich over poor. The elaborate rituals, expensive accoutrements, and intensive intellectual training provided wealthy citizens an opportunity to flaunt their refinement and sophistication. Fiddlers, however, sneered at these displays. Fighting fire with fire, they also used music, though of a very different kind, to argue that posturing rather than merit lay behind the claims of wealthy Atlantans. The only difference between fiddlers and violinists was the authenticity of the one and the pretensions of the other. Fritz Kreisler and Jan Kubelik had nothing on Red Neck Jim Lawson and Fiddlin' John Carson, nor was their companionship welcome should they ever seek to take up "Polly Put the Kettle On." The fiddling contest thus fostered a tense mixture of humor and hostility that mocked and challenged the presumed superiority of elite culture. When coupled with distinct memories of Georgia populism and the pangs of labor discontent at the Fulton Bag Mill, the fiddling contest's hilarity had an edge that threatened to cut in either direction.

"My Own Kind of Folks"

Atlanta's New South elite was determined that it cut to its advantage. Though Fiddlin' John Carson might be summarily divested of job and home for joining the strike, when the Georgia Old-Time Fiddlers' Contest began he was the toast of the town. Prominent whites stumbled over themselves expressing their admiration for old-time fiddlers and the Anglo-Saxon culture they preserved. While they certainly enjoyed the entertainment, they also found the fiddling contest a perfect opportunity to deflect working-class resentment away from themselves by reminding white city residents of their common values and common heritage. For all the differences in wealth, they said, fiddlers and bank presidents were still country folk at heart, and thus class disparities should never impede white unity.[131]

From the first time that "staid business men jumped up and yelled, 'Whee!'" the press never failed to remark on the large number of important locals in the audience.[132] The crowd included not only some of the city's wealthiest individuals, but also the municipal organist, the mayor, and occasionally even the governor. Just two years into the convention the *Journal* noted that more than a smattering of "society folk" had "taken blocks of seats"; the next day the *Constitution* wrote that these socialites had been "just as riotous in their applause as any of the visitors from the mountains."[133] By 1916 opening night became known as "Society night," and the *Constitution* ran a list of box holders and their parties, just as it did when opera came to town.[134] The next morning readers marveled that "the boxes resembled a night at the opera save that the gowns were hardly so elaborate." "Fiddler's parties" became a regular feature of the weekend's entertainment, promising socialites "a unique diversion."[135] By 1918 it had "become the fashionable thing in Atlanta to be a first-nighter at the fiddlers' frolic," and by 1919 the fiddlers had earned a spot on the *Journal's* society page.[136] Judging "from the chatter around the clubs," the column announced, it was "expected that hundreds of the fashionable set will join in the festivities to the tune of 'Turkey in the Straw.'"[137] The papers made a special effort to mention wealthy patrons by name and to report their actions in detail.

While some rich folks merely watched, others joined in the fun. In 1914 they "yelled and cheered as the spirit moved and became part of the performance."[138] "It has frequently been observed that dignified citizens have experienced a peculiar twitching in their toes which has forced them to step out into the aisle and cut a pigeon wing or a double shuffle."[139] Even that bastion of respectability, the United Daughters of the Confederacy (UDC), let down its collective hair and sponsored the event for four of the convention's initial five years.[140] Other well-known Atlantans played prominent roles as contest judges. Between 1913 and 1919 two bankers, a city councilman, an engineer, the city clerk, and two judges bent their skills toward deciding the winner. In 1916 the president of the Georgia Chamber of Commerce, Charles J. Haden, was invited to "lend official sanction and approval to the convention," and he responded by speaking "eloquently of fiddlers and fiddling."[141] After Haden finished, the audience cheered wildly for Judge Dick (not Richard) Russell, of the State Court of Appeals, who told the crowd that he was happy to be among "my own kind of folks, Georgia crackers and fiddlers."[142] Two years earlier, while in a similar position, he had taken the opportunity to congratulate "'you well-dressed folks' on 'not forgetting your raising.'"[143] Russell stayed on to decide the fiddling champion with help from Judge Andy (not Andrew) Calhoun of the city criminal court.

That Dick Russell, a distinguished jurist, newspaper editor, politician, and New South entrepreneur, who could read Caesar's *Commentaries* in Latin by age seven, knew Greek and spoke fluent French, and whose maternal and paternal ancestors were fixtures of South Carolina's aristocracy, could call himself a "cracker" reveals more than simply his political ambitions.[144] Russell imagined himself a "cracker" born and bred because to him the term bound white people together in ways that transcended class. The Atlanta papers eagerly took up Russell's call to white assembly. Just scratch the gilt surface of the city's most famous residents, they said, and you quickly strike Georgia clay. "There are many who go to grand opera and enjoy it who were raised on the 'hog and hominy' of country fiddling," a columnist wrote in 1914. There were even some in the city, he continued, who could recall the now-distinguished judge Andy Calhoun as a young man "at a country breakdown . . . with but one 'gallus' on his judicial back, jump in the middle of the room and cut the pigeon wing, to the delicious strains of 'Possum up the Gum Stump, Coonie in the Hollow.'"[145] An article in the *Constitution* similarly observed that the fiddling contest would feature many old tunes "your granddaddies used to dance to in the country cabins before they moved to Atlanta and got rich in real estate and turned to grand opera lovers."[146] Back of their wealth, learning, and status, everyone agreed, New South parvenus differed little from rural crackers. Fiddling brought out the cultural bonds of whiteness. As one rousing newspaper description of the 1914 fiddling contest related: "From front to back and high into the circles sat city folk, country folk, ladies in expensive furs, working folk, in plain attire, men tired from their labor, well-tailored magnates fresh from a dinner at the club—verily all kinds and conditions of men. They rubbed elbows, quarreled over the merits of rival favorites, and patted their feet as one man to the tune of "Run Nigger, Run, de Patter-Roller [Patrol Will] Git You."[147] Unified by race, if not by class, elites and poor whites could tap their feet, smile at one another, and know that they, at least, had no fear of being caught by "de Patter-Roll."[148]

For all their populism, however, the rich never exchanged their silk hats for wool.[149] Although they cheered on the fiddlers as avidly as any highland partisan, they did so from reserved boxes or from the judge's table. The constant press attention they received reaffirmed their elevated status and kept fiddlers at a respectful distance. Appalachian fiddlers, habituated to lives of poverty and simplicity, appeared content with this arrangement. Kephart had written that the mountaineer was neither "tempted by a display of good things all around him, nor is he embittered by the haughtiness and extravagance of the rich." The fiddlers appeared to confirm this assessment.[150] One fiddler who arrived at the 1920 contest by train seemed interested in "neither the lofty interior of the Terminal station, the honking automobiles in the plaza, nor the bright lights of Mitchell street." The humble highlander "accepted all these new things as a matter of course, like all the mountaineers, and seemed only interested in the convention."[151] Fiddlers wanted to have fun and saw no reason to get riled up about their poverty. New South boosters felt reassured that class relations would not take on the ugly character typical of the industrial Northeast and that the mountain minstrels wandering Atlanta's streets would not protest the disparities of wealth that confronted them. Rural crackers and urban parvenus shared an inseparable bond of race and culture that could never succumb to temporary class divisions. Atlanta's New South generation welded the "spirit of the mountains" to the "Atlanta spirit" and anchored them both on the rock of white superiority.[152]

The "Innate Soul of Music Undefiled"

Without question, the fiddling contest took its cues from the old-time blackface minstrel show. Nineteenth-century blackface minstrel shows often vented lower-class discontent against the well heeled, and the fiddling convention offered an almost identical form of class burlesque. Although the minstrel format never lost its popularity, watching blackface performers did. Upper- and middle-class audiences in the early twentieth century preferred seeing their minstrels with white faces. The Georgia Old-Time Fiddlers' Contest, therefore, signaled a move from mangled top hats and plantation rags to wool caps and backwoods homespun, but whiteness remained the common cause.[153]

Many tunes in the repertoire, like "Nigger in the Woodpile," "Possum up a Gum Stump," "Run Nigger Run," "Ole Dan Tucker," "Boil Them Cabbage Down," and "Turkey in the Straw" either had their origins on the minstrel stage or had achieved widespread popularity there.[154] The press even made clear the links between the fiddlers and their blackface counterparts, such as the *Journal* reporter who described Gid Tanner as possessing "a mouth as flexible as a minstrel show coons.'"[155] The *Georgian* marveled that one contestant could rattle the bones "in a way to make a minstrel end-man envious."[156] Blackface minstrel performers had largely conformed their skits to stock characters, and the fiddlers followed suit. Their heavy dialect, native eloquence, and simultaneous awe and contempt of urban life made these "Georgia minstrels of the soil" immediately recognizable.[157] Newspaper accounts paraded before their readers a chuckling cast of fiddlers, such as the one who accepted an offer for a free oyster supper with the blustering comment, "Well I'll come and do my share. We never could do no good raisin' 'em up in my neck of the woods."[158] Another fiddler merely "hitched up his trousers, before he sat down, and the audience laughed."[159] Though not yet "hillbillies," the fiddlers had begun to craft a white alternative to the minstrel "darkey."[160]

The fiddling contest filled a void left by the perceived decline of the old-time blackface minstrel show. An 1897 obituary for minstrel Billy Birch offered an increasingly common jeremiad about minstrelsy's late-nineteenth-century devolution. In Birch's early days, the *New York Tribune* reported, "there was none of the effort for gorgeous effect in costuming and stage setting that there is among the degenerate companies that call themselves negro minstrels." While conceding that "real negroes on a plantation" probably never "sat in a half circle and threw conundrums from the ends to the middle quite as old-time minstrels did," in the old shows "there was at least some attempt to act and talk like darkies and to have the songs of a character resembling real negro songs."[161] Similar complaints continued into the new century. A 1908 essay surveying the history of African American music, for example, noted that in modern minstrel shows "there was very little suggestion left of the music of the negro himself."[162] Atlantans joined in the grumbling. A 1910 *Journal* article declared that because of vaudeville, the "old-time negro show" increasingly relied on spectacle and consequently could not "keep within the bounds of the negro minstrel performance."[163] The perceived decline in old-time minstrelsy mirrored a similar fear throughout the white South that the simple, old-time "darkey" was also fast disappearing. Whether on stage or on the street, the New Negro was too sophisticated, too complicated, and too dangerous to any longer deserve white admiration, envy, and paternalistic condescension. Although the eulogies for blackface minstrelsy were much too early, they nevertheless signaled the loss of minstrelsy's respectable clientele at just the moment fiddling gained one.

If the old-time fiddler hearkened back to a well-worn stage persona, and if his tunes recalled minstrel performances of old, he nevertheless differed from his predecessor in a defiant commitment to racial segregation. The minstrel stage, crowded with "yaller gals," had testified to the prevalence of racial mixing, and the very act of blackface represented a titillating adventure into cross-racial identities. The fiddlers would have none of that. Unlike their forebears, they refused to hide their white faces or to imitate popular black musical styles among the "darkey's" modern descendants. "No rag-time is on the program," one 1913 article spat.[164] When jazz dethroned ragtime in popular affections, the *Journal* guaranteed fiddle fans that "no modern 'jazz' is permitted."[165] Indeed, jazz put fiddlers in a pugilistic mood, leading a *Constitution* headline to report, "King Jazz Given Knockout When Georgia Fiddlers Play."[166]

Their disdain was not simply aesthetic but was also linked to a chorus of condemnation that rained down upon ragtime and jazz as a threat to white people.[167] Of course, many whites expressed genuine enthusiasm for these innovative genres, convinced, as one music critic wrote, that these new musical forms "more nearly voice the fever of modern American life" than any other.[168] Yet critics were both vocal and numerous. They countered that through ragtime white Americans were "falling prey to the collective soul of the negro." Given the "primitive morality and perceptible moral limitations of the Negro type," listeners to black music were therefore susceptible to moral rot.[169] The ultimate aim of black music, critics claimed, was to inspire in white women a momentary lapse of their propriety and thereby open the door to miscegenation. "Its sole purpose and use is to cause us to forget ourselves, order, and decency."[170] In a vivid expression of disgust, members of Atlanta's Ku Klux Klan marched down Auburn Avenue to demonstrate against the white youngsters who frequented black nightclubs.[171] Gate City whites, like their counterparts elsewhere, feared that black music could literally tear down American society, reducing it to an idiotic, morally bankrupt state. Without vigilance, American society could dance itself to destruction.

Music, therefore, represented a real threat to the color line. But it also offered one of the best hopes for relief. The old-time fiddler and his antiquated repertoire provided aid to a white population threatened with sexual immorality and racial perfidy. Appalachia's interpreters took special note of the "high standard of morality which pervades the sex relationship" among the highlanders.[172] While jazz and ragtime could properly be labeled "an offence against womanly purity," fiddling music inspired no similar outrages.[173] Even when "a modern street-song succeeds in penetrating into the mountains," wrote ballad prospector Cecil Sharp, the song was "purified" and rendered fit for civilized ears.[174] Atlanta's fiddlers brought this mountain sensibility to the big city, insisting that they had no patience with the "the vile degrading suggestiveness of jazz."[175] Instead, the *Journal* observed with satisfaction, "the mountain musician's harmonies are healthy like the air he breathes. He

Fiddlin' John Carson. Courtesy of the Southern Folklife Collection, Wilson Library, University of North Carolina at Chapel Hill.

is no degenerate." Old-time fiddling was the "innate soul of music undefiled."[176]

Jews were not exempt from the fiddler's disdain. "Not even the conductor of the Boston Symphony Orchestra could look with more contempt on jazz" than did the fiddlers who scorned "the profane melodies which have come out of New York's Tin Pan Alley to compete with the tunes their grandads played."[177] At least one fiddler put rhetoric into action. When on August 17, 1915, a calculating mob lynched a prominent local Jew named Leo Frank for allegedly raping and murdering a young girl in his employ, Fiddlin' John Carson rushed to entertain the assembled crowd. Those at the Marietta courthouse who had been "deprived of the picture" of Frank "swinging" could nevertheless enjoy Carson's performance. The fiddling contest favorite had, the *Constitution* reported, "turned up with his fiddle at every Frank development within radius of thirty miles of Marietta since the day Mary Phagan's body was discovered," and today was no different. Standing at the courthouse steps he serenaded the excited throng with his ballad about "Little Mary Phagan," and they responded enthusiastically. "The crowd would cheer and applaud him lustily, and, inspirited by this show of appreciation, he would repeat his song, over and over again."[178] Those not present to hear Carson could purchase a sheet music version of the eight-verse ballad hawked on Atlanta's streets for ten cents.

Atlanta was only one of a host of cities and towns that turned to fiddling as a means of enforcing white supremacy. In 1923 residents of Huntsville, Alabama, enjoyed an old-time fiddling contest during which "no jazz disturbed the musical atmosphere" and "no commercial 'blues' sounded their decadent note."[179] In 1925 local chapters of the Ku Klux Klan sponsored fiddling contests in Birmingham, Alabama, and Mountain City, Tennessee.[180] Two years later Nashville commenced the "All Southern Old Fiddlers' Convention," which rivaled Knoxville's own contest.[181] Not to be outdone, both Joplin and Paris, Missouri, held fiddling contests, and North Carolina gave birth to one in Union Grove and another in Cliffside.[182] Old-time music also became a staple on radio stations cropping up across the South in the early to mid-1920s. In 1924, for instance, KFMQ from Fayetteville, Arkansas, broadcast an old-time fiddlers's match, and in the following year Nashville's WSM promised listeners that the evening's fare included some "old familiar tunes" that would delight those "parts of the country [where] jazz has not completely turned the tables."[183]

Old-time fiddling received a prominent boost from automobile mogul Henry Ford, who in 1926 sponsored a nationwide fiddling contest. He hoped that the contestants would provide suitable accompaniment for the old-time dances he aimed to revive, as well as some "melodious ammunition for his war" against the popular music industry.[184] Ford automobile dealerships sponsored local contests in New York, Pennsylvania, Washington, D.C., Ohio, Illinois, Minnesota, Wisconsin, the Dakotas, Iowa, Kansas, Nebraska, Oklahoma, Arkansas, Missouri, Kentucky, West Virginia, Tennessee, Mississippi, Alabama, and Florida, with the winner reporting to Detroit for the national championship. The fiddlers could check the combined influence of black musicians and Jewish middlemen, both of whom Ford accused of plotting to pervert the nation's moral standards.[185] Atlantans, in short, were hardly alone in seeing old-time music as a bulwark against perceived cultural threats to white supremacy.

Old-time mountain fiddlers comprised a relief force to rescue the encircled garrisons. The mountain musicians came from a backwoods culture that allegedly resorted to violence readily and with little moral compunction. Indeed, in the context of interracial conflict, white Atlantans took the propensity for violence as one of Appalachia's chief virtues, an image burnished by the region's admirers who frequently drew upon martial imagery to describe the highlanders. William Frost had called the mountaineers "one of God's grand divisions"; another writer had observed that this noble army was prepared to "preserve our civil and religious institutions unimpaired in the Armageddon with which the hordes of undesirable Americans and unAmericanized [*sic*] immigrants are threatening our nation."[186] Coupled with rumors that highlanders sometimes gouged and scraped each other for no better reason than entertainment, such rhetoric affirmed an already widespread conviction that mountain hollers and coves nurtured a particularly feisty lot. But when examined carefully, writers explained, the highlanders' was not an indiscriminate violence. Instead, it was directed at protecting their families, whatever the threat and whatever the cause. Trying to soften feuding's unpleasant reputation, Frost observed that it was merely "the reverse side of family affection."[187] It was a phrase destined to resonate with white Atlantans who, though distant from highland warfare, defended lynching as "a spontaneous outburst of emotions" based on "love for the home and wife and children."[188] Both lynching and feuding, therefore, were explained as natural, moral responses to barbaric, inhuman threats. Highlanders shared with New South elites a recognition that violence, though never employed lightly, was a reasonable means of self-preservation.

The mountain fiddler thus helped to fashion a stance of moderation that did not forsake violence as a legitimate weapon to maintain racial hierarchies. Just knowing that "one of God's grand divisions" stood unafraid upon the race's parapets comforted the city's elite. "I b'lieve in treatin' niggers squar," one level-headed mountain patriarch told Horace Kephart. "There'd orter be a place for them, but it's *some place else* —not around me!"[189] Atlanta whites who considered themselves moderate on the "race question" could hardly have put it better. It was precisely the reasoning they liked to employ whenever critics rolled into town with race relations on their mind. "Treatin' niggers squar" was fair enough, but woe be unto them who asked for more. There was hell to pay for pushing jolly fiddling minstrels too far. Fiddles and fisticuffs were never far apart, and the ramparts of white supremacy could hardly have found more inspiring soldiers.[190]

"We Raise Corn, Hell and Fiddlers"

Though the objects of a vigorous defense, white women were not expected to lend more than moral support to the cause. Violence, should it be required, was a masculine responsibility. In this way, mountain life pointed back to gender distinctions that city life seemed destined to make obsolete. In the mountains, spattered blood, dangling eyeballs, and broken bones still measured masculinity, and, rather than turning a disgusted eye on such behavior, women encouraged it. Even shy mountain Madonnas, Kephart reported, "would despise any man who took insult or injury without showing fight."[191] Hence, mountain violence and mountain music inspired titillated interest because it promised not only to protect the color line but also to forcefully reassert patriarchal authority.[192]

When Emilia Wells announced her intention to compete in the 1929 fiddlers' contest, the convention's secretary groaned that these days women seemed intent on "running men out of every kind of job." Mountaineers, he whined, "have always figured that the place for a woman is in the cabin," and so they were "certainly not used to women fiddlers."[193] It was a lament that Atlanta's New South men had been expressing for decades. They seized upon the fiddling contest's boisterous music and feisty performers as a weapon with which they could strike back at women who seemed intent on making men submit. They suffered through the opera season's innumerable parties, bewildering fashion rules, and strictly moderated decorum because they wished to demonstrate their gentility, but they would be damned if it meant sacrificing their masculinity.[194] Stuffed into their opera clothes and debating over roasted squab guineas the rival merits of Enrico Caruso and Giovanni Zenatello, these Georgia men could presumably only take so much. There came a point when peevish rage compelled them to blurt out that the "plain business men" cared "more for a good tune than for grand opera."[195] When it came right down to it, they preferred "Shorty Harper at his best to Caruso in his most inspired moments." And this "sob song" from *Il Pagliacci* that dissolved women into puddles of aesthetic ecstasy, well, hell, it "doesn't carry nearly the punch of 'Turkey in the Straw.'"[196] Damn me, they cried, warming to the subject, when those old fiddlers bore down on "Sugar in the Gourd," they "shook some dust off beams Caruso's voice never troubled."[197] Though men patronized opera, they did so with a measure of caution. Men who applied themselves too closely to a culture whose rules and customs were dictated by women endangered some vital aspect of their masculinity. By uniting their own sophisticated urban values with those of the primitive Anglo-Saxon mountain fiddler, however, they could forge a male culture with its own aesthetic standards and pantheon of heroes, knowing full well that in a Darwinian struggle of cultures theirs would win. Homespun fiddlers could always beat the stuffing out of sissy violinists. As Uncle Bud Littlefield noted in 1920 with a twinkle in his eye, "Yes, sir, we raise corn, hell and fiddlers, and we had a pretty good crop this year, all around."[198]

If anything delighted men in the audience more than the music, it was the great valley that separated the summits of art from the hilltops of Appalachia. Though it undoubtedly would have relieved many in the auditorium, there was never much chance that during an opera Enrico Caruso would just off and pop a rival in the jaw or, armed with his favorite barlow knife, launch himself at a surly member of the cast. Yet if at the fiddling contest no one drew a blade or if no one threatened to gouge out another's eye, journalists always tempered the disappointment by assuring readers that *tomorrow* evening might just be the night when it *would* happen. Whether it was "a war to a finish" or a "battle of the catgut,"[199] violence was sure to break out momentarily. In 1914 dozens of spectators no doubt thought twice about attending the event until a headline reassured them that "Fiddlers Will Check Weapons before Big Contest Begins." The papers reported that the contest's judges were experiencing "feelings of mingled pleasure and fear," because Georgia's legal history abounded in cases showing that "an adverse decision in a fiddling contest has proved that a man may be as handy with a gun as with a fiddle bow." The judges presumably took great comfort in knowing, however, that the fiddlers had "agreed to check all arms at the cloak room."[200] The *Georgian* reported in 1916 that during one caucus of fiddlers "it looked as though the fur would fly," while elsewhere in the auditorium two fiddlers almost fell to blows, causing one combatant to announce himself "ready to take up the challenge with anything from a barlow knife to plain flat and skull scraping."[201] Although opera week might experience temperamental artists indulging in snippy behavior, such antics seemed ludicrously effete when matched against the home-spun brawlers.

The audience also abandoned the dictates of civil behavior so scrupu-lously policed during opera week. Although no one expected Caruso's arias to cause more than a fluttering heart and a dewy brow, no fiddler could count himself a true master of the instrument if his tune did not have the potential to start a riot. During one contest the papers reported that fans from a particularly quarrelsome mountain county "grew so uproarous [*sic*] it appeared that the services of a police squad would be necessary."[202] Another fiddler "was not applauded. He was cheered loudly."[203] When Shorty Harper announced himself resigned to the decorum required of someone his age and to forsaking "monkey-shines" as "beneath his dignity," it took only a few tunes to make him for-get his vow.[204] The music, it was reported, made "a direct appeal to one's feet," and the proprieties of age or station were powerless against it.[205]

It was uncertain, however, that the proprieties of gender were in fact powerless to the fiddle's charms. Women in the audience seemed pecu-liarly unmoved by horsehair and catgut. A 1915 article in *Harper's* de-scribed the plight of one poor mountain fiddler who found religion and was forced to resign the fiddle and bow. To prevent backsliding, his ex-cursions into town always included the company of two female "stoop-shouldered, black-bonneted bodyguards who trailed him everywhere and rarely let him out of their sight." This "feminine surveillance" so "oppressed" the fiddler that he could only be induced to play on a bor-rowed fiddle in a locked room outside the hearing range of his body-guards. It took only a few tunes, however, for him to forget his oppres-sion and to begin "cutting loose." Disdaining the feminine restrictions that had followed him to town, he boldly announced before diving in to "Bonaparte's Retreat," "Now, boys, I'm a-going to make your hair stand up on end this time!"[206]

Though women valiantly insisted on maintaining the opera's stan-dards of civility, the press assured readers that it was a losing battle. Just a few contestants into the 1913 convention it became obvious that dras-tic measures would be needed, and "some wives all but sat upon their husbands' heads to keep them down."[207] Six years later a writer for the *Georgian* observed that things had not changed much since the first con-vention. It was still not unusual "to see a staid and dignified Atlantan succumb to the spell of the fiddle tunes and join in the square dance . . . dragging with him an unwilling wife."[208] When he began scraping out "Run Nigger Run," Fiddlin' John Carson got one benighted husband into a heap of trouble. Much to the audience's delight "William Swanson, of Kirkwood, rose from his seat, stepped into the middle aisle and began a hornpipe." The crowd ignited and clambered onto their seats to catch the terpsichorean demonstration. Cutting through a thicket of flying feet and excited hollers, however, rumbled an implacable Mrs. Swanson, who "reached gently up and pulled on her husband's coat. Mr. Swanson sat down and the show went on."[209] Whether on the stage or in the audience, men raucously defied the feminine standards of conduct and artistic appreciation so insistently advanced through opera week. Though women could have their opera, the fiddling contest was at least one musical event in the calendar at which men could, as a headline in the *Constitution* put it, "Make Merry in Ye Old Boys' Way."[210] Opera's grave conduct, aesthetic reveries, and precious singers were all overturned in a giddy carnival that celebrated a masculine realm of boisterous conduct, commonsense music, and plain-folk fiddlers.

The popularity of old-time fiddling in New South Atlanta initially defied logic. Contestants were celebrated for values squarely at odds with the things Atlantans prized in their New South. The Chamber of Commerce did not promote the city as a haven for drunken, truculent, hell-raising illiterates, nor did it aim to fashion a New South peopled with subsistence farmers stuck in the values and habits of a bygone era. Moreover, it was the magnolia-draped verandas of Old South plantations, not the pine-scented porches of Appalachian cabins, that formed the basis for encomiums to the South's "way of life." In short, there seemed little place for the highlanders or their culture in the making of a New South.

For a time in the 1910s and 1920s, however, the fiddlers captivated significant numbers of distinguished white Atlantans for complex but compelling reasons. The music should not be discounted as insignificant, to be sure. The old fiddle tunes played havoc with the nervous system, sending electrical jolts into stomping feet and clapping hands. And, of course, it took a stony heart to keep from chuckling over the gags and cracker-barrel philosophy liberally dispensed throughout the contest. Nor should nostalgia and a tinge of antimodernism be overlooked, for rural Appalachia took on added charms to men grown weary of cramped and dirty streets, craven moneygrubbing, and physical inertia. "Over there in the mountains," wrote one of the region's enthusiasts, "are men who do not live in cages: a million Americans who do not chase the dollar; who do not serve time machines; [and] who do not learn their manners from the movies."[211] It would seem, then, that the reasons for fiddling's popularity rest not far below the surface, and that a number of logical explanations immediately resolve the initial conundrum. Compelling as these attractions proved, however, they do not fully explain the sudden enthusiasm for old-time fiddling among a group of men at the vanguard of a New South. Alongside entertainment and nostalgia moved a number of equally forceful but far more unsettling specters that troubled their New South reveries.

At the center stood gnawing doubt. Atlanta's white New South men prided themselves on their patience, resourcefulness, and buoyancy, but they lived in times that tried their souls. They daily contended with a roiling, shadowy black population that required wearying vigilance. A swarming host of vociferous mothers, wives, sisters, and daughters raised a whole different set of challenges, and disturbing evidence of lower-class discontent further darkened optimistic dreams of making an orderly and harmonious New South. A cold listing of these anxieties does not do justice to how they piled upon one another and became so frighteningly entangled. Indeed, the trouble they caused lay in their eerie ability to work together and to defy a single solution.

Atlanta's New South men were not without hope, though it admittedly came from an unlikely source. Appalachia, dismissed by hostile critics as an ignorant and backward part of a modernizing South, nevertheless found itself in the early twentieth century with formidable defenders eager to overturn unfavorable stereotypes. Every strike against the region, they argued, turned in its favor when rightly reconsidered by fair-minded observers; crudeness became honest simplicity, ignorance became homely wisdom, savagery became rugged masculinity, and poverty became sterling frugality. In this imagined New Appalachia, as in the imagined New South itself, confounding social problems melted like mountain mists. The divisions and the conflicts, the animosities and the jealousies that so bedeviled efforts at crafting a harmonious New South held no sway in the New Appalachia. There a common purpose, a common past, a common race, a common culture, and a common identity all pointed to a common future. It was an enchanting idyll of social and cultural cohesion. Because these New Appalachians were imaginary, they rarely fought back in the way that New Southerners did. The unceasing demands from African Americans, women, and working-class southerners found no voice in the mountains. Even those fiddling mountaineers that Atlantans actually met and gave themselves over to every year seemed delightfully predictable. Thus when Atlanta's wealthy men broke cornpones with highland fiddlers, it seemed the fulfillment of their New South prophecies. All the disruptions, all the bitterness, all the confusion yielded to the certainty that, just as New Appalachia's flaws turned to gold, the New South's fissures could not obscure an underlying cohesion that rested on the leadership of upper-class, white, male Atlantans. In 1913 when Wiley Harper "played 'Polly Put the Kettle On' with such abandon that all trouble was forgotten," he undoubtedly had little conception of just how much trouble he temporarily relieved his jangled audience of.[212]

Epilogue

"Atlanta is a cosmopolitan town," marveled the *Journal* in 1916, "entertaining the fiddlers' convention and grand opera all in one season." Three years later the paper again beamed that the city was "exceptionally broad in its music tastes."[1] The *Journal* was right. City residents did enjoy a wide range of music, and the burgeoning market for "race" and "hillbilly" records and the programming on the city's WSM radio station would expand those interests even further. Yet the paper's self-congratulatory insight contained a hint of mild perplexity: *the fiddlers' convention and grand opera all in one season.*

Writing of a much different time and place, Robert Darnton has observed that "when we cannot get a proverb, or a joke, or a ritual, or a poem, we know we are on to something." By picking at that disjuncture, he continues, "we may be able to unravel an alien system of meaning."[2] Ironically, as the *Journal* makes clear, many New South Atlantans themselves possessed a vague sense of wonder about their musical habits and doings. They did not, however, pick at the disjuncture with much avidity, preferring merely to note it and pass on. I have made New South Atlantans (and us) pause and reflect a little longer on their own bemusement to examine what it revealed of that South's system of meaning.

Obviously, music was neither the only nor even the most important engine of social and cultural transformation in the making of a New South. But it was far from incidental. Attempts to inscribe opera, fiddling, and the spirituals with a single, public, fixed meaning connected to much larger struggles over the distribution of social, political, cultural, and economic power. The Colored Music Festival, for instance, signaled either the rise of a new black intelligentsia powered by the soulful wisdom gained through righteous suffering or the perpetuation of a servile underclass dedicated to serving the white community and committed to racial segregation. The spirituals were ambiguous enough to New South audiences to render neither interpretation untenable. Our own sentiments may rest easily with those of the festival's organizers, but clearly segregationist whites had little trouble listening to the same music and hearing an endorsement of their most optimistic Jim Crow fantasies. That opera, spirituals, and fiddling could simultaneously sanction conflicting visions made them far from soothing retreats from the rattle of daily discord. Instead, city residents charged these events with deep significance, turning an evening's entertainment into a struggle between rival claimants for the New South's soul.

Music is most frequently praised as a universal language that unites people. As one contemporary put it, music promotes "the social consciousness by effecting a sense of fellowship with others in a refined experience."[3] Music's influence thus extends beyond the concert hall to make a better, more humane world. Yet New South Atlantans also demonstrated that music's reach can just as easily generate hatred, suspicion, and resentment. They reinvented spirituals, fiddling, and opera, seeking to find in these venerable expressions something useful to them in the larger struggles that engaged their lives. Sometimes they heard fellowship and kindliness, but they also heard fear and disgust. Because they, too, considered music a "universal language" whose meanings were transparent and immutable, what they heard offered irrefutable, even divine, support for their inflexible New South creeds. Music's power, therefore, comes not from benign mysticism that breaks down barriers, but from its capacity to simultaneously "mean" numerous things.[4] The conflicts, debates, and contradictions that emerged when Atlantans articulated the meaning of what they heard revealed the sinews of a New South in the making.

Notes

Abbreviations

AC   *Atlanta Constitution*
AG   *Atlanta Georgian*
AHC   Atlanta History Center
AI   *Atlanta Independent*
AJ   *Atlanta Journal*
CB   *Atlanta City Builder*
MA   *Musical America*
SCHS South Carolina Historical Society

Introduction

1. For more on Grady, see Gaston, *New South Creed*, 83–116.

2. Weston Woman's Club, *History of Webster County*, 17.

3. Ibid., 47.

4. U.S. Bureau of the Census, *Agriculture of the United States in 1860: Compiled from the Original Returns of the Eighth Census* (Washington, D.C.: GPO, 1864), 26–29, and *The Statistics of Wealth and Industry of the United States: Compiled from the Original Returns of the 1870 Census* (Washington, D.C.: GPO, 1872), 3:124–27.

5. Russell, *Atlanta, 1847–1890*, 267.

6. "Our Atlanta Dudes," *The Georgia Major*, April 29, 1883, reprinted in *Atlanta Historical Bulletin* 5 (July 1940): 236.

7. Clarke, *Illustrated History of Atlanta*, 107 (emphasis in original).

8. McClure, *The South*, 58–60. "The Old South was feudal, chivalric," a 1917 Atlanta tourist pamphlet explained respectfully, but "the New South is ultra-modern." And, of course, Atlanta was the "true metropolis" and self-proclaimed capital of this New South. *Seeing Atlanta, Georgia, by the Photograph Route*, n.p.

9. Henry Grady at the New England Society of New York City in 1886, reprinted in Escott and Goldfield, *Major Problems in the History of the American South*, 2:71.

10. *AC*, August 15, 1880, 1.

11. *AJ*, November 1, 1916, quoted in Garrett, *Atlanta and Environs*, 2:687.

12. *AC*, May 3, 1914, 4F. Material on Peel's life was drawn from Thomas H. Martin, *Atlanta and Its Builders*; Knight, *Standard History of Georgia*, vol. 4; Glass, *Men of Atlanta*; MacDougald, "A Trip down Peachtree Street"; Williford, *Peachtree Street* and *Americus through the Years*; *AC*, February 3, 1927; Garrett, *Atlanta and Environs*; and Weston Woman's Club, *History of Webster County*. The scholarly debate over how "new" the region was during this period has inspired a great deal of superb work.

Necessary documents in the ongoing debate include Woodward, *Origins of the New South*; Gaston, *New South Creed*; Wiener, *Social Origins of the New South*; Billings, *Planters and the Making of a "New South"*; Russell, *Atlanta, 1847–1890*; Doyle, *New Men, New Cities*; Cobb, "Beyond Planters and Industrialists"; and Ayers, *Promise of the New South*.

13. Ray Stannard Baker, *Following the Color Line*, 65.

14. The role of contingency and uncertainty is particularly well examined throughout Ayers, *Promise of the New South*, esp. viii–ix, and again in Ayers, "Narrating a New South," 559. It is too, of course, an essential aspect of Woodward's analysis throughout *Origins of the New South*.

15. *Pioneer Citizens' History of Atlanta*, 9. The Pioneer Citizens' Society was formed in 1891. Members were required to have lived in Atlanta since 1860.

16. *AC*, July 3, 1913, 3. For more on the struggle to balance Old and New South, see Gaston, *New South Creed*.

17. *AC*, July 20, 1881, quoted in Garrett, *Atlanta and Environs*, 2:25.

18. *Atlanta Evening News*, September 25, 1906, quoted in Godshalk, "In the Wake of Riot," 244.

19. For more on black Atlanta and Georgia, see Du Bois, "Georgia"; John Hammond Moore, "Jim Crow in Georgia"; Porter, "Black Atlanta"; O'Connor, "Measurement and Significance of Racial Residential Barriers"; Dittmer, *Black Georgia in the Progressive Era*; Rabinowitz, *Race Relations in the Urban South*; Godshalk, "In the Wake of Riot"; Mixon, "Atlanta Riot of 1906" and "'Good Negro—Bad Negro'"; Hunter, *To 'Joy My Freedom*; and Leroy Davis, *Clashing of the Soul*.

20. Du Bois, "Georgia," 65.

21. Glenda Elizabeth Gilmore, *Gender and Jim Crow*; Bederman, *Manliness and Civilization*; Janiewski, "Southern Honor, Southern Dishonor"; Williamson, *Crucible of Race*; Fields, "Ideology and Race in American History"; Hall, *Revolt against Chivalry*; MacLean, *Behind the Mask of Chivalry*; Kantrowitz, *Ben Tillman*. Recent criticisms of "whiteness studies" have begun to demand greater awareness of splits within whites; see, e.g., Arnesen, "Whiteness and the Historians' Imagination," and Kolchin, "Whiteness Studies."

22. Haarsager, *Organized Womanhood*; Scott, *Natural Allies*; Blair, *The Clubwoman as Feminist*; Blair, *The Torchbearers*; Roth, *Matronage*; Sims, *Power of Femininity*.

23. McClure, *The South*, 59.

24. Ray Stannard Baker, *Following the Color Line*, 65.

25. Doyle, *New Men, New Cities*; Ayers, *Promise of the New South*.

26. Goodson, *Highbrows, Hillbillies*; Ayers, *Promise of the New South*, 375–408.

27. *AG*, September 27, 1921, 7. As Lawrence Levine ("Folklore of Industrial Society," 1393) has aptly pointed out, "We forget that going to a movie and listening to the radio are in and of themselves *events* and that we may have as much to learn from the process, the ritual, surrounding the expressive culture as from the content of the culture itself" (emphasis in original). For more on ritual and concertgoing, see Small, *Musicking*. Fortunately for historians, a rich body of theoretical literature has arisen that examines the interaction between music and

patterns of social organization. The works I have found most helpful are Small, *Musicking*; Kramer, *Music as Cultural Practice* and *Musical Meaning*; McClary, *Feminine Endings*; Shepherd and Wicke, *Music and Cultural Theory*; Peter J. Martin, *Sounds and Society*; and DeNora, *Music in Everyday Life*.

28. Diary of Josephine Joel, May 12, 1915, Herman Heyman Papers, Ida Pearle and Joseph Cuba Archives of the William Breman Jewish Heritage Museum, Atlanta.

29. As Keith Negus (*Popular Music in Theory*, 4) points out, "Music is created, circulated, recognized and responded to according to a range of conceptual assumptions and analytical activities that are grounded in quite particular social relationships, political processes and cultural activities."

Chapter One

1. *Atlanta Journal and Constitution*, July 7, 1963, 1C.
2. *Official Souvenir Program of the Atlanta Music Festival*, n.p.
3. *AJ*, February 14, 1909, 1. For more on the history of the Atlanta Music Festival Association, see the 1911 flier that accompanied the year's opera booklet, Katherine Wooten Scrapbooks, AHC.
4. *AJ*, February 14, 1909, 4L.
5. *AJ*, April 15, 1909, 7.
6. For ticket receipts, see *AJ*, May 7, 1909, 1; for "good music," see *AJ*, February 28, 1909, 4. For more on the inaugural festival, see Burton, "Music Festival of 1909."
7. The Met performed in Atlanta during 1910–17, 1919–30, 1940–42, and 1947–85. For more on the opera in Atlanta, see Burton, "First Season of Metropolitan Opera Presentations" and "Metropolitan Opera in Atlanta," and Goodson, *Highbrows, Hillbillies*, 108–36.
8. For some of the innumerable merchants hoping to reap financial rewards from the opera, see the program for the 1910 season in the Metropolitan Opera Collection, Emory University, Atlanta.
9. *AJ*, April 12, 1917, 11.
10. *CB*, March 1916, 8. Doyle, *New Men, New Cities*, 17–21, 136–38.
11. "Music and Manliness"; "Is Music an Effeminate Art?"; Randolph, "Why Do Not More Men Take Up Music?" For more on the concerns about the state of masculinity during this period, see Kasson, *Houdini, Tarzan*; Kimmel, *Manhood in America*, 81–188, and "Men's Response to Feminism"; Bederman, *Manliness and Civilization*; Rotundo, *American Manhood*; Lutz, *American Nervousness*; Peter Filene, *Him/Her/Self*, 74–99; and Gorn, *Manly Art*. For masculinity in the white South, see Ownby, *Subduing Satan*; MacLean, *Behind the Mask of Chivalry*, 98–124; Kantrowitz, *Ben Tillman*; Silber, *Romance of Reunion*, 159–96; and Williamson, *Crucible of Race*.
12. As Linda Kerber ("Separate Spheres," 18) has astutely pointed out, we need to pay attention to how "activities defined by women in their own sphere influenced and even set constraints and limitations on what men might choose to do."

For the decline of patriarchal power in the New South, see Williamson, *Crucible of Race*, 109–39 passim, and Hale, *Making Whiteness*, 114–19. For music and elite male power in Atlanta, see Doyle, *New Men, New Cities*, 189–225, and Goodson, *Highbrows, Hillbillies*, 108–10, 133–35.

13. For more on club work, see Haarsager, *Organized Womanhood*; Scott, *Natural Allies*; Blair, *The Clubwoman as Feminist* and *The Torchbearers*; Sims, *Power of Femininity*, 80–127; and Whitesitt, "Women as 'Keepers of Culture.'"

14. Chittenden Turner, "Music and the Woman's Crusade," 29.

15. The intersection between whiteness as embodied in women and in race purity has inspired a number of significant works, the most important including Hale, *Making Whiteness*; Glenda Elizabeth Gilmore, *Gender and Jim Crow*; Williamson, *Crucible of Race*; and Hall, *Revolt against Chivalry*.

16. *AC*, May 6, 1909, 8. For more on the role of armories in American public culture, see Fogelson, *America's Armories*.

17. *AC*, April 28, 1914, 6.

18. Farnham, *Education of a Southern Belle*, 26, 87–88; Blair, *The Torchbearers*, 12–28; Koza, "Music and the Feminine Sphere"; Roell, *The Piano in America*, 13–28. For the circumscription of women's other artistic efforts to the domestic sphere in the antebellum period, see McCarthy, *Women's Culture*, 3–34.

19. Maguire, "People to Whom a Girl Plays."

20. Hamilton, "Teachers' Round Table."

21. Block, "Women in American Music"; Tick, "Women in Music" and "Passed Away Is the Piano Girl." For women's orchestras, see Ammer, *Unsung*, 99–115; Tick, "Passed Away Is the Piano Girl," 328–32; and Neuls-Bates, "Women's Orchestras." For representative reviews of their performances, see *MA*, May 22, 1915, 27, June 3, 1922, 11. For the growing acceptance of women both in the audience and on the opera stage in the nineteenth century, see Ahlquist, *Democracy at the Opera*, 60–61, 90–97, and Dizikes, *Opera in America*, 50–52. A few of the more adventurous even attempted to add a female voice to the world of composition. For more on the first generation of women composers in America and the obstacles they faced, see Ammer, *Unsung*, 71–98.

22. *MA*, May 8, 1915, 41. See also Batchellor, "Woman's Sphere in Music-Teaching."

23. Koza, "'Missing Males.'" An interesting exception to this general rule was Frances Elliott Clark, whose remarkable career is recounted in Keene, *History of Music Education*, 244–69.

24. Tick, "Women in Music," 550–51, and "Passed Away Is the Piano Girl," 327; Henry J. Harris, "Occupation of Musician."

25. *MA*, June 1, 1912, 20.

26. Winn, "Woman as Musician." Another musician pointed to the example of Boston composer Amy Beach. "To those who believe that women who achieve greatness in any art or science must be masculine in mind and manner, unsexed phenomena," she reassured readers, "we say that Mrs. Beach is most womanly in all her ways." Elson, *History of American Music*, 305. For more on Beach's career, see Block, *Amy Beach*.

27. *MA*, June 22, 1912, 31.

28. *MA*, January 27, 1923, 26.

29. *MA*, May 12, 1917, 4.

30. *MA*, October 23, 1909, 5.

31. *MA*, November 6, 1909, 2.

32. *AC*, March 24, 1912, 6B. "The tradition that domesticity and art are unallied has long been proven fallacious by our prima donnas," claimed a similar article in *Musical America* that included a photo of Marguerite Sylva with her husband and two children by the hearth. *MA*, May 31, 1919, 9.

33. Useful bibliographies covering the wide-ranging interests of music clubs and of women in music generally include Block and Neuls-Bates, *Women in American Music*, and Skowronski, *Women in American Music*. For the role of women's clubs in promoting the work of female composers like Amy Beach, see Block, *Amy Beach*, 163–69; for their work promoting new music more generally, see Joseph Horowitz, *Wagner Nights*, as well as the essays in Locke and Barr, *Cultivating Music in America*. For an examination of the intersection of women and cultural philanthropy more broadly, see McCarthy, *Women's Culture*.

34. *MA*, July 18, 1914, 4.

35. Barnes, "Feminizing of Culture," 775.

36. Traquair, "Women and Civilization," 296.

37. *MA*, May 22, 1909, 1.

38. *AJ*, May 4, 1909, 1, 6.

39. Fanny Morris Smith, "Beginning of the Club Year." Local music clubs could affiliate with two national federations: the National Federation of Music Clubs or, beginning in 1910, the Music Division of the Federation of Women's Clubs. Whitesitt, "Women as 'Keepers of Culture,'" 65–86; Blair, *The Torchbearers*, 44–75.

40. Fanny Morris Smith, "Beginning of the Club Year."

41. Benedict, "Woman's Share in the Musical Civilization of the Public," 319. See also Robeson, "Woman's Work in Music," and Mrs. William D. Steele, "Relation of the Woman's Club," 124.

42. Kate Louise Roberts, *Club Woman's Handybook*, 11–12.

43. *MA*, May 10, 1919, 39.

44. Kate Louise Roberts, *Club Woman's Handybook*, 7.

45. McCarthy, *Women's Culture*; Scott, *Natural Allies*, 111–74.

46. Mrs. David Allen Campbell, "New Citizen's Work for Music."

47. Fairweather, "Psychological and Ethical Value of Music," 625.

48. Fryberger, *Listening Lessons in Music*, 15. For similar sentiments, see also Ripley, "Ideal Supervisor," 851; Newton, "Mysticism of Music," 185; Seymour, *What Music Can Do for You*, 174–75; Kempf, "From Harmonica to Symphony"; *MA*, October 8, 1910, 3; and *MA*, June 8, 1912, 22.

49. The notion of music's social utility was not exclusive to the twentieth century. For nineteenth-century precedents, see Stone, "Mid-Nineteenth-Century American Beliefs"; Musselman, *Music in the Cultured Generation*, esp. 36–51, 84–103; Ahlquist, *Democracy at the Opera*, 46–48, 82–116, 182–200; and Donakowski,

Muse for the Masses, esp. 188–215. For the Progressive Era, see Blair, *The Torchbearers*, 63–73; Roell, *The Piano in America*; and Gavin James Campbell, "'A Higher Mission.'" For other efforts at reform through cultural philanthropy not solely relying on music, see Trachtenberg, *Incorporation of America*, 140–81; Levine, *Highbrow, Lowbrow*, 200–219; Helen Lefkowitz Horowitz, *Culture and the City*; and McCarthy, *Noblesse Oblige*, 75–96.

50. Committee on Education, House of Representatives, 68th Cong., 1st sess., Hearing on H.R. 7011 (March 25, 1924), 14.

51. "America owes its women a debt of gratitude," one music teacher wrote in a common refrain, for without them "there simply would be no art in America." *MA*, January 25, 1913, 35. See also Sternberg, "Are Girls Taught Music to the Exclusion of Boys?"; Finck, "Women in Music To-day"; *MA*, March 30, 1912, 29; and *MA*, November 25, 1922, 11.

52. *MA*, March 1, 1913, 15.

53. Seymour, *What Music Can Do for You*, 174, 171.

54. Peter Filene, *Him/Her/Self*, 16–18; Sims, *Power of Femininity*, 80–127; Blair, *The Torchbearers* and *The Clubwoman as Feminist*.

55. Wood, *History of the General Federation*, 305.

56. Huneker, "Feminism in Modern Music," 694.

57. Mason, *Music as a Humanity*, 15.

58. "Human Need for Music," 9.

59. Goepp, "Musical Appreciation," 31. For a concurring opinion, see Hanh, "The Business Man and Good Music."

60. Goepp, "Musical Appreciation," 33.

61. Rogers, "Do Men Lack Culture?," 127.

62. *MA*, March 16, 1912, 22.

63. Traquair, "Women and Civilization," 290.

64. Randolph, "Why Do Not More Men Take Up Music?"

65. Charles Edward Locke, "Music as a Factor in Culture," 647. The conflict between an older model of refined manliness and a newer model of rugged masculinity is expertly discussed throughout Gail Bederman's *Manliness and Civilization*.

66. Dickinson, *Education of a Music Lover*, 25. These cautions extended, of course, back to ancient Rome. For an examination of this issue in an earlier context, see Austern, "'Alluring the Auditorie to Effeminacie.'"

67. Huneker, "Feminism in Modern Music," 692–93. See also Huneker, "The Girl Who Plays Chopin," 466.

68. *MA*, May 22, 1909, 14. "I think we men would be likely to agree," wrote another of Chopin, "that for a steady diet, he would for us be likely to prove a bit cloying." Randolph, "Why Do Not More Men Take Up Music?," 300.

69. Mason, *Music as a Humanity*, 9.

70. Erb, *Music Appreciation for the Student*, 3.

71. *MA*, June 15, 1918, 3.

72. *Houston Post*, May 17, 1903, quoted in Neil Harris, "John Philip Sousa," 24.

73. Hanh, "The Business Man and Good Music," 570. The bands, wrote an-

other critic, were generally "not considered so high-class as the regular 'Symphony orchestras.'" Gustav L. Becker, "Recent Notable Progress," 15.

74. *MA*, June 29, 1918, 30. One educator warned, however, against overemphasizing "the kind of music men now sing, which is chiefly associated with sports and conviviality." Surette, *Music and Life*, 136.

75. Randolph, "Why Do Not More Men Take Up Music?," 300.

76. Bridge, "How Industry and Common Sense Help."

77. Randolph, "Why Do Not More Men Take Up Music?," 299. This article is a reprint of an address Randolph made in 1922 to the Music Teachers' National Association under the title "The Feminization of Music."

78. Cooke, "The Business Side of Making an Artist," 499.

79. "Art and Money."

80. Bridge, "How Industry and Common Sense Help." Violinist Micha Elman once received a typical reply to the admission that he was a musician: "Why I thought all big musical bugs had funny names and long hair." *MA*, May 8, 1915, 23.

81. Baltzell, "The Business of Being an Artist," 414. For similar sentiments, see Baltzell, "The American College Man in Music," 633, as well as "Business Men and High Art."

82. Law, "Captains of Music," 470. For similar sentiments, see *MA*, August 10, 1912, 13.

83. *MA*, May 15, 1915, 38. Even so notable a financier as Otto Kahn advised boys that although "the day of the industrial pioneer in America . . . is about over," the day of the "pioneer of culture and idealism has come." "Mobilizing Our Millionaires." For more on the connections between music and business, see "Business Men and High Art," and Tapper, "What Should the Musician Know about Business."

84. Randolph, "Why Do Not More Men Take Up Music?," 299.

85. Upton, *Theodore Thomas*, 1:215. Thomas had "repressed force" and "latent power," marveled a Chicago paper, yet he looked "more like a substantial banker than one of the four most renowned conductors in the world." *Chicago Evening Post*, December 21, 1895, quoted in Schabas, *Theodore Thomas*, 219. For more on Thomas as a figure of discipline, see Kasson, *Rudeness and Civility*, 234–39, and Levine, *Highbrow, Lowbrow*, 112–19, 187–88. For more on his life and career, see Schabas, *Theodore Thomas*.

86. *Musical America* bubbled with admiration in 1912, reporting that Sousa was currently on a trap-shooting vacation and that afterward "he will be in fine condition to resume the strenuous work of touring through the country." *MA*, May 11, 1912, 28. For more on Sousa's image as a robust man of music, see Bierley, *John Philip Sousa*, 110–15. For the equation of his music with American expansionism, see Hess, "Sousa's *El Capitan*."

87. Quoted in Joseph Horowitz, *Understanding Toscanini*, 65. See especially Horowitz's treatment of the contrasting public opinion regarding the styles of Toscanini and Wilhelm Furtwängler. The cultural power of conductors is a subject that Christopher Small takes up in *Musicking*, 75–86.

88. *MA*, August 21, 1909, 9.

89. *MA*, March 1, 1913, 15.

90. *MA*, June 26, 1909, 2.

91. Smith, "Music and Manliness," 12, quoted in Koza, "'Missing Males,'" 221 (emphases in original).

92. "How I Came to Love Music," 235.

93. Randolph, "Why Do Not More Men Take Up Music?," 299. See also Erb, *Music Appreciation for the Student*, 2. Even those students who signed up for music classes in college did not do so "for any love of the art," one commentator observed, but "because the course is reputed easy." *MA*, July 13, 1912, 23. Proving his masculinity became a dominant theme in the work of composer Charles Ives and can be examined more carefully in Rossiter, *Charles Ives and His America*, 31–37, 79–83, and Tick, "Charles Ives and Gender Ideology."

94. Editorial, *Etude*.

95. Ibid., 582.

96. *MA*, March 16, 1912, 22.

97. "The Uncultured Sex," 1100. I am not ignoring the significant financial contributions women made to a variety of musical organizations, but, rather, I am suggesting that men overlooked those contributions. For the role of women in financially backing music, see the essays in Locke and Barr, *Cultivating Music in America*.

98. *AC*, May 1, 1914, 1.

99. *Los Angeles Graphic* 10 (November 19, 1904), quoted in Catherine Parsons Smith, "Inventing Tradition," 314.

100. *MA*, June 19, 1909, 14.

101. Squire, "Status of the Musician."

102. I have used "Mrs." throughout to name Oates's wife only because the newspaper delicately and politely refused to print her name.

103. *AG*, April 23, 1913, 1.

104. Blackwelder, "Mop and Typewriter," 24; Hall, "Private Eyes, Public Women," 260–61. For more on the transformation of white women's lives in the South during this period, see Scott, *Southern Lady*; Hall, *Revolt against Chivalry*; Wedell, *Elite Women and the Reform Impulse*; Roth, *Matronage*; Glenda Elizabeth Gilmore, *Gender and Jim Crow*; and Sims, *Power of Femininity*.

105. *AC*, September 26, 1915, 10M.

106. *CB*, May 1924, 31. For more on club work in Atlanta, see Roth, *Matronage*.

107. Barbara J. Harris, *Beyond Her Sphere*; Kessler-Harris, *Out to Work*; Dumenil, *Modern Temper*, 98–144.

108. *MA*, May 11, 1912, 26.

109. Scrapbook, 1917, Atlanta Music Club, AHC.

110. For more on Atlanta's early concert life, see Orr, *Alfredo Barili*, and Goodson, *Highbrows, Hillbillies*, 108–20. For an earlier retrospective, see *AC*, February 4, 1912, 3G.

111. *AC*, November 23, 1902, 1. For more on lackluster attendance at classical performances, see Goodson, *Highbrows, Hillbillies*, 128–33.

112. "Brief History and Report of the Atlanta Musical Association; Read before the Federation of Women's Clubs in Atlanta, Georgia, May 27, 1910," Bertha Harwood-Arrowood Papers, AHC.

113. *AC*, April 25, 1910, 2.

114. "Brief History and Report," Bertha Harwood-Arrowood Papers, AHC. A local directory of music and musicians characterized the association's membership as comprising "over two hundred of the best professional and amateur musicians of the best social element." *The Musical Directory of Atlanta*, 115.

115. *AC*, July 17, 1910, 3.

116. *AC*, June 15, 1913, 11M.

117. *AC*, January 26, 1911, 8.

118. *MA*, May 18, 1912, 20.

119. *AC*, February 4, 1912, 3G.

120. Ibid., 3G. To follow some of the controversy surrounding forming the symphony, see *MA*, July 31, 1909, 22; *MA*, August 7, 1909, 1; and *MA*, September 4, 1909, 14.

121. *AG*, February 21, 1911, Bertha Harwood-Arrowood Papers, AHC. For an appeal to the city's business interests in creating and maintaining a symphony, see *AC*, January 12, 1913, 4F.

122. The latest mention I have found for it was in *AC*, June 15, 1913, 11M. In later years Harwood blamed the organization's demise on "selfish greed" brought on by "unscrupulous members." Bertha Harwood-Arrowood to Rena Barickman, May 7, 1942, Harwood-Arrowood Papers, AHC.

123. Tucker, *Atlanta Music Club*, 21.

124. "Club History," Atlanta Music Study Club Programs and Recitals, 1919–20, Atlanta Music Club Papers, AHC.

125. *AJ*, October 7, 1923, 7.

126. *AC*, September 12, 1915, 6M.

127. Tucker, *Atlanta Music Club*, 19.

128. For more on Carroll, see *MA*, May 26, 1917, 13.

129. Mrs. Armond [Annie May] Carroll to Wolfsohn Musical Bureau, February 26, 1918, Atlanta Music Club Papers, AHC.

130. Minutes of the Atlanta Music Club, September 24, 1919, Atlanta Music Club Papers, AHC.

131. *AJ*, October 8, 1923, 2.

132. *AJ*, October 21, 1923, 1B.

133. Mrs. Armond [Annie May] Carroll to Hansell Crenshaw, October 14, 1917, Atlanta Music Club Papers, AHC. For Crenshaw's article, see *AC*, October 14, 1917, 4A.

134. Minutes of the Atlanta Music Club, December 9, 1919, Atlanta Music Club Papers, AHC.

135. Undated clipping [1923?], Scrapbook, Nana Tucker Collection, AC 66-440M, Georgia Division of Archives and History, Atlanta.

136. *AC*, April 27, 1923, 9. There was, during this period, a conscious effort in

Atlanta and nationwide to reclaim prisoners through music. In 1911, for instance, the warden at Atlanta's prison had announced that the prison orchestra would "give a concert each day and play for an hour or so at the helpless inmates." *Musical Courier*, December 20, 1911, 20. For examples outside Atlanta, see Crawford, "'Pirates' and Prisoners"; "A Prison 'Sing'"; Amey, "Music Hath Power"; and Van de Wall, *Utilization of Music in Prisons* and *Music in Institutions*.

137. The ministers could not "but view with concern and deep regret [the proposal] to give so-called sacred concerts in the Auditorium, thus breaking the sacredness of God's day." In all, they considered the idea an "unscriptural innovation in this fair city." *AJ*, May 10, 1909, 3.

138. "Atlanta," Harwood recalled of her campaign to allow Sunday concerts, "was not especially religious but exceedingly churchy and laws were made according to that standard regardless of its merits." "Motives behind the Atlanta Musical Association," Bertha Harwood-Arrowood Papers, AHC.

139. *CB*, May 1924, 31.

140. *AJ*, February 25, 1909, 1.

141. *AC*, May 2, 1915, 8C.

142. *AC*, January 26, 1911, 8.

143. *AC*, May 1, 1910, 7. An advertisement in the Metropolitan Opera program for Redfern Corsets implied a similar feminine ease. "She is chic, well-tailored — grace itself, with an easy swinging walk that conveys an impression of graciousness." Metropolitan Opera program, 1910, in Bertha Harwood-Arrowood Papers, AHC.

144. *AJ*, May 2, 1909, 7B.

145. *AC*, April 25, 1915, 3A.

146. Ibid., 5A.

147. Metropolitan Opera program, Metropolitan Opera Collection, Emory University, Atlanta.

148. *AJ*, May 1, 1910, 2. For Caruso at Cloud-Stanford, see *AJ*, May 3, 1910, 1.

149. *AJ*, April 6, 1909, 4.

150. *AJ*, April 27, 1914, 5.

151. *CB*, August 1922, 22, 41.

152. *AC*, April 30, 1916, 11B; *AC*, May 3, 1914, 5M.

153. *AC*, April 30, 1916, 11B.

154. Ibid.

155. *AC*, May 6, 1909, 7.

156. *AC*, May 7, 1909, 5.

157. *AC*, April 30, 1916, 11B.

158. *CB*, May 10, 1917, 7.

159. *AC*, May 5, 1919, 9.

160. *CB*, March 1919, 5.

161. *AC*, April 25, 1919, 10.

162. Ibid., 12.

163. Quaintance Eaton, *Opera Caravan*, 152.

164. *CB*, February 1924, 13.

165. *AC*, April 24, 1916, 6.

166. *AC*, May 3, 1914, 4F.

167. *AC*, April 27, 1915, 1.

168. *AC*, May 1, 1910, 4.

169. *AC*, April 21, 1913, 6.

170. *AC*, April 27, 1915, 1.

171. *AJ*, May 9, 1909, 5B. See also *AC*, May 6, 1909, 2.

172. *AC*, May 3, 1914, 5M.

173. *AC*, April 25, 1919, 10.

174. *AC*, April 22, 1919, 11.

175. *AJ*, May 4, 1909, 1. See also *AJ*, May 3, 1910, 4, and *AC*, April 23, 1913, 2.

176. *AC*, April 28, 1914, 1.

177. *AC*, April 23, 1919, 12. For other examples, see *AJ*, May 5, 1910, 9; *AJ*, April 28, 1914, 3; and *AC*, April 27, 1915, 1.

178. *AJ*, February 24, 1909, 3.

179. *AC*, May 5, 1909, 6.

180. *AC*, May 2, 1915, 1.

181. *AC*, April 25, 1916, 10.

182. *AJ*, May 5, 1909, 10.

183. *AC*, May 5, 1909, 6.

184. The literature on the intersection between classical music and social class is voluminous, but major works include Broyles, *Music of the Highest Class* and "Music and Class Structure"; Kasson, *Rudeness and Civility*; Levine, *Highbrow, Lowbrow*; McConachie, "New York Operagoing"; DiMaggio, "Cultural Entrepreneurship in Nineteenth-Century Boston" and "Cultural Entrepreneurship in Nineteenth-Century Boston, Part II"; and Helen Lefkowitz Horowitz, *Culture and the City*. Several of these studies take as their base the influential work of French sociologist Pierre Bourdieu, particularly his book, *Distinction*. For a survey of some of the more recent work on classical music and social hierarchy, see Peter J. Martin, *Sounds and Society*. For a critique of the class model of cultural "sacralization," see Ralph P. Locke, "Music Lovers, Patrons." For the formation of class identities in Atlanta through such rituals as opera, see Doyle, *New Men, New Cities*, 189–225, and Goodson, *Highbrows, Hillbillies*, 108–36.

185. *AC*, April 27, 1913, 7F.

186. *AJ*, May 1, 1910, 6A.

187. *AJ*, May 6, 1910, 8.

188. *AC*, December 16, 1925, 3.

189. Glass, "Grand Opera in Atlanta," 26–27.

190. *CB*, March 1924, 14.

191. *CB*, April 1916, 11.

192. *AC*, April 21, 1913, 6.

193. *AC*, April 28, 1914, 1 (first quotation); *AC*, April 22, 1919, 11 (second quotation).

194. Harvey Johnson, "Atlanta," 7.

195. *AC,* May 1, 1914, 1.

196. *AJ,* February 14, 1909, 4L.

197. Goodson, *Highbrows, Hillbillies,* 121–24; Doyle, *New Men, New Cities,* 222–23.

198. *AJ,* May 4, 1909, 8.

199. *AJ,* February 23, 1909, 3.

200. *AJ,* January 27, 1915, 10.

201. *CB,* March 1924, 13–14.

202. *AC,* April 26, 1916, 10.

203. *MA,* July 31, 1909, 22.

204. *MA,* May 17, 1919, 47.

205. *AC,* May 3, 1914, 4F.

206. *AC,* May 5, 1919, 9.

207. Bourne, "Trans-National America," 90.

208. Magill, "A Georgian at the Opera," 136–37. This sketch is clearly inspired by an earlier, widely circulated humorous account of a southerner (this time a Virginian) attending a piano recital in New York starring Anton Rubinstein. Bagby, *Old Virginia Gentleman.*

209. *MA,* March 15, 1913, 8.

210. *AC,* February 19, 1905, 5D.

211. *MA,* May 12, 1917, 40. The selection was apparently a popular one with the Russian Symphony Orchestra in its southern appearances, as it landed on the program again in Birmingham in 1922; see *MA,* May 27, 1922, 26.

212. *AJ,* February 4, 1917, 2H.

213. *AC,* April 1, 1917, 3M.

214. *AC,* April 30, 1916, 11B. For similar sentiments, see *AC,* April 30, 1911, 8M; *AJ,* April 28, 1914, 3; and *AJ,* May 2, 1914, 5.

215. *AJ,* May 8, 1910, 4A.

216. *AC,* April 28, 1917, 1.

217. *AC,* April 28, 1911, 9.

218. *AC,* April 1, 1917, 3M.

219. *AC,* February 19, 1905, 5D.

220. Kasson, *Rudeness and Civility,* 251; Goodson, *Highbrows, Hillbillies,* 130–31.

221. Henry J. Harris, "Occupation of Musician," 307. The last nineteen slots (in descending order) were Wyoming, Idaho, Texas, South Dakota, Kentucky, Louisiana, Florida, North Dakota, Tennessee, Oklahoma, Virginia, Alaska, West Virginia, Arkansas, Georgia, Alabama, Mississippi, South Carolina, and North Carolina.

222. Notices for these and other annual music festivals in the South can be found interspersed in *Musical America;* see, e.g., May 15, 1909 (p. 1), September 4, 1909 (p. 17), October 2 (p. 9), 16 (pp. 71, 75–76).

223. Annie K. Steele, "Music of Our South," 263.

224. *MA,* August 31, 1912, 28.

225. *AC,* May 5, 1910, 5.

226. *AC*, March 7, 1915, 2F (emphasis in original).

227. Program, 1920, Scrapbook, Metropolitan Opera Collection, AHC.

228. *AJ*, May 1, 1911, 1.

229. Program, 1915, Scrapbook, Metropolitan Opera Collection, AHC.

230. *AJ*, May 8, 1910, 1A.

231. *AC*, April 23, 1913, 2.

232. *AC*, April 30, 1911, 14B.

233. *AC*, April 28, 1911, 9.

234. *AJ*, April 23, 1917, 1.

235. *AC*, April 30, 1911, 8M.

236. *AJ*, May 8, 1909, 2.

237. *AJ*, February 14, 1909, 1.

238. *AC*, May 1, 1911, 1.

239. "The Atlanta Music Festival Association," flier, Katherine Wooten Scrapbooks, AHC.

240. *AC*, May 5, 1910, 10.

241. *AC*, April 28, 1911, 1.

242. *AC*, April 23, 1913, 5.

243. *AC*, May 1, 1914, 8.

244. Sectional reconciliation based on a shared embrace of white supremacy was recognized early on. See, e.g., Ray Stannard Baker, "Gathering Clouds along the Color Line," 233. For more recent examinations, see Williamson, *Crucible of Race*, 339–40, 414–58; Hale, *Making Whiteness*, 67–84; Silber, *Romance of Reunion*; O'Leary, *To Die For*, 110–49; and Blight, *Race and Reunion*.

245. E. Davidson Washington, *Selected Speeches of Booker T. Washington*, 36.

246. *AI*, May 8, 1909, 4.

247. *CB*, March 1917, 13.

248. *AC*, August 15, 1910, 5.

249. Kuhn, Joye, and West, *Living Atlanta*, 284–85; *AJ*, May 7, 1909, 7.

250. *AC*, April 26, 1919, 1, 7.

251. *AJ*, May 5, 1909, 3.

252. *AJ*, December 19, 1909, quoted in Garrett, *Atlanta and Environs*, 2:543.

253. *AC*, June 15, 1913, 3F. For more on Decatur Street, see Newman, "Decatur Street."

254. *AC*, May 2, 1909, 2.

255. *AC*, April 23, 1913, 7. Even more titillating, the papers earlier reported that soprano Johanna Gadski had spent one pleasant Atlanta evening singing African American songs. "Gadski," the paper gasped in mock horror, "the incomparable Gadski, singing coon songs!" *AC*, May 4, 1910, 11.

256. *AJ*, May 4, 1910, 5.

257. *AJ*, April 24, 1917, 6.

258. *AJ*, April 26, 1914, 8H. For more on the sacralization of opera and other forms of "high" culture, see Levine, *Highbrow, Lowbrow*, and Kasson, *Rudeness and Civility*.

259. *CB*, February 1924, 11. See also *AJ*, April 26, 1914, 8H, and *AJ*, April 24, 1917, 7.

260. *AJ*, May 5, 1910, 9.

261. *AJ*, February 18, 1909, 2.

262. *AC*, May 4, 1910, 6. Caruso followed her example three years later; *AC*, April 24, 1913, 7.

263. *AC*, May 2, 1914, 4.

264. *AC*, May 5, 1910, 9.

265. *AC*, May 2, 1909, 1. See also *AC*, May 5, 1909, 7.

266. *AC*, May 5, 1909, 7.

267. *AC*, May 1, 1910, 10M.

268. *AC*, April 22, 1919, 11. See also *AC*, May 3, 1910, 9.

269. *AC*, May 2, 1909, 2M.

270. *AI*, May 8, 1909, 4.

271. *AC*, April 23, 1913, 2.

272. Grant, *Passing of the Great Race*, 28.

273. *AC*, April 29, 1911, 16; *AJ*, April 27, 1911, 15; Williamson, *Crucible of Race*, 414–58.

274. Traquair, "Women and Civilization," 294.

275. Elson, *Woman's Work in Music*, 234.

276. *AJ*, April 5, 1914, L10.

277. Atlanta Music Club Programs and Recitals, 1919–20, Atlanta Music Club Papers, AHC.

278. *AC*, September 25, 1906, 6.

Chapter Two

1. *AI*, July 23, 1910, 1.

2. *AJ*, February 16, 1909, 1.

3. *AI*, August 5, 1911, 6.

4. *AI*, July 23, 1910, 1. Even the white papers reported that "Negroes are looking upon Burleigh as did the white people on Caruso." *AJ*, August 2, 1910, 4.

5. *AI*, July 30, 1910, 2.

6. *AI*, July 29, 1911, 1.

7. For overviews of the Colored Music Festival, see Porter, "Black Atlanta," 265–66; Johns, "Henry Hugh Proctor"; and Goodson, *Highbrows, Hillbillies*, 154–60. For a list of the festival's officers, see *AJ*, August 12, 1912, 3. For more on black Atlanta during the Jim Crow period, see Goodson, *Highbrows, Hillbillies*, 137–83; Leroy Davis, *Clashing of the Soul*; Hunter, *To 'Joy My Freedom*; Bayor, *Race and the Shaping of Twentieth-Century Atlanta*, 3–12; Dittmer, *Black Georgia in the Progressive Era*; Porter, "Black Atlanta"; and John Hammond Moore, "Jim Crow in Georgia."

8. Rathbun, "Negro Music of the South," 174. See also Gaines, *Uplifting the Race*, 76–77.

9. Gonzales, *With Aesop*, xiv. One of the most common manifestations of the

white sorrow over the "darkey's" passing was the effort to celebrate the Old Black Mammy. See, e.g., Deborah Gray White, *Ar'n't I a Woman*, 46–61; Thurber, "Development of the Mammy Image"; and Hale, *Making Whiteness*, 98–119. For white memorials to slaves more generally, see Savage, *Standing Soldiers, Kneeling Slaves*, 129–61. For evidence from Atlanta, see Goodson, *Highbrows, Hillbillies*, 142–45.

10. Gaston, *New South Creed*, 153–86; Woodward, *Origins of the New South*, 157–58.

11. Ray Stannard Baker, *Following the Color Line*, 44.

12. Murphy, "True Negro Music," 1723.

13. Kerlin, "Canticles of Love and Woe," 63–64.

14. Fredrickson, *Black Image in the White Mind*, 283–319; Williamson, *Crucible of Race*, 254–55, 414–58.

15. *AG*, August 17, 1912, 6.

16. Savage, *Standing Soldiers, Kneeling Slaves*, 160.

17. Jefferson, *Notes on the State of Virginia*, 266.

18. Shaler, *The Neighbor*, 153–54.

19. Conrad, *Reminiscences of a Southern Woman*, 8 (originally published serially in *Southern Workman*, 1901). For a similar sentiment, see "Passing of a Picturesque People," 126.

20. Ray Stannard Baker, *Following the Color Line*, 28. For a similar lament about black folk tales, see Parsons, "Joel Chandler Harris."

21. *MA*, January 1, 1910, 20.

22. Williamson, *Crucible of Race*; Hale, *Making Whiteness*; Jack E. Davis, *Race against Time*.

23. Gonzales, *With Aesop*, ix.

24. Bronner, *American Folklore Studies* and *Following Tradition*; Zumwalt, *American Folklore Scholarship*; Bendix, *In Search of Authenticity*.

25. The author continued: "To have the hopes and passions, joys and sorrows of a race crystallized into certain melodic expressions preserving all the ethnographic colors and typical traits visualizes the soul of a people more intimately than all the books of history." *MA*, June 1, 1912, 19. For some concurring opinions, see Burlin, *Hampton Series*, 3; Work, "Negro Folk Song," 293; Krehbiel, *Afro-American Folksongs*, 2–4; and Faulkner, *What We Hear in Music*, 32.

26. Murphy, "Survival of African Music in America," 328. See also Joseph Hutchison Smith, "Folk Songs of the American Negro," 211, and Grant, *Passing of the Great Race*, 16.

27. *MA*, January 1, 1910, 20. Lawrence Levine (*Black Culture and Black Consciousness*, 19–25) and Charles Joyner ("Single Southern Culture") have both attempted to lay the subject of interracial cultural exchange to rest (though, given the scholarly and popular attention still given the question, obviously with minimal success).

28. Cooley, "Aunt Jane and Her People," 429. For some pioneering nineteenth-century studies of the region's black folklore, see Jones, *Negro Myths from the Georgia Coast* and Christensen, *Afro-American Folk Lore*.

29. Cooley, "Aunt Jane and Her People," 432. For concurring opinions from the

Black Belt, see Hallowell, *Calhoun Plantation Songs*; Burlin, "Negro Music at Birth," 86–89; and "Negro Spirituals," *New York Times*, January 27, 1924, sec. 7, 4.

30. Postell, "Tales Told Out of School," 43.

31. Murphy, "True Negro Music," 1723.

32. Seroff, "Polk Miller," 147; *Confederate Veteran* 2 (October 1894): 321. For a similar lecture from the 1880s, see Bagby, *Old Virginia Gentleman.*

33. *Confederate Veteran* 2 (August 1894): 230; *Confederate Veteran* 3 (January 1895): 7. For similar sentiments, see *Confederate Veteran* 3 (April 1895): 120, and *Confederate Veteran* 21 (December 1913): 598. For more on Miller, see Savage, *Standing Soldiers, Kneeling Slaves*, 159–60.

34. For more on the Old South Quartette, see Seroff, "Polk Miller," and Lornell, *Virginia's Blues*, 134–36. They made two recordings — one with and one without Miller. Document Records has reissued these early releases. "The Earliest Negro Vocal Quartets: Complete Recorded Works, 1894–1928," DOCD-5061.

35. Reproduced in Seroff, "Polk Miller," 148 (emphases in original).

36. Reproduced in Lornell, *Virginia's Blues*, 135.

37. Haskell, "Negro Spirituals," 577.

38. *Confederate Veteran* 6 (July 1898): 344. The article described Murphy as a repository of the "wit, pathos, superstitions, and eccentricities of the genuine Southern negro." Murphy herself reported with great satisfaction that one old black woman told her, "You does shore sing 'em good; and for a white lady you is got a good deal of de Holy Spirit in you, honey." Murphy, "Survival of African Music in America," 331.

39. *MA*, May 7, 1921, 19.

40. *MA*, March 16, 1912, 24.

41. *MA*, July 6, 1912, 23.

42. *MA*, May 11, 1912, 36. For more on Cheatham's remarkably successful career, see *MA*, July 27, 1912 (p. 10), March 15, 1913 (p. 10), July 10, 1915 (p. 29), August 14, 1915 (p. 18), and December 9, 1922 (p. 25), and Aldrich, *Concert Life in New York*, 311. For praise from the black community, see *Crisis* 10 (September 1915): 215–16, and Work, *Folk Song of the American Negro*, 97–98.

43. *Savannah Press*, February 23, 1924, Scrapbook, Papers of the Society for the Preservation of Spirituals, SCHS, Charleston. The society later released a book of spirituals (Smythe, *Carolina Low-Country*), made several recordings, and in 1935 performed at the Roosevelt White House.

44. *Charleston News and Courier*, May 2, 1923, Scrapbook, Papers of the Society for the Preservation of Spirituals, SCHS, Charleston.

45. Howe, "Song of Charleston."

46. *Savannah Press* [?], February 19, 1924, Scrapbook, Papers of the Society for the Preservation of Spirituals, SCHS, Charleston. For a concurring opinion, see Whaley, *Old Type Passes*, 9–10.

47. Murphy, "True Negro Music," 1723–24.

48. *MA*, December 9, 1922, 28.

49. Work, *Folk Song of the American Negro*, 93.

50. Williamson, *Crucible of Race*; Hale, *Making Whiteness*.

51. Anna Julia Cooper, quoted in Lee D. Baker, "Research, Reform, and Racial Uplift," 57. See also Gaines, *Uplifting the Race*, 179–208, and Anderson, *Deep River*, 36–37.

52. Perkins, "Negro Spirituals from the Far South," 224.

53. "Plantation Melody," 61. For a more complete treatment, see Levine, *Black Culture and Black Consciousness*, 161–70, and Benjamin Filene, *Romancing the Folk*, 29–30.

54. Henry M. Field, *Bright Shadows and Dark Shadows*, quoted in Housewright, *History of Music and Dance in Florida*, 277.

55. Moton, *Finding a Way Out*, 57–61. Composer William Grant Still, who had had a middle-class upbringing in Little Rock, Arkansas, "laughed heartily" at the music he heard as a boy in the state's rural black congregations. He recalled considering the whole service "a hilarious show put on just for my benefit." Still, "My Arkansas Boyhood," 248.

56. Work, *Folk Song of the American Negro*, 118; Meier, *Negro Thought in America*, 265; Wolters, *New Negro on Campus*, 37–38, 75, 249–55; Levine, *Black Culture and Black Consciousness*, 155–74.

57. Haskell, "Negro Spirituals," 581.

58. Cuney-Hare, *Negro Musicians*, 240.

59. Hurston, "Hue and Cry," 315.

60. Kelly Miller to Booker T. Washington, December 27, 1909, in Harlan and Smock, *Booker T. Washington Papers*, 10:255. See also Davenport, *Azalia*, 153.

61. Benjamin J. Davis, *Communist Councilman from Harlem*, quoted in Goodson, *Highbrows, Hillbillies*, 159.

62. James Weldon Johnson, *Book of American Negro Spirituals*, 49.

63. Huggins, *Harlem Renaissance*; David Levering Lewis, *When Harlem Was in Vogue*. For material specifically relating to music, see Floyd, *Black Music in the Harlem Renaissance*; Spencer, *New Negroes and Their Music*; and Anderson, *Deep River*.

64. *MA*, July 22, 1922, 24.

65. James Weldon Johnson, *Book of American Negro Spirituals*, 14.

66. Work, *Folk Song of the American Negro*, 118. For similar sentiments, see Moton, *Religious Folk Songs of the Negro*, vi; and "The Negro's Contribution to Art."

67. Du Bois, *The Souls of Black Folk*, 545. See also David Levering Lewis, *W. E. B. Du Bois*, 278, 286, and Anderson, *Deep River*, 13–57.

68. Dvořák, "The Real Value of *Negro Melodies*," *New York Herald*, May 21, 1893, reprinted in Tibbetts, *Dvořák in America*, 356. For more on the search for an American style of music, see Howard, *Our American Music*, 404–46; Hitchcock, *Music in the United States*, 143–44; Musselman, *Music in the Cultured Generation*, 104–23; Levy, *Musical Nationalism* and "Search for Identity in American Music"; Tischler, *An American Music*; and Tawa, *Mainstream Music*, 103–40. For similar trends in other art forms, including music, see Alexander, *Here the Country Lies*.

69. Howard, "Our Folk-Music," 170.

70. *MA*, August 11, 1906, 2. For further criticisms, see James Creelman, "Dvo-

rák's Negro Symphony," *Pall Mall Budget,* June 21, 1894, reprinted in Beckerman, *Dvořák and His World*; Hughes and Elson, *American Composers,* 22; Elliott, "Our Musical Kinship with the Spaniards"; and *MA,* July 24 (p. 8), 31 (p. 14).

71. *Colored American Magazine* 11 (July 1906): 59. For a similar statement, see Burlin, *Hampton Series, Negro Folk-Songs,* 3:6.

72. For a brief overview of this output, see Southern, *Music of Black Americans,* 265–312, and Anderson, *Deep River,* 22–23.

73. Booker T. Washington, Introduction to *Twenty-Four Negro Melodies* by Coleridge-Taylor, ix.

74. *MA,* January 5, 1918, 48.

75. Burlin, "Negro Music at Birth," 89.

76. *AC,* May 6, 1909, 7.

77. *AC,* November 29, 1894, 7.

78. Walter G. Cooper, *The Cotton States and International Exposition and South Illustrated,* quoted in Rydell, *All the World's a Fair,* 91.

79. *AJ,* May 2, 1910, 3.

80. *AC,* March 25, 1912, 4.

81. For more on the riot, see Leroy Davis, *Clashing of the Soul,* 164–73; Godshalk, "In the Wake of Riot"; Williamson, *Crucible of Race,* 209–23; Mixon, "Atlanta Riot of 1906"; and Dittmer, *Black Georgia in the Progressive Era,* 123–31.

82. *AC,* February 6, 1914, 5.

83. Ibid., 1, 6.

84. Mays, *Born to Rebel,* 75, 80 (emphasis in original). For more on the everyday level of racial anxieties, see Goodson, *Highbrows, Hillbillies,* 138–41, and Hunter, *To 'Joy My Freedom.*

85. McKelway, "Atlanta Riots," 562.

86. Mays, *Born to Rebel,* 72 (emphasis in original).

87. *AC,* July 4, 1910, 1.

88. *AC,* July 5, 1910, 1. For a more detailed analysis of the fight and nationwide riots, see Litwack, *Trouble in Mind,* 440–44; Bederman, *Manliness and Civilization,* 1–10, 41–42; Randy Roberts, *Papa Jack*; Levine, *Black Culture and Black Consciousness,* 429–33; and Al-Tony Gilmore, *Bad Nigger!.* For the response in Georgia, see Dittmer, *Black Georgia in the Progressive Era,* 69–71.

89. *AC,* July 7, 1910, 1, 4.

90. *AC,* September 26, 1906, 6.

91. Godshalk, "In the Wake of Riot," 158 (quotation); Williamson, *Crucible of Race,* 79–108, 259–84.

92. *AC,* July 31, 1910, 7A.

93. *AG,* August 4, 1910, 7; *AI,* July 23, 1910, 1.

94. *AC,* July 31, 1910, 7A.

95. Ibid.

96. *AC,* August 4, 1910, 4.

97. *AC,* August 10, 1910, 10.

98. *AI,* July 30, 1910, 2. For black embarrassment about Johnson's victory, see Al-Tony Gilmore, *Bad Nigger!,* 51–54, and Litwack, *Trouble in Mind,* 443.

99. *AI,* July 23, 1910, 1.

100. Proctor, *Between Black and White,* 108; *AC,* March 4, 1918, 5.

101. *AJ,* June 29, 1913, 7H.

102. *AI,* August 5, 1911, 6. See also Gaines, *Uplifting the Race,* 2–5.

103. *AI,* August 4, 1911, 6; *AC,* August 16, 1912, 2.

104. Proctor, *Between Black and White,* 91.

105. Proctor, "Atlanta Riot," 424; Leroy Davis, *Clashing of the Soul,* 141, 171.

106. Clement Richardson, *National Cyclopedia of the Colored Race,* 136; Hunter, *To Joy My Freedom,* 143–44; Gatewood, *Aristocrats of Color,* 290–92.

107. Proctor, *Between Black and White,* 52, 87, 85–86.

108. *AJ,* August 16, 1912, 3. For more on historical pageantry, see Glassberg, *American Historical Pageantry.* W. E. B. Du Bois wrote a pageant similar in theme to Proctor's, but from a very different perspective; see O'Leary, *To Die For,* 201–3, and Blight, *Race and Reunion,* 375–77.

109. *AC,* August 16, 1912, 2.

110. *AJ,* August, 12, 1912, 3.

111. *AC,* June 29, 1913, 6B.

112. Proctor, *Between Black and White,* 177–78.

113. *AJ,* August 17, 1912, 5; *AC,* August 10, 1911, 10.

114. *AG,* August 10, 1911, 5.

115. *AJ,* August 12, 1912, 3.

116. *AC,* August 10, 1911, 10; *AJ,* August 5, 1910, 5. In his autobiography, Proctor notes that "one of the things that greatly helped me . . . in . . . things I attempted to do in a public way, was the courtesy of the press. They never failed to give due publicity to any matter I wanted to get before the public." He marks the *Constitution* for special mention, and that paper indeed gave more attention to the festival than any of the others. Proctor, *Between Black and White,* 120.

117. *AC,* August 4, 1910, 4.

118. *AJ,* August 5, 1910, 4.

119. *AC,* August 5, 1910, 14.

120. *AC,* August 6, 1911, 7C.

121. *AG,* August 10, 1911, 5.

122. *AC,* August 11, 1912, 4B.

123. *AC,* August 17, 1912, 5.

124. *AC,* August 6, 1911, 7C.

125. *AC,* June 29, 1913, 6B.

126. *AC,* July 31, 1910, 7A.

127. *AJ,* August 5, 1910, 8.

128. *AC,* August 5, 1910, 14.

129. *AC,* July 10, 1914, 12.

130. *AC,* June 29, 1913, 6B; *AC,* July 4, 1913, 3.

131. *AG,* August 5, 1910, 5.

132. *AG,* August 10, 1911, 5.

133. *AC,* August 5, 1910, 14. The same story was repeated in the *Independent;* see *AI,* August 6, 1910, 8.

134. *AC,* July 10, 1914, 12.

135. *AC,* August 5, 1910, 14. This article was reprinted in *AI,* August 6, 1910, 8.

136. *AC,* August 17, 1912, 5.

137. *AJ,* August 16, 1912, 4.

138. *AC,* August 16, 1912, 2; *AC,* August 11, 1912, 4B.

139. *AJ,* May 6, 1910, 8.

140. *AC,* August 14, 1912, 4. See also Gaines, *Uplifting the Race,* 69–70.

141. *AC,* August 17, 1912, 5. "It seemed," wrote the *Journal,* "as though the song had invoked the spirit of the past." *AJ,* August 17, 1912, 5.

142. McEwen, "First Congregational Church, Atlanta," 138.

143. *AI,* August 31, 1912, 6; Goodson, *Highbrows, Hillbillies,* 150–60.

144. For the importance of blues in Atlanta, see Lowry, "Black Sound"; Oakley, *Devil's Music,* 135–42; Bastin, *Red River Blues,* 125–49; and Barlow, *Looking Up at Down,* 191–98. For classical music at the universities, see Cureau, "Kemper Harreld and Willis James"; Jeffrey Green, "Conversation with Josephine Harreld Love"; and Dittmer, *Black Georgia in the Progressive Era,* 67–68. For the intersection of classical and popular music in Atlanta's black community, see Michael W. Harris, *Rise of Gospel Blues,* 26–46. For popular amusements available to the city's black working class, see Goodson, *Highbrows, Hillbillies,* 166–69, 176–78, and Hunter, *To 'Joy My Freedom,* 145–86 passim.

145. *AC,* July 31, 1911, 3; Hunter, *To 'Joy My Freedom,* 154.

146. Goodson, "'South of the North,'" 323–26.

147. Litwack, *Trouble in Mind,* 418–22.

148. Proctor, *Between Black and White,* 181.

149. Gaston, *New South Creed,* 136; Goodson, *Highbrows, Hillbillies,* 159–60.

150. Murphy, "True Negro Music," 1730 (emphasis in original).

Chapter Three

1. *AC,* April 4, 1913, 14. For a list of the association's officers, see *AJ,* April 4, 1913, 11.

2. The description of the 1914 contest is derived from *AJ,* February 19, 4; *AC,* February 18 (p. 3), 19 (p. 9); and *AG,* February 19, 12.

3. *AC,* February 5, 1914, 7. For evidence of fiddling's wide social appeal, see, e.g., *AG,* January 28, 1916, 7, November 16, 1919, 3A, October 1, 1921, 2; *AC,* January 27, 1916, 6, April 6, 1917, 12, March 7, 1919, 12, November 16, 1919, 8A; *AJ,* February 2, 1915, 2, January 27, 1916, 10, November 17, 1920, 7; and Daniel, "Old Time Georgians Recall," 10. For background on the convention, see Meade, "From the Archives"; Burrison, "Fiddlers in the Alley"; Daniel, "The Georgia Old-Time Fiddlers' Convention," "Old Time Georgians Recall," "'Shorty' Harper," "Women's Lib," "Georgia Old Time Fiddlers' Conventions—'A Pleasant Time Was Had by All,'" and *Pickin' on Peachtree;* Wiggins, *Fiddlin' Georgia Crazy,* 46–61; Wolfe, "Atlanta Fiddling Contests, 1913–1916" and "Atlanta Contests, 1921–1934"; Kuhn, Joye, and West, *Living Atlanta,* 282–83; and Goodson, *Highbrows, Hillbillies,* 163–66.

4. *AC*, October 31, 1925, 12.

5. *AG*, February 19, 1914, 12.

6. *AC*, April 2, 1913, 1.

7. *AJ*, February 19, 1914, 4.

8. *New York Times*, July 26, 1885, quoted in Waller, "Feuding in Appalachia," 356. See also Dawley, "Our Southern Mountaineers."

9. Some of the most important monographs include Fox, *Little Shepherd of Kingdom Come* and *Trail of the Lonesome Pine*; Miles, *Spirit of the Mountains*; Samuel Tyndale Wilson, *Southern Mountaineers*; Kephart, *Our Southern Highlanders*; Campbell and Sharp, *English Folk Songs*; John C. Campbell, *Southern Highlander*; and Raine, *Land of Saddle-Bags*. An excellent bibliography of regional writings can be found in Shapiro, *Appalachia on Our Mind*, 309–40. Some of the more important essays and articles have been collected in McNeil, *Appalachian Images in Folk and Popular Culture*. For the changing nature of Appalachia's image, see Hsiung, *Two Worlds in the Tennessee Mountains*; Batteau, *Invention of Appalachia*; Whisnant, *All That Is Native and Fine*; Shapiro, *Appalachia on Our Mind*; Silber, *Romance of Reunion*; and Benjamin Filene, *Romancing the Folk*, 15–27.

10. Frost, "Our Contemporary Ancestors," 315.

11. Ibid., 313.

12. Stephenson, "Segregation of the White and Negro Races in Cities"; John Hammond Moore, "Jim Crow in Georgia"; Dittmer, *Black Georgia in the Progressive Era*, 13–14; Doyle, *New Men, New Cities*, 260–89; Bayor, *Race and the Shaping of Twentieth-Century Atlanta*, 3–12.

13. For an overview of the recent scholarship overturning such popular images, see Ronald L. Lewis, "Beyond Isolation and Homogeneity." For more on African Americans in the region, see William H. Turner, "Demography of Black Appalachia"; Klotter, "Black South and White Appalachia"; and Inscoe, *Mountain Masters* and "Race and Racism in Nineteenth-Century Southern Appalachia."

14. For more on Frost's role in fashioning a new image for Appalachia, see Shapiro, *Appalachia on Our Mind*, 113–32, and Batteau, *Invention of Appalachia*, 74–85.

15. Frost, "Southern Mountaineer," 308.

16. Frost, "Our Contemporary Ancestors," 311.

17. Ibid., 313, 315, 311.

18. Frost, "Three Million American Highlanders," 9, 12. See also Frost, "Our Contemporary Ancestors," 316.

19. Frost, "Our Contemporary Ancestors," 313.

20. Frost, "Historical Museum," 9; see also Frost, "Appalachian America."

21. "Race Conservation."

22. For more on nativism, see Higham, *Strangers in the Land*, and Jacobson, *Whiteness of a Different Color* and *Barbarian Virtues*.

23. Kephart, *Our Southern Highlanders*, 385.

24. Semple, "Anglo-Saxons of the Kentucky Mountains," 150–51. See also Samuel Tyndale Wilson, *Southern Mountaineers*, 44–45. Although Semple's conclusions

about Anglo-Saxonism received widespread approval, not everyone agreed with her. William Aspenwall Bradley, for instance, believed that the region's racial makeup was much more complicated than she suggested. He accused Semple and others like her of "Anglo-Saxon chauvinism." Bradley, "Folk Culture of the Cumberlands," 96.

25. Kephart, *Our Southern Highlanders*, 385. For a similar statement, see Miles, *Spirit of the Mountains*, 200–201.

26. For a sampling of writing attempting to work out an ethnographic name for Appalachian people, see Samuel Tyndale Wilson, *Southern Mountaineers*, 24–25; Frost, "Our Contemporary Ancestors," 311; Hartt, "The Mountaineers," 397; Johnston, "Romance of the Kentucky Feuds," 110; Grant, *Passing of the Great Race*, 99; Kephart, *Our Southern Highlanders*, 430–34; and Brockway, "Quest of the Lonesome Tunes," 228. The region's most sophisticated observer, sociologist John C. Campbell, attempted to avoid the fracas altogether, deeming the mountain people too heterogeneous to make any one label satisfactory. Nevertheless, even Campbell could not escape the issue, devoting twenty-one pages of his book to the question of ancestry. He attempted to cut the Gordian knot by arguing that, in the end, all that could be said was that the environment had homogenized the various ethnic elements into "the type which has come to be called 'American,'" but his definition of the "American" type necessarily excluded anyone who was not white. Campbell, *Southern Highlander*, 50–71.

27. For the increased popular and academic interest in folklore in America, see Bronner, *American Folklore Studies* and *Following Tradition*; Zumwalt, *American Folklore Scholarship*; Kammen, *Mystic Chords of Memory*, 407–43; and Bendix, *In Search of Authenticity*.

28. Samuel Tyndale Wilson, *Southern Mountaineers*, 161, 18.

29. Raine, *Land of Saddle-Bags*, 16.

30. Frost, "Our Contemporary Ancestors," 316.

31. Fox, "Southern Mountaineer," 150.

32. Semple, "Anglo-Saxons of the Kentucky Mountains," 151.

33. "Mountain Minstrelsy."

34. For more on Child, see Kittredge, Introduction; Hustvedt, *Ballad Books and Ballad Men*, 205–25; Bendix, *In Search of Authenticity*, 81–88; and Benjamin Filene, *Romancing the Folk*, 12–15.

35. Bradley, "Song-Ballets," 905.

36. These statewide folklore societies were established in Missouri (1906), Texas (1909), Kentucky (1912), North Carolina (1913), South Carolina (1913), Virginia (1913), and West Virginia (1915). Tennessee also had folklore societies during this period but could not sustain a long-term organization until 1934. Mississippi formed a group in 1927. Hand, "North American Folklore Societies." For an analysis of the interest in mountain folk song, see Wilgus, *Anglo-American Folksong Scholarship*; Bronson, "Folk-Song in the United States"; Shapiro, *Appalachia on Our Mind*, 244–65; Whisnant, *All That Is Native and Fine*, 183–252; Linn, *That Half-Barbaric Twang*, 116–44; and Benjamin Filene, *Romancing the Folk*, 15–26.

37. The resulting state collections with Appalachian material include Arthur Kyle Davis, *Traditional Ballads of Virginia*; Reed Smith, *South Carolina Ballads*; and Brown, *North Carolina Folklore*. Other important collections compiled during this period include Shearin and Combs, *Syllabus of Kentucky Folk-Songs*; Wyman and Brockway, *Lonesome Tunes*; Campbell and Sharp, *English Folk Songs*; Combs, *Folk-Songs of the Southern United States*; and Cox, *Folk-Songs of the South*.

38. Charles Alphonso Smith, "A Great Movement."

39. Bradley, "Song-Ballets," 903.

40. McGill, "'Following Music,'" 383.

41. One of the few to see continuities in the old and newer ballads was Miles, *Spirit of the Mountains*, 163. Collector Cecil Sharp (*English Folk Songs from the Southern Appalachians*, ix) wrote of the singers he met that "very often they misunderstood our requirements and would give us hymns instead of the secular songs and ballads which we wanted." For more on the selective manner of folk song collecting, see Whisnant, *All That Is Native and Fine*, 51–56, 110–27; Malone, *Singing Cowboys*, 44–45; and Benjamin Filene, *Romancing the Folk*, 12–20.

42. Campbell and Sharp, *English Folk Songs*, xx. For a fuller explication of these ideas, see Sharp, *English Folk-Song*, and Stekert, "Tylor's Theory of Survivals," 228–32.

43. Campbell and Sharp, *English Folk Songs*, xx.

44. Sharp, *English Folk-Song*, 136.

45. Campbell and Sharp, *English Folk Songs*. For an overview of Sharp's work in the mountains, see Karpeles, *Cecil Sharp*, 140–71, and Benjamin Filene, *Romancing the Folk*, 20–25.

46. Campbell and Sharp, *English Folk Songs*, vii. For more on Sharp's racial theories and his work in the Appalachians, see Whisnant, *All That Is Native and Fine*, 110–27, and Benjamin Filene, *Romancing the Folk*, 20–25.

47. Olive Dame Campbell, "Songs and Ballads," 374.

48. Raine, *Land of Saddle-Bags*, 107; Reed Smith, *South Carolina Ballads*, 74; see also p. 73.

49. McGill, "'Following Music,'" 384.

50. Brockway, "Quest of the Lonesome Tunes," 228.

51. Quoted in Hart and Ferleger, *Theodore Roosevelt Cyclopedia*, 364. For more on Roosevelt's fears about overcivilization, see Dyer, *Theodore Roosevelt and the Idea of Race*, 123–67.

52. Kasson, *Houdini, Tarzan*; Kimmel, *Manhood in America*, 81–188; Bederman, *Manliness and Civilization*; Slotkin, *Gunfighter Nation*; Ownby, *Subduing Satan*; Peter Filene, *Him/Her/Self*, 74–99; Rotundo, *American Manhood*; Gorn, *Manly Art*, 179–206.

53. Kephart, *Our Southern Highlanders*, 308. For more on mountain masculinity, see Silber, *Romance of Reunion*, 148–52.

54. Frost, "Our Contemporary Ancestors," 312.

55. Samuel Tyndale Wilson, *Southern Mountaineers*, 20–21.

56. Frost, "How To Make Something Out of This Fighting Stock," 11–12. For

more on the development of the feudist stereotype, see Waller, "Feuding in Appalachia," and Blee and Billings, "Where 'Bloodshed is a Pastime.'" For an excellent study of the economic and social roots of feuding, see Waller, *Feud*.

57. Kephart, *Our Southern Highlanders*, 348, 465.

58. Ibid., 267 (quotation); John C. Campbell, *Southern Highlander*, 124. Bederman, *Manliness and Civilization*; Silber, *Romance of Reunion*, 167–78.

59. Kephart, *Camping and Woodcraft*, 19.

60. Kephart, *Our Southern Highlanders*, 281; see also *Camping and Woodcraft*, 18.

61. Kephart, *Our Southern Highlanders*, 89.

62. Kephart, *Camping and Woodcraft*, 19–20.

63. Kephart, *Our Southern Highlanders*, 379.

64. Ibid., 268. For more on Kephart's life, see Kephart, "Horace Kephart"; Ellison, Introduction; and Batteau, *Invention of Appalachia*, 89–91.

65. Raine, *Land of Saddle-Bags*, 16, 260.

66. For a concise overview of the New Woman phenomenon, see Dumenil, *The Modern Temper*, 98–144.

67. Mrs. William Frost, "The Women of the Mountains," 7.

68. Kephart, *Our Southern Highlanders*, 330–32.

69. Raine, *Land of Saddle-Bags*, 91.

70. McGill, "'Following Music,'" 372.

71. Grant, *Passing of the Great Race*, 47. See also "Childless Women of Cities."

72. Combs, *Kentucky Highlanders*, 19. See also Frost, "Our Contemporary Ancestors," 318; Samuel Tyndale Wilson, *Southern Mountaineers*, 58–61; and Roosevelt, "Race Decadence," 764.

73. Raine, *Land of Saddle-Bags*, 91.

74. McGill, "'Following Music,'" 371.

75. MacKaye, "Untamed America," 327.

76. Frost, "Our Contemporary Ancestors," 318, 311.

77. Frost, "Historical Museum," 8.

78. Raine, *Land of Saddle-Bags*, 62.

79. Frost, "Our Contemporary Ancestors," 318; Samuel Tyndale Wilson, *Southern Mountaineers*.

80. *AC*, July 31, 1910, 7.

81. These issues are treated extensively in Whisnant, *All That Is Native and Fine*, and Shapiro, *Appalachia on Our Mind*, 133–243. See also Whisnant, *Modernizing the Mountaineer*, 3–18, and Jane S. Becker, *Selling Tradition*.

82. Gaston, *New South Creed*, 117–50; Silber, *Romance of Reunion*, 143–58; Klotter, "Black South and White Appalachia"; Shannon H. Wilson, "Lincoln's Sons and Daughters."

83. Kephart, *Our Southern Highlanders*, 427.

84. Fox, "Southern Mountaineer," 143. See also Hartt, "The Mountaineers," 403, and "Foreign Missions, Continued," 488.

85. Gielow, "Call of the Race," 215, 218.

86. Grant, *Passing of the Great Race*, 49.

87. *AJ*, April 20, 1909, 8; *AC*, May 9, 1909, 4B.

88. Thomas H. Martin, *Atlanta and Its Builders*, 12.

89. *AG*, June 25, 1911, 3A. For more on the mountain schools in Georgia, see Allen H. Eaton, *Handicrafts of the Southern Highlands*, 71–72; "The School at Rabun Gap"; and Roth, *Matronage*, 116–19. For more on Atlanta's attitudes toward mountain people, see Goodson, *Highbrows, Hillbillies*, 162–63.

90. *AC*, May 13, 1906, 8M. For an editorial supporting Ritchie's work, see *AC*, June 21, 1907, 6.

91. *AC*, August 28, 1910, 5.

92. *AC*, November 12, 1911, 10M.

93. Ibid.

94. *AJ*, October 5, 1923, 10; *AC*, May 9, 1909, 7A. See also the editorial in *AC*, June 21, 1907, 6.

95. *AJ*, January 26, 1916, 8; *AC*, March 1, 1918, 7.

96. *AC*, April 2, 1913, 1.

97. *AJ*, April 2, 1913, 11. See also *MA*, March 21, 1914, 29.

98. *AC*, February 15, 1914, 4B. For similar stories, see *AJ*, June 21, 1914, Magazine, 3; *AG*, February 22, 1914, 3A; and *AJ*, September 10, 1922, 8B.

99. For more on Carson's life, see Wiggins, *Fiddlin' Georgia Crazy*.

100. *AJ*, April 3, 1913, 9.

101. *AC*, March 7, 1919, 12.

102. *AC*, January 27, 1916, 6.

103. *AC*, January 25, 1916, 3.

104. Hoeptner and Pinson, "Clayton McMichen Talking," Part 1:19. For more on McMichen's career, see Cohen, "Clayton McMichen," and Wolfe, *Devil's Box*, 81–98.

105. Hoeptner and Pinson, "Clayton McMichen Talking," Part 3:14. For an account of the kind of showmanship that McMichen criticized, see *AC*, April 4, 1913, 4. Fiddler Gordon Tanner, whose father was a convention favorite, was less critical of Smart: "He was a good manager. He kept things going and some fiddlers they just fiddle away and never did get tired and finally he would have to get right up at them with that cowbell eight inches long and that thing made a fuss. He'd ring them out, get them to quit." Interview with Gordon Tanner, Living Atlanta Collection, AHC.

106. Hoeptner and Pinson, "Clayton McMichen Talking," Part 4:20. For biographical information on some of the other contest's participants, see Cohen, "'Fiddlin' John Carson'"; Daniel, "Georgia Fiddling Champion," "'Shorty' Harper," and "Women's Lib"; Wolfe, "Bill Shores"; Wolfe, Bulger, and Wiggins, "Roba Stanley"; Wiggins, "Gordon Tanner" and *Fiddlin' Georgia Crazy*; and LaRose, "Interview with Lowe Stokes."

107. Perhaps not surprisingly, McMichen was named an officer of the new organization. See *AJ*, September 29, 1921, 4; *AC*, September 29, 1921, 13; *AG*, September 29, 1921, 7; *AC*, September 30, 1921, 7.

108. Quoted in Kuhn, *Contesting the New South Order*, 40.

109. Kephart, *Our Southern Highlanders* (emphasis added).

110. See, e.g., the map accompanying William Goodell Frost's essay "Southern

Mountaineer," 303, which shows the mountains ending abruptly at the Pennsylvania border.

111. *CB*, February 1923, 36, quoted in Garofalo, "Sons of Henry Grady," 189.

112. Silber, *Romance of Reunion*, 143–52.

113. "Southern Problem." See also Mayo, "Educational Opportunity at Berea," 312.

114. Samuel H. Thompson, *Highlanders of the South*, 55, 46.

115. *AC*, September 25, 1906, 6.

116. Tompkins, "Mountain Whites as an Industrial Factor," 61. Contemporary observers took a great deal of interest in the makeup of the mill labor force, especially its reliance on white workers. See, e.g., Holland Thompson, *From the Cotton Field to the Cotton Mill*, 96–118, and Mitchell, *Rise of Cotton Mills*, 160–232. For more recent examinations, see Carlton, *Mill and Town in South Carolina*; Williamson, *Crucible of Race*, 429–44; Hall et al., *Like a Family*; and Newby, *Plain Folk in the New South*.

117. Horner, "Educational Work in the Mountains," 590.

118. Fink, *Fulton Bag and Cotton Mills Strike*, 64–90; Hall, "Private Eyes, Public Women"; Kuhn, *Contesting the New South Order*.

119. *CB*, March 1916, 8 (emphasis in original).

120. *AC*, November 19, 1920, 7. See also *AG*, October 1, 1921, 2.

121. *AC*, February 7, 1914, 5A.

122. *AJ*, November 18, 1919, 19.

123. *AG*, November 18, 1920, 8. For another comparison, see *AJ*, February 15, 1914, Magazine, 7. Atlanta's fiddlers were not the only ones to make such jabs. The nation's premier old-time music show was, after all, Nashville's "Grand Ole Opry."

124. *AJ*, March 1, 1918, 10.

125. *AC*, March 1, 1918, 7.

126. *AG*, March 1, 1918, 10. See also *AJ*, January 26, 1916, 8.

127. *AG*, November 16, 1920, 6. See also *AG*, February 19, 1914, 12, and *MA*, March 21, 1914, 29.

128. *AJ*, January 26, 1916, 8; *AJ*, November 18, 1920, 20.

129. *AC*, February 21, 1914, 6. See also *AG*, January 27, 1916, 4, and *AC*, October 1, 1921, 6.

130. *AJ*, January 31, 1915, Magazine, 7.

131. Williamson, *Crucible of Race*, 414–58; Janiewski, "Southern Honor, Southern Dishonor."

132. *AG*, February 19, 1914, 12.

133. *AJ*, February 2, 1915, 2; *AC*, February 6, 1915, 8.

134. *AC*, January 26, 1916, 4; *AC*, January 27, 1916, 6.

135. *AC*, January 27, 1916, 6, 1.

136. *AC*, February 28, 1918, 9.

137. *AJ*, November 21, 1919, 32. See also *AC*, February 7, 1915, 2M, and *AJ*, March 6, 1919, 12.

138. *AJ*, February 19, 1914, 4.

139. *AJ*, November 14, 1920, Magazine, 9.

140. The UDC passed the money along to its Tallullah Falls Industrial School

for mountain children. For a UDC-sponsored fiddling convention in Fayette County, Ala., see Cauthen, *With Fiddle and Well-Rosined Bow*, 184–86. Other recipients of proceeds from the Atlanta contests included the Georgia National Guard's Fifth Infantry Regiment (1913), the Commission on Training Camp Activities (1918), the Scottish Rite Hospital for Crippled Children (1919), the fiddlers themselves (1920–21), the Atlanta Convention Bureau (1922), and the Maple Grove Circle, No. 39, Woodmen of the World (1923).

141. *AC*, January 26, 1916, 1; *AG*, January 27, 1916, 4.

142. *AC*, January 27, 1916, 6. See also *AG*, January 27, 1916, 4, and *AJ*, January 27, 1916, 8.

143. *AC*, February 19, 1914, 9; *AJ*, February 19, 1914, 4.

144. Russell was the father of the more famous man of the same name who became a U.S. senator. Biographical information on the elder Russell is based on Knight, *Standard History of Georgia*, 6:3301; Jack White, *Bench and Bar of Georgia*, 274; Turbeville, *Eminent Georgians*, 1:12–16; Kelly, "Richard B. Russell," 1–47; and Fite, *Richard B. Russell, Jr.*, 1–15. For his KKK membership, see MacLean, *Behind the Mask of Chivalry*, 17.

145. *AJ*, February 15, 1914, Magazine, 7.

146. *AC*, April 1, 1913, 9.

147. *AJ*, February 19, 1914, 4. For an early examination of the manipulation of whiteness to trump class, see Du Bois, "Georgia: Invisible Empire State." For later studies, see MacLean, *Behind the Mask of Chivalry*, 125–48, and Kantrowitz, *Ben Tillman*.

148. Goodson, *Highbrows, Hillbillies*, 165–66.

149. As Barbara Fields ("Ideology and Race in American History," 158) has noted, "Each class of whites [has] its particular variety of racialist ideology."

150. Kephart, *Our Southern Highlanders*, 327. For similar assessments, see Semple, "Anglo-Saxons of the Kentucky Mountains," 170; Raine, *Land of Saddle-Bags*, 34, 53; and Kephart, *Our Southern Highlanders*, 326–27, 455. John Fox ("Southern Mountaineer," 141) asserted that Methodists and Baptists had gained so many converts among the mountain people precisely because "they were more democratic" than competing denominations. For modern studies disputing this contention of classless Appalachian society, see Waller, *Feud*, and Pudup, Billings, and Waller, *Appalachia in the Making*.

151. *AC*, November 14, 1920, 8A.

152. I have taken this phrase from Miles, *Spirit of the Mountains*.

153. The literature on minstrelsy is large but unfortunately focuses heavily on the antebellum period, with less attention to twentieth-century manifestations. Major works include Wittke, *Tambo and Bones*; Nathan, *Dan Emmet*; Toll, *Blacking Up*; Boskin, *Sambo*, 65–94; Lott, *Love and Theft*; Hamm, *Putting Popular Music in Its Place*; Bean, Hatch, and McNamara, *Inside the Minstrel Mask*; Cockrell, *Demons of Disorder*; Roediger, *Wages of Whiteness*, 115–31; and Mahar, *Behind the Burnt Cork Mask*. For the minstrel's influence on John Carson, see Wiggins, *Fiddlin' Georgia Crazy*, 155–57.

154. This does not mean that these tunes had not become "folk" songs in impor-

tant ways by the beginning of the twentieth century. Indeed, the cross-fertilization between southern vernacular musicians and minstrel performers is enormously complex. Yet the minstrel shows, as evidenced by the repertoire at the Atlanta convention, clearly provided a great deal of inspiration for the fiddlers. For some examination of the intersection between minstrelsy and vernacular traditions, see Talley, *Negro Folk Rhymes*; Scarborough, *On the Trail of Negro Folk-Songs*; Newman Ivey White, *American Negro Folk-Songs* and "White Man in the Woodpile"; Newman Ivey White et al., *Frank C. Brown Collection*, 3:480–568; Toll, *Blacking Up*, 42–51; Levine, *Black Culture*, 192–95; Winans, "The Folk, the Stage"; Epstein, *Sinful Tunes and Spirituals*, 241–42; Cantwell, *Bluegrass Breakdown*, 249–74; Linn, *That Half-Barbaric Twang*, 116–18; Abrahams, *Singing the Master*, 131–53; Malone, *Singing Cowboys*, 50–56; and Conway, *African Banjo Echoes*, 84–159.

155. *AJ*, February 19, 1914, 4.

156. *AG*, November 20, 1920, 2.

157. *AJ*, January 26, 1916, 8. See also *AG*, January 26, 1916, 2; *AC*, February 26, 1918, 7; and *AJ*, June 25, 1922, Magazine, 5.

158. *AG*, November 19, 1920, 17.

159. *AJ*, April 3, 1913, 9.

160. The term "hillbilly" seems not to have come into popular currency until the mid-1920s. Before then, as Archie Green notes, white rural music was simply sold on records as old-time tunes or old hill music. For the origins of the hillbilly stereotype and its appropriation by commercial musicians, see Green, "Hillbilly Music"; Daniel, "George Daniell's Hill Billies"; Linn, *That Half Barbaric Twang*, 141–42; Malone, *Singing Cowboys*, 69–90; Harkins, "The Significance of 'Hillbilly' in Early Country Music"; and Peterson, *Creating Country Music*, 67–80.

161. *New York Tribune*, March 28, 1897, sec. 3:5.

162. "Negro Music and Minstrelsy," 69. For more on this, see Matthews, "Rise and Fall of Negro-Minstrelsy," and the editorials collected from sources across America in "Passing of the Minstrels." For a slightly later account, see Wittke, *Tambo and Bones*, 103–34.

163. *AJ*, May 1, 1910, 12H.

164. *AC*, March 30, 1913, 5B.

165. *AJ*, October 23, 1923, 4.

166. *AC*, October 1, 1921, 6.

167. For overviews on the debates surrounding ragtime's social impact, see Leonard, "Reaction to Ragtime," and Berlin, *Ragtime*, 32–96. For jazz, see Leonard, *Jazz and the White Americans*; MacDonald Smith Moore, *Yankee Blues*; and Ogren, *Jazz Revolution*.

168. Howard, *Our American Music*, 427. For other contemporary defenses, see *MA*, June 22, 1912, 24, and July 22, 1922, 23. For a later assessment of white enthusiasm for jazz, see Berger, "Jazz," and Leonard, *Jazz and the White Americans*, 47–72.

169. Kenilworth, "Demoralizing Rag Time Music," *Musical Courier* 66 (28 May 1913), quoted in Berlin, *Ragtime*, 107–8.

170. *MA*, May 13, 1922, 41.

171. Kuhn, *Living Atlanta*, 316.

172. Ashworth, "Virginia Mountaineers," 197.

173. Quoted in Leonard, *Jazz and the White Americans*, 37.

174. Campbell and Sharp, *English Folk Songs*, ix.

175. *AJ*, June 25, 1922, Magazine, 5.

176. *AJ*, February 15, 1914, 7.

177. *AC*, November 16, 1927, 2.

178. *AC*, August 18, 1915, 7. For more on Carson's role in the Frank case and the composition and texts of his ballads about Frank and Phagan, see Wiggins, *Fiddlin' Georgia Crazy*, 26–44. For more on the ballad, see Snyder, "Leo Frank and Mary Phagan"; Keyes, "'Little Mary Phagan'"; and Wilgus and Hurvitz, "'Little Mary Phagan.'" For the Frank case, see Golden, *A Little Girl Is Dead*; Dinnerstein, *The Leo Frank Case*; and MacLean, "The Leo Frank Case."

179. *Metronome* 39 (February 1923): 27.

180. Cauthen, *With Fiddle and Well-Rosined Bow*, 192–95. For other Alabama conventions, see ibid., 163–200, and Archie Green, "Hillbilly Music," 214.

181. Wolfe, "The Great 1927 Nashville Fiddlers' Convention," "Old-Time Fiddling Contests at Knoxville's Market Hall," and "The 1926 Tennessee State Championship Contest."

182. *Metronome* 34 (July 1923): 19; *Talking Machine World* 22 (March 15, 1926): 59; Brotherton, "Early Fiddling Contests." Most of these conventions were, like Atlanta's, highly publicized and theatrical affairs. Fiddling contests thrived in vernacular settings as well, though they lacked the same self-consciousness that was a staple of the urban contests. For evidence of vernacular contests, see Bascom, "Ballads and Songs of Western North Carolina." Some late-nineteenth-century contests perhaps leading the way from vernacular to more commercial versions are covered briefly in Wolfe, *Tennessee Strings*, 20–22, and *Kentucky Country*, 12.

183. Cochran, *Our Own Sweet Sounds*, 18; *Nashville Tennesseean*, December 20, 1925, reprinted in *John Edward Memorial Foundation Newsletter* 4 (September 1968): 111; Daniel, "Old-Time Fiddler's Contests on Early Radio." See also Cauthen, "D. Dix Hollis," and Grundy, "'We Always Tried to Be Respectable People.'"

184. "Fiddling to Henry Ford."

185. For a fuller account of Ford's critique, see "Jewish Jazz Becomes Our National Music," 177–85. For more on the Ford contests, see Blaustein, "Traditional Music and Social Change," 35–53; David L. Lewis, *Public Image of Henry Ford*, 227–78; Wells, "Mellie Dunham"; Daniel, "Mechanics and Musicians"; Meade, "Fiddles and Fords"; Sutherland, "Beware of Old-Time Music Revivals"; Linn, *That Half-Barbaric Twang*, 144; and Peterson, *Creating Country Music*, 59–62. For the popularity of old-time fiddling generally during the period, see Braine, "Country Fiddler," and Blaustein, "Traditional Music and Social Change," 25–55.

186. Frost, "Our Contemporary Ancestors," 311; Samuel Tyndale Wilson, *Southern Mountaineers*, 195.

187. Frost, "Our Contemporary Ancestors," 316. In a similar vein, Kephart (*Our*

Southern Highlanders, 389) called it a "chivalrous, self-sacrificing fidelity to family and to clan leader."

188. *AC*, August 3, 1897.

189. Kephart, *Our Southern Highlanders*, 454 (emphasis in original). "Race purity," another chronicler noted, is "zealously preserved. The cohabitation of whites and negroes would not be tolerated by the whites of the remotest mountain sections." Ashworth, "Virginia Mountaineers," 197.

190. Williamson, *Crucible of Race*, 291–95.

191. Kephart, *Our Southern Highlanders*, 417; see also 419.

192. Ownby, *Subduing Satan*, 38–55.

193. *AJ*, September 22, 1929, 10B. As Wayne Daniel has pointed out, women had been involved in the contest all along, but they had received little notice by the press. Despite the newspapers's propensity for exaggeration, it appears that the opposition to female fiddlers was not entirely fabricated. Anita Sorrells Wheeler recalled that in 1930, when she entered the contest, "John Carson didn't want me to play because I was a woman. . . . So the other fiddlers said, 'Well, o.k., if she don't play, we don't play.' So I played." Daniel, "Women's Lib," 14. For contemporary evidence that men dominated fiddling, see Semple, "Anglo-Saxons of the Kentucky Mountains," 174; Bascom, "Ballads and Songs of Western North Carolina," 239; William Anspenwall Bradley, "Song-Ballets," 913; and Josephine McGill, "'Following Music' in a Mountain Land," 368. See also Jabbour, "Fiddle Music," 253–56. For popular representation of gender and mountain music, see Linn, *That Half-Barbaric Twang*, 130–33, and Whisnant, *All That Is Native and Fine*, 97–101.

194. For the conflict between female evangelical culture and the emerging (male) mass culture in the turn-of-the-century South, see Ownby, *Subduing Satan*, 194–212.

195. *AJ*, November 17, 1920, 7.

196. That is, the aria "Vesti la giubba." *AJ*, April 8, 1917, Magazine, 6.

197. *AJ*, November 20, 1920, 2.

198. *AC*, November 14, 1920, 8A.

199. *AC*, October 30, 1925, 12; *AJ*, February 19, 1914, 4.

200. *AC*, February 18, 1914, 3.

201. *AG*, January 27, 1916, 4.

202. *AC*, April 2, 1913, 1.

203. *AJ*, April 2, 1913, 11.

204. *AC*, March 2, 1918, 4.

205. *AJ*, November 16, 1919, 4A.

206. Bradley, "Song-Ballets," 913–14; Ownby, *Subduing Satan*, 1–18.

207. *AJ*, April 2, 1913, 11.

208. *AG*, November 16, 1919, 3A.

209. *AC*, April 2, 1913, 1.

210. *AC*, April 11, 1917, 16.

211. MacKaye, "Untamed America," 327.

212. *AC*, April 2, 1913, 1.

Epilogue

1. *AJ*, January 27, 1916, 10; *AJ*, November 21, 1919, 32.
2. Darnton, *Great Cat Massacre*, 5.
3. Dickinson, *Education of a Music Lover*, 281.
4. Kramer, *Musical Meaning*, 1–9.

Bibliography

Manuscript Collections

Atlanta, Georgia
    Atlanta History Center
        Atlanta Music Club Papers
        Bertha Harwood-Arrowood Papers
        Living Atlanta Collection
        Metropolitan Opera Collection
        Music Collection
        Katherine Wooten Scrapbooks
    Emory University, Special Collections, Robert W. Woodruff Library
        Metropolitan Opera Collection
    Georgia Department of Archives and History, Office of Secretary of State
        Nana Tucker Collection
    Ida Pearle and Joseph Cuba Archives of the William Breman Jewish
      Heritage Museum
        Herman Heyman Papers
Charleston, South Carolina
    South Carolina Historical Society
        Papers of the Society for the Preservation of Spirituals

Newspapers

Atlanta City Builder	*Atlanta Independent*
Atlanta Constitution	*Atlanta Journal*
Atlanta Georgian	*Musical America*

Books and Articles

Abrahams, Roger D. *Singing the Master: The Emergence of African American Culture in the Plantation South.* New York: Pantheon Books, 1992.

Ahlquist, Karen. *Democracy at the Opera: Music, Theater, and Culture in New York City, 1815–1860.* Urbana: University of Illinois Press, 1997.

Aldrich, Richard. *Concert Life in New York, 1902–1923.* New York: G. P. Putnam's Sons, 1941.

Alexander, Charles C. *Here the Country Lies: Nationalism and the Arts in Twentieth-Century America.* Bloomington: Indiana University Press, 1980.

Amey, Ellen. "Music Hath Power." *The Survey* 48 (April 22, 1922): 109–11.

Ammer, Christine. *Unsung: A History of Women in American Music.* Westport,
    Conn.: Greenwood Press, 1980.

Anderson, Paul Allen. *Deep River: Music and Memory in Harlem Renaissance Thought.*
    Durham: Duke University Press, 2001.

Arnesen, Eric. "Whiteness and the Historians' Imagination." *International Labor
    and Working-Class History* 60 (Fall 2001): 3–32.

"Art and Money." *Etude* 12 (March 1894): 63.

"Art from the Cabin Door." *Outlook* 141 (October 21, 1925): 268–69.

Ashworth, John H. "The Virginia Mountaineers." *South Atlantic Quarterly* 12 (July
    1913); reprinted in *Appalachian Images in Folk and Popular Culture,* 2d ed.,
    edited by W. K. McNeil, Knoxville: University of Tennessee Press, 1995.

Austern, Linda Phyllis. "'Alluring the Auditorie to Effeminacie': Music and the
    Idea of the Feminine in Early Modern England." *Music and Letters* 74 (August
    1993): 343–54.

Ayers, Edward L. *The Promise of the New South: Life after Reconstruction.* New York:
    Oxford University Press, 1992.

———. "Narrating a New South." *Journal of Southern History* 61 (August 1995):
    555–66.

Bacon, A. M. "Proposal for Folk-Lore Research at Hampton, V.A." *Journal of
    American Folklore* 6 (October–December 1893): 305–9.

Bagby, George William. *The Old Virginia Gentleman and Other Sketches.* 4th ed.
    Richmond: Dietz Press, 1943.

Baker, Lee D. *From Savage to Negro: Anthropology and the Construction of Race, 1896–
    1954.* Berkeley: University of California Press, 1998.

———. "Research, Reform, and Racial Uplift: The Mission of the Hampton Folk-
    Lore Society, 1893–1899." In *Excluded Ancestors, Inevitable Traditions: Essays
    toward a More Inclusive History of Anthropology,* edited by Richard Handler.
    Madison: University of Wisconsin Press, 2000.

Baker, Ray Stannard. *Following the Color Line: American Negro Citizenship in the
    Progressive Era.* 1908. Reprint, New York: Harper Torchbooks, 1964.

———. "Gathering Clouds along the Color Line." *World's Work* 32 (June 1916):
    232–36.

Baltzell, W. J. "The American College Man in Music." *Musical Quarterly*
    1 (October 1915): 623–36.

———. "The Business of Being an Artist." *Musician* 22 (June 1917): 414–15.

Barlow, William. *"Looking Up at Down": The Emergence of Blues Culture.*
    Philadelphia: Temple University Press, 1989.

Barnes, Earl. "The Feminizing of Culture." *Atlantic Monthly* 109 (June 1912):
    770–76.

Bartholomew, E. F. *Relation of Psychology to Music.* 2d ed. Revised. Rock Island,
    Ill.: New Era Publishing Co., 1902.

Bascom, Louise Rand. "Ballads and Songs of Western North Carolina." *Journal of
    American Folklore* 22 (April–June 1909): 238–40.

Bastin, Bruce. *Red River Blues: The Blues Tradition in the Southeast.* Urbana:
    University of Illinois Press, 1986.

Batchellor, Daniel. "Woman's Sphere in Music-Teaching." *Etude* 19 (September 1901): 319.

Batteau, Alan. *The Invention of Appalachia*. Tucson: University of Arizona Press, 1990.

Bayor, Ronald H. *Race and the Shaping of Twentieth-Century Atlanta*. Chapel Hill: University of North Carolina Press, 1996.

Bean, Annemarie, James V. Hatch, and Brooks McNamara, eds. *Inside the Minstrel Mask: Readings in Nineteenth-Century Blackface Minstrelsy*. Hanover, N.H.: University Press of New England, 1996.

Becker, Gustav L. "Recent Notable Progress in American Music." *Etude* 33 (January 1915): 15–16.

Becker, Jane S. *Selling Tradition: Appalachia and the Construction of an American Folk, 1930–1940*. Chapel Hill: University of North Carolina Press, 1998.

Beckerman, Michael. *Dvořák and His World*. Princeton: Princeton University Press, 1993.

Bederman, Gail. *Manliness and Civilization: A Cultural History of Gender and Race in the United States, 1880–1917*. Chicago: University of Chicago Press, 1995.

Bendix, Regina. *In Search of Authenticity: The Formation of Folklore Studies*. Madison: University of Wisconsin Press, 1997.

Benedict, Marie. "Woman's Share in the Musical Civilization of the Public." *Etude* 19 (September 1901): 318–19.

Berger, Morroe. "Jazz: Resistance to the Diffusion of a Culture-Pattern." *Journal of Negro History* 32 (October 1947): 461–94.

Berlin, Edward. *Ragtime: A Musical and Cultural History*. Berkeley: University of California Press, 1980.

Bierley, Paul E. *John Philip Sousa: American Phenomenon*. Revised. Westerville, Ohio: Integrity Press, 1986.

Billings, Dwight B., Jr. *Planters and the Making of a "New South": Class, Politics, and Development in North Carolina, 1865–1900*. Chapel Hill: University of North Carolina Press, 1979.

Billings, Dwight B., Gurney Norman, and Katherine Ledford, eds. *Confronting Appalachian Stereotypes: Back Talk from an American Region*. Lexington: University of Kentucky Press, 1999.

Birge, Edward Baily. *History of Public School Music in the United States*. 2d ed. Philadelphia: Oliver Ditson Co., 1937.

"Black Music and Its Future Transmutation into Real Art." *Current Opinion* 63 (July 1917): 26–27.

"Black Voices." *Nation* 119 (September 17, 1924): 278.

Blackwelder, Julia. "Mop and Typewriter: Women's Work in Early-Twentieth-Century Atlanta." *Atlanta Historical Journal* 27 (Fall 1983): 21–30.

Blair, Karen J. *The Clubwoman as Feminist: True Womanhood Redefined, 1868–1914*. New York: Holmes and Meier, 1980.

———. *The Torchbearers: Women and Their Amateur Arts Associations in America, 1890–1930*. Bloomington: Indiana University Press, 1994.

Blaustein, Richard J. "Traditional Music and Social Change: The Old Time Fiddlers Association Movement in the United States." Ph.D. diss., Indiana University, 1975.

Blee, Kathleen M., and Dwight B. Billings. "Where 'Bloodshed Is a Pastime': Mountain Feuds and Appalachian Stereotyping." In *Confronting Appalachian Stereotypes: Back Talk from an American Region,* edited by Dwight B. Billings, Gurney Norman, and Katherine Ledford. Lexington: University of Kentucky Press, 1999.

Blight, David W. *Race and Reunion: The Civil War in American Memory.* Cambridge: Harvard University Press, 2001.

Block, Adrienne Fried. "Women in American Music, 1800–1918." In *Women and Music: A History,* edited by Karin Pendle. Bloomington: Indiana University Press, 1991.

———. *Amy Beach, Passionate Victorian: The Life and Work of an American Composer, 1867–1944.* New York: Oxford University Press, 1998.

Block, Adrienne Fried, and Carol Neuls-Bates, eds. *Women in American Music: A Bibliography of Music and Literature.* Westport, Conn.: Greenwood Press, 1979.

Boskin, Joseph. *Sambo: The Rise and Demise of an American Jester.* New York: Oxford University Press, 1986.

Bourne, Randolph S. "Trans-National America." *Atlantic Monthly* 118 (July 1916): 86–97.

Bowers, Jane M. "Feminist Scholarship in the Field of Musicology." Parts 1 and 2. *College Music Symposium* 29 (1989): 81–92; 30 (Spring 1990): 1–13.

Bradley, William Aspenwall. "Song-Ballets and Devil's Ditties." *Harper's Magazine* 130 (May 1915): 901–14.

———. "In Shakespeare's America." *Harper's Magazine* 131 (August 1915): 436–46.

———. "The Folk Culture of the Cumberlands." *Dial* 64 (January 31, 1918): 95–98.

Braine, Robert. "The Country Fiddler." *Etude* 40 (February 1922): 132.

Bridge, Frederick. "How Industry and Common Sense Help the Musician." *Etude* 29 (January 1910): 20.

Britan, Halbert H. "Music and Morality." *International Journal of Ethics* 15 (October 1904): 48–63.

Brockway, Howard. "The Quest of the Lonesome Tunes." *Art World* 2 (June 1917): 227–30.

Bronner, Simon J. *American Folklore Studies: An Intellectual History.* Lawrence: University of Kansas Press, 1986.

———. *Old-Time Music Makers of New York State.* Syracuse: Syracuse University Press, 1987.

———. *Following Tradition: Folklore in the Discourse of American Culture.* Logan: Utah State University Press, 1998.

Bronson, Bertrand Harris. "Folk-Song in the United States, 1910–1960." In *The*

Ballad as Song, by Bertrand Harris Bronson. Berkeley: University of California Press, 1969.

Brotherton, Terry. "Early Fiddling Contests." *Devil's Box* 9 (July 1969): 15.

Brower, Edith. "Is the Musical Idea Masculine?." *Atlantic Monthly* 73 (March 1894): 332–39.

Brown, Frank C., ed. *North Carolina Folklore.* 7 vols. Durham, N.C.: Duke University Press, 1952–64.

Broyles, Michael. "Music and Class Structure in Antebellum Boston." *Journal of the American Musicological Society* 44 (Fall 1991): 451–93.

———. *Music of the Highest Class: Elitism and Populism in Antebellum Boston.* New Haven: Yale University Press, 1992.

Buchanan, Charles L. "The National Music Fallacy." *Arts and Decoration* 20 (February 1924): 26, 62.

Burlin, Natalie Curtis. *Hampton Series, Negro Folk-Songs.* Books 1–4. New York: G. Schirmer, 1918.

———. "Negro Music at Birth." *Musical Quarterly* 5 (January 1919): 86–89.

Burrison, John A. "Fiddlers in the Alley: Atlanta as an Early Country Music Center." *Atlanta Historical Bulletin* 21 (Summer 1977): 59–87.

Burton, Eldin. "Music Festival of 1909." *Atlanta Historical Bulletin* 4 (July 1939): 199–202.

———. "The First Season of Metropolitan Opera Presentations." *Atlanta Historical Bulletin* 4 (October 1939): 270–74.

———. "The Metropolitan Opera in Atlanta." *Atlanta Historical Bulletin* 5 (January 1940): 37–61.

———. "The Metropolitan Opera in Atlanta, Part 2." *Atlanta Historical Bulletin* 5 (April 1940): 146–69.

———. "The Metropolitan Opera in Atlanta, Part 3." *Atlanta Historical Bulletin* 5 (October 1940): 285–95.

"Business Men and High Art." *Etude* 40 (December 1922): 801.

Cameron, Ian. "Negro Songs." *Musical Times* 63 (June 1, 1922): 431–32.

Campbell, Gavin James. "'A Higher Mission Than Merely to Please the Ear': Music and Social Reform in America, 1900–1925." *Musical Quarterly* 84 (Summer 2000): 259–86.

Campbell, John C. *The Southern Highlander and His Homeland.* New York: Russell Sage Foundation, 1921.

Campbell, Mrs. David Allen. "The New Citizen's Work for Music." *Papers and Proceedings of the Music Teachers' National Association,* 1918, 83.

Campbell, Olive Dame. "Songs and Ballads of the Southern Mountaineers." *The Survey* 33 (January 2, 1915): 371–74.

Campbell, Olive Dame, and Cecil J. Sharp. *English Folk Songs from the Southern Appalachians.* New York: G. P. Putnam's Sons, 1917.

Cantwell, Robert. *Bluegrass Breakdown: The Making of the Old Southern Sound.* Urbana: University of Illinois Press, 1984.

Carlton, David L. *Mill and Town in South Carolina, 1880–1920.* Baton Rouge: Louisiana State University Press, 1982.

182 ::: *Bibliography*

Cauthen, Joyce H. "D. Dix Hollis—Early Paramount Recording Artist and Fiddler Who Challenged the World." *John Edwards Memorial Foundation Quarterly* 21 (Spring–Summer 1985): 17–19.

———. *With Fiddle and Well-Rosined Bow: Old-Time Fiddling in Alabama.* Tuscaloosa: University of Alabama Press, 1989.

"The Childless Women of Cities." *World's Work* 10 (October 1905): 6701.

Christensen, A. M. H. *Afro-American Folk Lore Told Round Cabin Fires on the Sea Islands of South Carolina.* Boston: J. G. Cupples Co., 1892.

Clark, Mrs. Frances E. "The Message of the Schools." *National Federation of Music Clubs Bulletin* 2 (February 1923): 5.

Clarke, E. Y. *Illustrated History of Atlanta.* 1877. Reprint, Atlanta: Cherokee Publishing Co., 1971.

Clements, William C. "The 'Offshoot' and the 'Root': Natalie Curtis and Black Expressive Culture in Africa and America." *Western Folklore* 54 (October 1995): 277–301.

Cobb, James C. "Beyond Planters and Industrialists: A New Perspective on the New South." *Journal of Southern History* 54 (February 1988): 45–68.

Cochran, Robert. *Our Own Sweet Sounds: A Celebration of Popular Music in Arkansas.* Fayetteville: University of Arkansas Press, 1996.

Cockrell, Dale. *Demons of Disorder: Early Blackface Minstrels and Their World.* Cambridge: Cambridge University Press, 1997.

Cohen, Norm. "Clayton McMichen: His Life and Music." *John Edwards Memorial Foundation Quarterly* 11 (Autumn 1975): 117–24.

———. "'Fiddlin' John Carson: An Appreciation and a Discography." *John Edwards Memorial Foundation Quarterly* 10 (Winter 1976): 175–84.

Coleridge-Taylor, Samuel. *Twenty-four Negro Melodies Transcribed for the Piano.* Boston: Oliver Ditson Co., 1905.

Combs, Josiah Henry. *The Kentucky Highlanders from a Native Mountaineer's Viewpoint.* Lexington, Ky.: J. L. Richardson and Co., 1913.

———. *Folk-Songs of the Southern United States.* 1925. Reprint, Austin: University of Texas Press, 1967.

Conger-Kaneko, Josephine. "The 'Effeminization' of the United States." *World's Work* 12 (May 1906): 7521–24.

Conrad, Georgia Bryan. *Reminiscences of a Southern Woman.* Hampton, Va.: Institute Press, n.d. [192?].

Conway, Cecelia. *African Banjo Echoes in Appalachia: A Study of Folk Traditions.* Chapel Hill: University of North Carolina Press, 1995.

Cooke, James Francis. "The Business Side of Making an Artist." *Etude* 25 (August 1907): 499–500.

Cooley, Rossa B. "Aunt Jane and Her People: The Real Negroes of the Sea Islands." *Outlook* 90 (October 24, 1908): 424–32.

Cox, John Harrington. *Folk-Songs of the South.* Cambridge: Harvard University Press, 1925.

Crawford, Mary Caroline. "'Pirates' and Prisoners: Music as a Reforming Influence." *The Survey,* July 11, 1914, 393.

Crowe, Charles. "Racial Violence and Social Reform: Origins of the Atlanta Riot of 1906." *Journal of Negro History* 53 (July 1968): 249–54.

Cuney-Hare, Maud. *Negro Musicians and Their Music.* Washington, D.C.: Associated Publishers, 1936.

Cureau, Rebecca T. "Kemper Harreld and Willis James: Music at Atlanta University, Morehouse College, and Spelman College." *Black Music Research Bulletin* 11 (Spring 1989): 5–8.

Daniel, Wayne W. "The Georgia Old-Time Fiddlers' Convention: 1920 Edition." *John Edwards Memorial Foundation Quarterly* 16 (Summer 1980): 67–73.

———. "Old Time Georgians Recall the Georgia Old Time Fiddlers' Conventions." *Devil's Box* 15 (March 1981): 7–16.

———. "'Shorty' Harper: Georgia State Fiddling Champion of 1915 and 1916." *Devil's Box* 15 (June 1981): 43–48.

———. "Old-Time Fiddler's Contests on Early Radio." *John Edwards Memorial Foundation Quarterly* 17 (Fall 1981): 159–65.

———. "Women's Lib and the Georgia Old-Time Fiddlers' Conventions: The Story of Mrs. J. P. Wheeler, Georgia's Reigning Fiddle Champion." *Devil's Box* 16 (March 1982): 10–19.

———. "The Georgia Old Time Fiddlers' Conventions—'A Pleasant Time Was Had by All.'" *Bluegrass Unlimited* 17 (August 1982): 42–47.

———. "George Daniell's Hill Billies: The Band That Named the Music?." *John Edwards Memorial Foundation Quarterly* 19 (Summer 1983): 81–84.

———. "Georgia Fiddling Champion: A. A. Gray." *Old Time Music* 41 (Spring 1985): 9–13.

———. "Mechanics and Musicians: Henry Ford and Old-Time Music." *Devil's Box* 20 (Fall 1986): 17–24.

———. *Pickin' on Peachtree: A History of Country Music in Atlanta, Georgia.* Urbana: University of Illinois Press, 1990.

Darnton, Robert. *The Great Cat Massacre and Other Episodes in French Cultural History.* New York: Basic Books, 1984.

Davenport, M. Marguerite. *Azalia: The Life of E. Azalia Hackley.* Boston: Chapman and Grimes, 1947.

Davis, Arthur Kyle, ed. *Traditional Ballads of Virginia.* Cambridge: Harvard University Press, 1929.

Davis, Jack E. *Race against Time: Culture and Separation in Natchez since 1930.* Baton Rouge: Louisiana State University Press, 2001.

Davis, Leroy. *A Clashing of the Soul: John Hope and the Dilemma of African American Leadership and Black Higher Education in the Early Twentieth Century.* Athens: University of Georgia Press, 1998.

Dawley, Thomas R., Jr. "Our Southern Mountaineers: Removal the Remedy for the Evils That Isolation and Poverty Have Brought." *World's Work* 19 (March 1910): 12704–14.

Deaton, Thomas Mashburn. "Atlanta during the Progressive Era." Ph.D. diss., University of Georgia, 1969.

Dennison, Sam. *Scandalize My Name: Black Imagery in American Popular Music.* New York: Garland Publishing, 1982.

DeNora, Tia. *Music in Everyday Life.* Cambridge: Cambridge University Press, 2000.

"Desecration of 'Spirituals.'" *Southern Workman* 51 (November 1921): 501–3.

Dett, R. Nathaniel. "The Development of Negro Religious Music." *Journal of Black Sacred Music* 5 (Fall 1991): 34–41.

Dick, Ernst S. "The Folk and Their Culture: The Formative Concepts and the Beginnings of Folklore." In *The Folk: Identity, Landscapes and Lores,* edited by Robert J. Smith and Jerry Stannard. Lawrence: Department of Anthropology, University of Kansas, 1989.

Dickinson, Edward. *The Education of a Music Lover.* New York: Charles Scribner's Sons, 1911.

DiMaggio, Paul. "Cultural Entrepreneurship in Nineteenth-Century Boston: The Creation of an Organizational Base for High Culture in America." *Media Culture and Society* 4 (January 1982): 33–50.

———. "Cultural Entrepreneurship in Nineteenth-Century Boston, Part II: The Classification and Framing of American Art." *Media Culture and Society* 4 (October 1982): 303–22.

Dinnerstein, Leonard. *The Leo Frank Case.* New York: Columbia University Press, 1968.

Dittmer, John. *Black Georgia in the Progressive Era, 1900–1920.* Urbana: University of Illinois Press, 1977.

Dizikes, John. *Opera in America: A Cultural History.* New Haven: Yale University Press, 1993.

Donakowski, Conrad L. *A Muse for the Masses: Ritual and Music in an Age of Democratic Revolution, 1770–1870.* Chicago: University of Chicago Press, 1972.

Dorman, James H. "Shaping the Popular Image of Post-Reconstruction Blacks: The 'Coon Song' Phenomenon of the Gilded Age." *American Quarterly* 40 (December 1988): 450–71.

Douglas, Ann. *The Feminization of American Culture.* New York: Alfred A. Knopf, 1977.

Douglass, Frederick. *My Bondage and My Freedom.* 1855. Reprint, New York: Dover Publications, 1969.

Downes, Olin. *The Lure of Music.* 2d ed. New York: Harper and Brothers, 1922.

Doyle, Don H. *New Men, New Cities, New South: Atlanta, Nashville, Charleston, Mobile, 1860–1910.* Chapel Hill: University of North Carolina Press, 1990.

Du Bois, W. E. B. "Georgia: Invisible Empire State." *Nation* 120 (January 21, 1925): 63–67.

———. *The Souls of Black Folk,* in *W. E. B. Du Bois: Writings.* New York: Library of America, 1986.

Dumenil, Lynn. *The Modern Temper: American Culture and Society in the 1920s.* New York: Hill and Wang, 1995.

Dyer, Thomas G. *Theodore Roosevelt and the Idea of Race.* Baton Rouge: Louisiana State University Press, 1980.

Eaton, Allen H. *Handicrafts of the Southern Highlands*. New York: Russell Sage Foundation, 1937.

Eaton, Quaintance. *Opera Caravan: Adventures of the Metropolitan on Tour, 1883–1956*. 1957. Reprint, New York: Da Capo Press, 1978.

Ebel, Otto. *Women Composers: A Biographical Handbook of Woman's Work in Music*. Brooklyn: F. H. Chandler, 1902.

Editorial. *Etude* 25 (September 1907): 582.

Edmunds, Pocahontas Wight. *Virginians Out Front*. Richmond: Whittet and Shepperson, 1972.

Elliott, Gilbert, Jr. "Our Musical Kinship with the Spaniards." *Musical Quarterly* 8 (July 1922): 413–18.

Ellison, George. Introduction to *Our Southern Highlanders*, by Horace Kephart. 1922. Reprint, Knoxville: University of Tennessee Press, 1976.

Elson, Louis C. *The National Music of America, and Its Sources*. Boston: L. C. Page and Co., 1900.

———. *Woman's Work in Music*. Boston: L. C. Page and Co., 1913.

———. *The History of American Music*. 1925. Reprint, New York: Burt Franklin, 1971.

Epstein, Dena J. *Sinful Tunes and Spirituals: Black Folk Music to the Civil War*. Urbana: University of Illinois Press, 1977.

———. "A White Origin for the Black Spiritual? An Invalid Theory and How It Grew." *American Music* 1 (Summer 1983): 53–59.

Erb, J. Lawrence. *Music Appreciation for the Student*. New York: G. Schirmer, 1926.

Fairweather, Elizabeth K. "The Psychological and Ethical Value of Music." *Journal of the Proceedings and Addresses of the National Education Association*, 1902.

Farnham, Christie Anne. *The Education of a Southern Belle: Higher Education and Student Socialization in the Antebellum South*. New York: New York University Press, 1994.

Faulkner, Anne Shaw. "Does Jazz Put the Sin in Syncopation?." *Ladies' Home Journal* 38 (August 1921): 16, 34.

———. *What We Hear in Music*. Camden, N.J.: Victor Talking Machine Co., 1921.

Fay, Amy. "The Woman Music-Teacher in a Large City." *Etude* 20 (January 1902): 14.

"Fiddling to Henry Ford." *Literary Digest* 88 (January 2, 1926): 33.

Fields, Barbara J. "Ideology and Race in American History." In *Region, Race, and Reconstruction: Essays in Honor of C. Vann Woodward*, edited by J. Morgan Kousser and James M. McPherson. New York: Oxford University Press, 1982.

Filene, Benjamin. "'Our Singing Country': John and Alan Lomax, Leadbelly, and the Construction of an American Past." *American Quarterly* 43 (December 1991): 602–24.

———. *Romancing the Folk: Public Memory and American Roots Music*. Chapel Hill: University of North Carolina Press, 2000.

Filene, Peter. *Him/Her/Self: Sex Roles in Modern America*. 3d ed. Baltimore: Johns Hopkins University Press, 1998.

Finck, Henry T. "Women in Music To-day." *Nation* 106 (June 1, 1918): 664.

Fink, Gary M. *The Fulton Bag and Cotton Mills Strike of 1914–1915: Espionage, Labor Conflict, and New South Industrial Relations.* Ithaca, N.Y.: ILR Press, 1993.

Finkelstein, Sidney. *Composer and Nation: The Folk Heritage in Music.* 2d ed. New York: International Publishers, 1989.

Fite, Gilbert C. *Richard B. Russell, Jr., Senator for Georgia.* Chapel Hill: University of North Carolina Press, 1991.

Floyd, Samuel A., Jr., ed. *Black Music in the Harlem Renaissance.* Westport, Conn.: Greenwood Press, 1990.

Fogelson, Robert M. *America's Armories: Architecture, Society, and Public Order.* Cambridge: Harvard University Press, 1988.

"Foreign Missions, Continued." *Watson's Jeffersonian Magazine* 3 (July 1909): 487–509.

Fox, John, Jr. "The Southern Mountaineer." *Scribner's Magazine* 29 (April–May 1901); reprinted in *Appalachian Images in Folk and Popular Culture,* 2d ed., edited by W. K. McNeil, Knoxville: University of Tennessee Press, 1995.

———. *The Little Shepherd of Kingdom Come.* New York: Charles Scribner's Sons, 1903.

———. *The Trail of the Lonesome Pine.* New York: Charles Scribner's Sons, 1908.

Fredrickson, George M. *The Black Image in the White Mind: The Debate on Afro-American Character and Destiny, 1817–1914.* New York: Harper and Row, 1971.

Frost, Mrs. William. "The Women of the Mountains." *Berea Quarterly* 18 (January 1915): 5–16.

Frost, William Goodell. "Our Contemporary Ancestors." *Atlantic Monthly* 83 (March 1899): 311–19.

———. "The Southern Mountaineer: Our Kindred of the Boone and Lincoln Type." *American Review of Reviews* 21 (March 1900): 303–12.

———. "An Historical Museum." *Berea Quarterly* 11 (April 1907): 8–11.

———. "Appalachian America." *Berea Quarterly* 9 (January 1910): 21–25.

———. "Three Million American Highlanders." *Berea Quarterly* 15 (January 1912): 9.

———. "How to Make Something Out of This Fighting Stock." *Berea Quarterly* 16 (January 1913): 9–16.

Fryberger, Agnes Moore. *Listening Lessons in Music.* New York: Silver, Burdette and Co., 1916.

Gaines, Kevin K. *Uplifting the Race: Black Leadership, Politics, and Culture in the Twentieth Century.* Chapel Hill: University of North Carolina Press, 1996.

Garofalo, Charles Paul. "The Sons of Henry Grady: Atlanta Boosters in the 1920s." *Journal of Southern History* 42 (May 1976): 187–204.

Garrett, Franklin M. *Atlanta and Environs: A Chronicle of Its People and Events.* 3 vols. Athens: University of Georgia Press, 1969.

Garst, John F. "Mutual Reinforcement and the Origins of the Spirituals." *American Music* 4 (Winter 1986): 390–406.

Gaston, Paul. *The New South Creed: A Study in Southern Mythmaking.* New York: Alfred A. Knopf, 1970.

Gatewood, Willard B. *Aristocrats of Color: The Black Elite, 1880–1920.* Bloomington: Indiana University Press, 1990.

Gielow, Martha Sawyer. "The Call of the Race." *Journal of American History* 11 (May–June 1917): 215–19.

Gilmore, Al-Tony. *Bad Nigger!: The National Impact of Jack Johnson.* Port Washington, N.Y.: Kennikat Press, 1975.

Gilmore, Glenda Elizabeth. *Gender and Jim Crow: Women and the Politics of White Supremacy in North Carolina, 1896–1920.* Chapel Hill: University of North Carolina Press, 1996.

Glass, Dudley. "Grand Opera in Atlanta." *Opera Magazine* (April 1914): 26–29.
———. *Men of Atlanta.* Atlanta: Blosser Williams Co., 1924.

Glassberg, David. *American Historical Pageantry: The Uses of Tradition in the Early Twentieth Century.* Chapel Hill: University of North Carolina Press, 1990.

Godshalk, David Fort. "In the Wake of Riot: Atlanta's Struggle for Order, 1899–1919." Ph.D. diss., Yale University, 1992.

Goepp, Philip H. "Musical Appreciation in America as a National Asset." In *Papers and Proceedings of the Music Teachers' National Association,* 1911, 31–33.

Golden, Harry Lewis. *A Little Girl Is Dead.* Cleveland: World Publishing Co., 1965.

Gonzales, Ambrose E. *The Black Border: Gullah Stories of the Carolina Coast.* Columbia, S.C.: The State Co., 1922.
———. *The Captain: Stories of the Black Border.* Columbia, S.C.: The State Co., 1924.
———. *With Aesop along the Black Border.* Columbia, S.C.: The State Co., 1924.

Goodson, Howard Steven. "'South of the North, North of the South': Public Entertainment in Atlanta, 1880–1930." Ph.D. diss., Emory University, 1995.

Goodson, Steve. *Highbrows, Hillbillies, and Hellfire: Public Entertainment in Atlanta, 1880–1930.* Athens: University of Georgia Press, 2002.

Gorn, Elliott J. *The Manly Art: Bare-Knuckle Prize Fighting in America.* Ithaca, N.Y.: Cornell University Press, 1986.

Gossett, Thomas F. *Race: The History of an Idea in America.* Dallas: Southern Methodist University Press, 1963.

Graham, Alice. "Original Plantation Melodies as One Rarely Hears Them." *Etude* 40 (November 1922): 744.

Grant, Madison. *The Passing of the Great Race, or the Racial Basis of European History.* 3d ed. Revised. New York: Charles Scribner's Sons, 1920.

Green, Archie. "Hillbilly Music: Source and Symbol." *Journal of American Folklore* 78 (July–September 1965): 204–28.

Green, Jeffrey. "Conversation with Josephine Harreld Love: Reminiscences of Times Past." *Black Perspective in Music* 18 (1990): 179–213.

Griswold, Philip A. "Sex-Role Associations of Music Instruments and Occupations by Gender and Major." *Journal of Research in Music Education* 29 (Spring 1981): 57–62.

Grundy, Pamela. "'We Always Tried to Be Respectable People': Respectability, Crazy Water Crystals, and Hillbilly Music on the Air, 1933–1935." *Journal of American History* 81 (March 1995): 1591–1620.

Haarsager, Sandra. *Organized Womanhood: Cultural Politics in the Pacific Northwest, 1840–1920.* Norman: University of Oklahoma Press, 1997.

Hahn, George. "The Business Man and Good Music." *Etude* 25 (September 1907): 570.

Hale, Grace Elizabeth. *Making Whiteness: The Culture of Segregation in the South, 1890–1940.* New York: Pantheon Books, 1998.

Hall, Jacquelyn Dowd. *Revolt against Chivalry: Jessie Daniel Ames and the Women's Campaign against Lynching.* New York: Columbia University Press, 1979.

———. "Private Eyes, Public Women: Images of Class and Sex in the Urban South, Atlanta, Georgia, 1913–1915." In *Work Engendered: Toward a New History of American Labor,* edited by Ava Baron. Ithaca, N.Y.: Cornell University Press, 1991.

Hall, Jacquelyn Dowd, et al. *Like a Family: The Making of a Southern Cotton Mill World. With a New Afterword by the Authors. Foreword by Michael Frisch.* Chapel Hill: University of North Carolina Press, 2000.

Hallowell, Emily, ed. *Calhoun Plantation Songs.* Revised. Boston: C. W. Thompson and Co., 1907.

Hamilton, Clarence G. "The Teachers' Round Table." *Etude* 41 (March 1923): 165.

Hamm, Charles. *Music in the New World.* New York: W. W. Norton, 1983.

———. *Putting Popular Music in Its Place.* Cambridge: Cambridge University Press, 1995.

Hand, Wayland D. "North American Folklore Societies: A Survey." *Journal of American Folklore* (July–September 1943): 161–91.

Hanh, George. "The Business Man and Good Music." *Etude* 25 (September 1907): 570.

Harkins, Anthony. "The Significance of 'Hillbilly' in Early Country Music, 1924–1945." *Journal of Appalachian Studies* 2 (Fall 1996): 299–322.

Harlan Louis R., and Raymond W. Smock, eds. *The Booker T. Washington Papers.* Vol. 10. Urbana: University of Illinois Press, 1981.

Harris, Barbara J. *Beyond Her Sphere: Women and the Professions in American History.* Westport, Conn.: Greenwood Press, 1978.

Harris, Henry J. "The Occupation of Musician in the United States." *Musical Quarterly* 1 (April 1915): 299–311.

Harris, Joel Chandler. "Plantation Music." *Critic* 3 (December 15, 1883): 506.

Harris, Michael W. *The Rise of Gospel Blues: The Music of Thomas Andrew Dorsey in the Urban Church.* Oxford University Press, 1992.

Harris, Neil. "John Philip Sousa and the Culture of Reassurance." In *Perspectives on John Philip Sousa,* edited by Jon Newsom. Washington, D.C.: Music Division, Library of Congress, 1983.

Harris, T. S. "Music in the Public Schools." *Proceedings of the Music Supervisors' National Conference,* 1922, 165–68.

Hart, Albert Bushnell, and Herbert Ronald Ferleger. *Theodore Roosevelt Cyclopedia.* New York: Stratford Press, 1941.

Hartt, Rollin Lynde. "The Mountaineers: Our Own Lost Tribes." *Century* 95 (January 1918): 395–404.

Harvey, Paul. *Redeeming the South: Religious Cultures and Racial Identities among Southern Baptists, 1865–1925.* Chapel Hill: University of North Carolina Press, 1997.

Haskell, Marion Alexander. "Negro Spirituals." *Century* 58 (August 1899): 577–81.

Hertzberg, Steven. *Strangers within the Gate City: The Jews of Atlanta, 1845–1915.* Philadelphia: Jewish Publication Society of America, 1978.

Hess, Carol A. "John Philip Sousa's *El Capitan*: Political Appropriation and the Spanish-American War." *American Music* 16 (Spring 1998): 1–24.

Higham, John. *Strangers in the Land: Patterns of American Nativism, 1860–1925.* 2d ed. New Brunswick, N.J.: Rutgers University Press, 1988.

Hirsch, Jerrold. "Modernity, Nostalgia, and Southern Folklore Studies: The Case of John Lomax." *Journal of American Folklore* 105 (Spring 1992): 183–207.

Hitchcock, H. Wiley. *Music in the United States: An Historical Introduction.* 2d ed. Englewood Cliffs, N.J.: Prentice-Hall, 1974.

Hoeptner, Fred, and Bob Pinson. "Clayton McMichen Talking." *Old Time Music,* Part 1 (Summer 1971): 8–10; Part 2 (Autumn 1971): 13–15; Part 3 (Winter 1971–72): 14–15, 19; Part 4 (Spring 1972): 19–20, 30.

Horner, Junius M. "Educational Work in the Mountains of North Carolina." *Outlook* 94 (March 12, 1910): 589–90.

Horowitz, Helen Lefkowitz. *Culture and the City: Cultural Philanthropy in Chicago from the 1880s to 1917.* Chicago: University of Chicago Press, 1976.

Horowitz, Joseph. *Understanding Toscanini: How He Became an American Culture-God and Helped Create a New Audience for Old Music.* New York: Alfred A. Knopf, 1987.

———. *Wagner Nights: An American History.* Berkeley: University of California Press, 1994.

Hough, Robin. "Choirs of Angels Armed for War: Reverend Marshall W. Taylor's *A Collection of Revival Hymns and Plantation Melodies.*" In *Feel the Spirit: Studies in Nineteenth-Century Afro-American Music,* edited by George R. Keck and Sherrill V. Martin. Westport, Conn.: Greenwood Press, 1988.

Housewright, Wiley L. *A History of Music and Dance in Florida, 1565–1865.* Tuscaloosa: University of Alabama Press, 1991.

Howard, John Tasker. "Our Folk-Music and Its Probable Impress on American Music of the Future." *Musical Quarterly* 7 (April 1921): 167–71.

———. *Our American Music: Three Hundred Years of It.* New York: Thomas Y. Crowell, 1929.

Howe, M. A. DeWolfe. "The Song of Charleston." *Atlantic Monthly* 146 (July 1930): 108–11.

Howell, Fletcher Mae. "Community Life!" *The Competitor* 3 (June 1921): 29.

"How I Came to Love Music." *Etude* 43 (April 1925): 235–36.

Hoxie, Albert N. "Reaching the Boy through Good Music." *Etude* 43 (June 1925): 393–94.

Hoyt, F. S. Introduction to *A Collection of Revival Hymns and Plantation Melodies*, edited by Marshall W. Taylor. Cincinnati: Curts and Jennings, 1882.

Hsiung, David C. *Two Worlds in the Tennessee Mountains: Exploring the Origins of Appalachian Stereotypes.* Lexington: University of Kentucky Press, 1997.

Huggins, Nathan Irvin. *Harlem Renaissance.* New York: Oxford University Press, 1971.

Hughes, Rupert. "Women Composers." *Century* 55 (March 1898): 768–79.

Hughes, Rupert, and Arthur Elson. *American Composers.* 2d ed. Revised. Boston: The Page Co., 1914.

"The Human Need for Music in Daily Life." *Etude* 33 (January 1915): 9–10.

Huneker, James. "The Girl Who Plays Chopin." *Harper's Bazar* 33 (June 23, 1900): 466–68.

———. *Overtones: A Book of Temperaments.* New York: Charles Scribner's Sons, 1904.

———. "Feminism in Modern Music." *Harper's Bazar* 39 (August 1905): 691–94.

Hunter, Tera W. *To 'Joy My Freedom: Southern Black Women's Lives and Labors after the Civil War.* Cambridge: Harvard University Press, 1997.

"Hunting the Lonesome Tunes in the Wilds of Kentucky." *Current Opinion* 62 (February 1917): 100–101.

Hurston, Zora Neal. "The Hue and Cry about Howard University." *The Messenger* 7 (September 1925): 315–19, 338.

Hustvedt, Sigurd Bernhard. *Ballad Books and Ballad Men: Raids and Rescues in Britain, America, and the Scandinavian North since 1800.* Cambridge: Harvard University Press, 1930.

Inscoe, John. *Mountain Masters: Slavery and the Sectional Crisis in Western North Carolina.* Knoxville: University of Tennessee Press, 1989.

———. "Race and Racism in Nineteenth-Century Southern Appalachia: Myths, Realities, and Ambiguities." In *Appalachia in the Making: The Mountain South in the Nineteenth Century*, edited by Mary Beth Pudup, Dwight B. Billings, and Altina L. Waller. Chapel Hill: University of North Carolina Press, 1995.

———, ed. *Appalachians and Race: The Mountain South from Slavery to Segregation.* Lexington: University of Kentucky Press, 2001.

"Is Music an Effeminate Art?" *Current Opinion* 75 (November 1923): 586–87.

Jabbour, Alan. "Fiddle Music." In *American Folklore: An Encyclopedia*, edited by Jan Harold Brunvard. New York: Garland Publishing, 1996.

Jackson, Bruce, ed. *The Negro and His Folklore in Nineteenth-Century Periodicals.* Austin: University of Texas Press, 1967.

Jackson, George Pullen. *White and Negro Spirituals.* New York: J. J. Augustin, 1944.

Jacobs, Harriet. *Incidents in the Life of a Slave Girl, Written by Herself.* Cambridge: Harvard University Press, 2000.

Jacobson, Matthew Frye. *Whiteness of a Different Color: European Immigrants and the Alchemy of Race.* Cambridge: Harvard University Press, 1998.

————. *Barbarian Virtues: The United States Encounters Foreign Peoples at Home and Abroad, 1876–1917.* New York: Hill and Wang, 2000.

Janiewski, Dolores. "Southern Honor, Southern Dishonor: Managerial Ideology and the Construction of Gender, Race, and Class Relations in Southern Industry." In *Work Engendered: Toward a New History of American Labor,* edited by Ava Baron. Ithaca, N.Y.: Cornell University Press, 1991.

Jefferson, Thomas. *Notes on the State of Virginia,* in *Writings: Thomas Jefferson,* edited by Merrill Peterson. New York: Literary Classics of the United States, 1984.

Jervey, Huger W. "Negro Music." In *The South in the Building of the Nation.* Vol. 3. Richmond: Southern Historical Publication Society, 1909.

"Jewish Jazz Becomes Our National Music." In *The Jewish Question,* edited by Louis Marshall. London: Militant Christian Patriots Publications, 1937.

Johns, Altona Trent. "Henry Hugh Proctor." *Black Perspective in Music* 3 (Spring 1975): 25–32.

Johnson, Harvey. "Atlanta, the Gate City of the South." *American City* 5 (July 1911): 3–8.

Johnson, J. Rosamond. "Why They Call American Music Ragtime." Reprinted in *Black Perspective in Music* 4 (July 1976): 260–65.

Johnson, James Weldon. *The Book of American Negro Spirituals.* New York: Viking Press, 1925.

Johnston, Josiah Stoddard. "Romance of the Kentucky Feuds." *Cosmopolitan* 27 (September 1899); reprinted in *Appalachian Images in Folk and Popular Culture,* 2d ed., edited by W. K. McNeil, Knoxville: University of Tennessee Press, 1995.

Jones, Charles C., Jr. *Negro Myths from the Georgia Coast Told in the Vernacular.* Boston: Houghton, Mifflin, 1888.

Joyner, Charles. "A Single Southern Culture: Cultural Interaction in the Old South." In *Black and White Cultural Interaction in the Antebellum South,* edited by Ted Ownby. Jackson: University Press of Mississippi, 1993.

Kammen, Michael. *Mystic Chords of Memory: The Transformation of Tradition in American Culture.* New York: Alfred A. Knopf, 1991.

Kantrowitz, Stephen. *Ben Tillman and the Reconstruction of White Supremacy.* Chapel Hill: University of North Carolina Press, 2000.

Karpeles, Maud. *Cecil Sharp, His Life and Work.* Chicago: University of Chicago Press, 1967.

Kasson, John F. *Rudeness and Civility: Manners in Nineteenth-Century Urban America.* New York: Hill and Wang, 1990.

————. *Houdini, Tarzan, and the Perfect Man: The White Male Body and the Challenge of Modernity in America.* New York: Hill and Wang, 2001.

Keene, James A. *A History of Music Education in America.* Hanover, N.H.: University Press of New England, 1982.

Kelly, Karen K. "Richard B. Russell: Democrat for Georgia." Ph.D. diss, University of North Carolina at Chapel Hill, 1979.

Kempf, Paul. "From Harmonica to Symphony." *Musician* 30 (January 1925): 17.

Kennedy, R. Emmet. "The Poetic and Melodic Gifts of the Negro." *Etude* 41 (March 1923): 159–60.

———. *Mellows: A Chronicle of Unknown Singers.* New York: Albert and Charles Bone, 1925.

Kephart, Horace. *Camping and Woodcraft: A Handbook for Vacation Campers and for Travelers in the Wilderness.* 2d ed. Revised. New York: Macmillan, 1921.

———. "Horace Kephart." *North Carolina Library Bulletin* 5 (June 1922): 49–52.

———. *Our Southern Highlanders.* 2d ed. Revised and enlarged. New York: Macmillan, 1922.

Kerber, Linda K. "Separate Spheres, Female Worlds, Woman's Place: The Rhetoric of Women's History." *Journal of American History* 75 (June 1988): 9–39.

Kerlin, Robert T. "Canticles of Love and Woe." *Southern Workman* 50 (February 1921): 62–64.

Kessler-Harris, Alice. *Out to Work: A History of Wage-Earning Women in the United States.* New York: Oxford University Press, 1982.

Keyes, Saundra. "'Little Mary Phagan': A Native American Ballad in Context." *Journal of Country Music* 3 (Spring 1972): 1–16.

Kimmel, Michael S. "Men's Response to Feminism at the Turn of the Century." *Gender and Society* 1 (September 1987): 261–83.

———. *Manhood in America: A Cultural History.* New York: Free Press, 1996.

Kirkland, Winifred. "Mountain Music." *Outlook* 123 (December 31, 1919): 593.

Kittredge, George Lyman. Introduction to *English and Scottish Popular Ballads*, edited by Helen Child Sargent and George Lyman Kittredge, 1904. Reprint, Boston: Houghton Mifflin, 1932.

Klotter, James C. "The Black South and White Appalachia." *Journal of American History* 66 (March 1980): 832–49.

Knight, Lucian Lamar. *A Standard History of Georgia and Georgians.* Vols. 4, 6. Chicago: Lewis Publishing, 1917.

Kolchin, Peter. "Whiteness Studies: The New History of Race in America." *Journal of American History* 89 (June 2002): 154–73.

Koza, Julia Eklund. "Music and the Feminine Sphere: Images of Women as Musicians in *Godey's Lady's Book.*" *Musical Quarterly* 75 (Summer 1991): 103–29.

———. "The 'Missing Males' and Other Gender Issues in Music Education: Evidence from the *Music Supervisors' Journal*, 1914–1924." *Journal of Research in Music Education* 41 (Fall 1993): 212–32.

Kramer, Lawrence. *Music as Cultural Practice, 1800–1900.* Berkeley: University of California Press, 1990.

———. *Musical Meaning: Toward a Critical History.* Berkeley: University of California Press, 2002.

Krehbiel, Henry Edward. *Afro-American Folksongs: A Study in Racial and National Music.* New York: G. Schirmer, 1914.

Kuhn, Clifford M. *Contesting the New South Order: The 1914–1915 Strike at Atlanta's Fulton Mills.* Chapel Hill: University of North Carolina Press, 2001.

Kuhn, Clifford M., Harlon E. Joye, and Bernard E. West, eds. *Living Atlanta: An Oral History of the City, 1914–1948*. Athens: University of Georgia Press, 1990.

Kushner, David Z. "John Powell of Virginia." *Journal of the American Liszt Society* 16 (December 1984): 98–108.

Ladd, George Trumbull. "Why Women Cannot Compose Music." *Yale Review* 6 (July 1917): 789–806.

Lahee, Henry C. *Famous Pianists of Today and Yesterday*. Boston: L. C. Page and Co., 1900.

LaRose, Joe. "An Interview with Lowe Stokes." *Old Time Music* 39 (Spring 1984): 6–11.

Law, Frederic S. "Captains of Music." *Etude* 21 (December 1903): 470–71.

Lears, T. J. Jackson. *No Place of Grace: Antimodernism and the Transformation of American Culture, 1880–1920*. New York: Pantheon Books, 1981.

Leloudis, James L. *Schooling the New South: Pedagogy, Self, and Society in North Carolina, 1880–1920*. Chapel Hill: University of North Carolina Press, 1996.

Leonard, Neil. *Jazz and the White Americans: The Acceptance of a New Art Form*. Chicago: University of Chicago Press, 1962.

———. "The Reaction to Ragtime." In *Ragtime: Its History, Composers, and Music*, edited by John Edward Hasse. New York: Schirmer Books, 1985.

Levine, Lawrence W. *Black Culture and Black Consciousness: Afro-American Folk Thought from Slavery to Freedom*. Oxford University Press, 1977.

———. *Highbrow, Lowbrow: The Emergence of Cultural Hierarchy in America*. Cambridge: Harvard University Press, 1988.

———. "The Folklore of Industrial Society: Popular Culture and Its Audiences." *American Historical Review* 97 (December 1992): 1369–99.

Levy, Alan Howard. *Musical Nationalism: American Composer's Search for Identity*. Westport, Conn.: Greenwood Press, 1983.

———. "The Search for Identity in American Music, 1890–1920." *American Music* 2 (Summer 1984): 70–81.

Lewis, David L. *The Public Image of Henry Ford: An American Folk Hero and His Company*. Detroit: Wayne State University Press, 1976.

Lewis, David Levering. *When Harlem Was in Vogue*. New York: Alfred A. Knopf, 1991.

———. *W. E. B. Du Bois: Biography of a Race, 1868–1919*. New York: Henry Holt, 1993.

Lewis, Ronald L. "Beyond Isolation and Homogeneity: Diversity and the History of Appalachia." In *Confronting Appalachian Stereotypes: Back Talk from an American Region*, edited by Dwight B. Billings, Gurney Norman, and Katherine Ledford. Lexington: University of Kentucky Press, 1999.

Linn, Karen. *That Half-Barbaric Twang: The Banjo in American Popular Culture*. Urbana: University of Illinois Press, 1991.

Litwack, Leon. *Trouble in Mind: Black Southerners in the Age of Jim Crow*. New York: Alfred A. Knopf, 1998.

Locke, Alain. "The Negro Spirituals." In *The New Negro: An Interpretation*, edited by Alain Locke. 1925. Reprint, New York: Johnson Reprint Corp., 1968.

Locke, Charles Edward. "Music as a Factor in Culture." *Journal of Proceedings and Addresses of the National Education Association* (1905): 644–50.

Locke, Ralph P. "Music Lovers, Patrons, and the 'Sacralization' of Culture in America." *Nineteenth-Century Music* 17 (Fall 1993): 149–73.

Locke, Ralph P., and Cyrilla Barr, eds. *Cultivating Music in America: Women Patrons and Activists since 1860.* Berkeley: University of California Press, 1997.

Lomax, John A. "Some Types of American Folk-Song." *Journal of American Folklore* 28 (January–March 1915): 1–17.

———. "Self-Pity in Negro Folk-Songs." *Nation* 105 (August 9, 1917): 141–45.

Lornell, Kip. *Virginia's Blues, Country, and Gospel Records, 1902–1943: An Annotated Discography.* Lexington: University Press of Kentucky, 1989.

Lott, Eric. *Love and Theft: Blackface Minstrelsy and the American Working Class.* New York: Oxford University Press, 1993.

Lowry, Pete. "Black Sound: A Survey of Black Music from Atlanta during the Twentieth Century." *Atlanta Historical Bulletin* 21 (Summer 1977): 88–113.

Lutz, Tom. *American Nervousness, 1903: An Anecdotal History.* Ithaca, N.Y.: Cornell University Press, 1991.

MacDougald, Louise Black. "A Trip down Peachtree Street in 1886." *Atlanta Historical Bulletin* 5 (April 1940): 135–45.

MacKaye, Percy. "Untamed America: A Comment on a Sojourn in the Kentucky Mountains." *Survey* 51 (January 1, 1924): 327–41, 360–63.

MacLean, Nancy. "The Leo Frank Case: Gender and Sexual Politics in the Making of Reactionary Populism." *Journal of American History* 78 (December 1991): 917–48.

———. *Behind the Mask of Chivalry: The Making of the Second Ku Klux Klan.* New York: Oxford University Press, 1994.

Macleod, Beth Abelson. "'Whence Comes the Lady Tympanist?': Gender and Instrumental Musicians in America, 1853–1990." *Journal of Social History* 27 (Winter 1993): 291–308.

MacLeod, Bruce A. "The Musical Instruments of North American Slaves." *Mississippi Folklore Register* 11 (Spring 1977): 34–49.

Magill, Mary Tucker. "A Georgian at the Opera." *Harper's New Monthly Magazine* 71 (June 1885): 135–39.

Maguire, Helena M. "The People to Whom a Girl Plays." *Etude* 18 (March 1900): 94.

Mahar, William J. *Behind the Burnt Cork Mask: Early Blackface Minstrelsy and Antebellum American Popular Culture.* Urbana: University of Illinois Press, 1999.

Malone, Bill C. *Singing Cowboys and Musical Mountaineers: Southern Culture and the Roots of Country Music.* Athens: University of Georgia Press, 1993.

Martin, Peter J. *Sounds and Society: Themes in the Sociology of Music.* New York: St. Martin's Press, 1995.

Martin, Thomas H. *Atlanta and Its Builders: A Comprehensive History of the Gate City of the South.* Vol. 1. Atlanta: Century Memorial Publication Co., 1902.

Martin, Tony. *Race First: The Ideological and Organizational Struggles of Marcus Garvey and the Universal Negro Improvement Association.* Westport, Conn.: Greenwood Press, 1976.

Mason, Daniel Gregory. *Music as a Humanity.* New York: H. W. Gray Co., 1921.

———. *Music in My Time and Other Remembrances.* New York: Macmillan, 1938.

Matthews, Brander. "The Rise and Fall of Negro-Minstrelsy." *Scribner's* 57 (June 1915): 754–59.

Mayo, A. D. "The Educational Opportunity at Berea." *American Review of Reviews* 21 (March 1900): 311–12.

Mays, Benjamin E. *Born to Rebel: An Autobiography of Benjamin E. Mays.* New York: Charles Scribner's and Sons, 1971.

McArthur, Alexander. "Women and Originality." *Etude* 20 (February 1902): 53.

McCarthy, Kathleen D. *Noblesse Oblige: Charity and Cultural Philanthropy in Chicago, 1849–1929.* Chicago: University of Chicago Press, 1982.

———. *Women's Culture: American Philanthropy and Art, 1830–1930.* Chicago: University of Chicago Press, 1991.

McClary, Susan. *Feminine Endings: Music, Gender, and Sexuality.* Minneapolis: University of Minnesota Press, 1991.

McClure, Alexander. *The South: Its Industrial, Financial, and Political Conditions.* Philadelphia: J. B. Lippincott, 1886.

McConachie, Bruce A. "New York Operagoing, 1825–1850: Creating an Elite Social Ritual." *American Music* 6 (Summer 1988): 181–92.

McEwen, H. C. "First Congregational Church, Atlanta: 'For the Good of Man and the Glory of God.'" *Atlanta Historical Bulletin* 21 (Spring 1977): 129–42.

McGill, Josephine. "'Following Music' in a Mountain Land." *Musical Quarterly* 3 (July 1917): 364–84.

McKelway, A. J. "The Atlanta Riots: A Southern White Point of View." *Outlook* 84 (November 3, 1906): 557–62.

McNeil, W. K., ed. *Appalachian Images in Folk and Popular Culture.* 2d ed. Knoxville: University of Tennessee Press, 1995.

Meade, Guthrie T. "From the Archives: 1914 Atlanta Fiddle Convention." *John Edwards Memorial Foundation Quarterly* 5 (Spring 1969): 27–30.

———. "Fiddles and Fords." *Journal of Country Music* 12, no. 3 (1989): 37–45.

Meier, August. *Negro Thought in America, 1880–1915: Racial Ideologies in the Age of Booker T. Washington.* Ann Arbor: University of Michigan Press, 1963.

Merwin, Henry Childs. "On Being Civilized Too Much." *Atlantic Monthly* 79 (June 1897): 838–46.

Miles, Emma Bell. "Some Real American Music." *Harper's Monthly Magazine* 109 (June 1904): 118–23.

———. *The Spirit of the Mountains.* 1905. Reprint, Knoxville: University of Tennessee Press, 1975.

Miller, Kelly. "The Artistic Gifts of the Negro." *Voice of the Negro* 3 (April 1906): 252–57.

Minton, John. "West African Fiddles in Deep East Texas." In *Juneteenth Texas: Essays in African-American Folklore,* edited by Francis Edward Abernethy,

Patrick B. Mullen, and Alan B. Govenar. Denton: University of North Texas Press, 1996.

Mitchell, Broadus. *The Rise of Cotton Mills in the South*. Baltimore: Johns Hopkins University Press, 1921.

Mixon, Gregory Lamont. "The Atlanta Riot of 1906." Ph.D. diss., University of Cincinnati, 1989.

———. "'Good Negro—Bad Negro': The Dynamics of Race and Class in Atlanta during the Era of the 1906 Riot." *Georgia Historical Quarterly* 81 (Fall 1997): 593–621.

"Mobilizing Our Millionaires in the Cause of American Art." *Current Opinion* 62 (January 1917): 54.

Moore, John Hammond. "Jim Crow in Georgia." *South Atlantic Quarterly* 66 (Fall 1967): 554–65.

Moore, MacDonald Smith. *Yankee Blues: Musical Culture and American Identity*. Bloomington: Indiana University Press, 1985.

Moton, Robert Russa. *Finding a Way Out: An Autobiography*. Garden City, N.Y.: Doubleday, Page, 1921.

———, ed. *Religious Folk Songs of the Negro as Sung on the Plantations*. 2d ed. Revised. Hampton, Va.: Institute Press, 1909.

"Mountain Minstrelsy." *Berea Quarterly* 9 (April 1905): 5.

Murphy, Jeannette Robinson. "The True Negro Music and Its Decline." *Independent* 55 (July 1923): 1723–30.

———. "Survival of African Music in America." In *The Negro and His Folklore in Nineteenth-Century Periodicals*, edited by Bruce Jackson. Austin: University of Texas Press, 1967.

"The Music of America Tomorrow." *Etude* 31 (March 1913): 165.

"Music and Labor." *Etude* 43 (June 1925): 367.

"Music and Manliness." *Nation* 75 (July 24, 1902): 66.

The Musical Directory of Atlanta and Georgia. Atlanta: Arno Music Co., 1909.

Musselman, Joseph A. *Music in the Cultured Generation: A Social History of Music in America, 1870–1900*. Evanston, Ill.: Northwestern University Press, 1971.

Nathan, Hans. *Dan Emmett and the Rise of Early Negro Minstrelsy*. Norman: University of Oklahoma Press, 1962.

"A Negro Explains Jazz." *Literary Digest* 61 (April 26, 1919): 28–9.

"Negro Music in the Land of Freedom." *Outlook* 106 (March 21, 1914): 611–12.

"Negro Music and Minstrelsy." In *The American History and Encyclopedia of Music: History of American Music*, edited by W. L. Hubbard. London: Irving Squire, 1908.

"The Negro's Contribution to Art." *Literary Digest* 55 (October 20, 1917): 26–27.

"Negro Spiritual Contest in Columbia." *Southern Workman* 55 (1926): 372–73.

"A Negro Spiritual Contest in Columbus." *Playground* 20 (May 1926): 90–2.

"Negro Spirituals." *New York Times*, January 27, 1924.

"Negro Spirituals Again in Columbus." *Playground* 20 (February 1927): 605–6.

Negus, Keith. *Popular Music in Theory: An Introduction*. Cambridge [U.K.]: Polity Press, 1996.

Neuls-Bates, Carol. "Women's Orchestras in the United States, 1925–45."
    In *Women Making Music: The Western Art Tradition, 1150–1950*, edited by Jane
    Bowers and Judith Tick. Urbana: University of Illinois Press, 1986.
————, ed. *Women in Music: An Anthology of Source Readings from the Middle Ages to
    the Present*. Revised. Boston: Northeastern University Press, 1996.
Newby, I. A. *Plain Folk in the New South: Social Change and Cultural Persistence,
    1880–1915*. Baton Rouge: Louisiana State University Press, 1988.
Newell, William Wells. "On the Field and Work of a Journal of American
    Folk-Lore." *Journal of American Folklore* 1 (April–June 1888): 3–7.
Newman, Harvey K. "Decatur Street: Atlanta's African American Paradise Lost."
    Atlanta History 64 (Summer 2000): 5–20.
Newton, R. Heber. "The Mysticism of Music as the Mystery of Religion." *Current
    Opinion* 59 (September 1915): 185–86.
Oakley, Giles. *The Devil's Music: A History of the Blues*. New York: Taplinger
    Publishing Co., 1977.
O'Connor, Michael James. "The Measurement and Significance of Racial
    Residential Barriers in Atlanta, 1890–1970." Ph.D. diss., University of
    Georgia, 1977.
Odum, Howard W., and Guy B. Johnson. *The Negro and His Songs*. Chapel Hill:
    University of North Carolina Press, 1925.
Official Souvenir Program of the Atlanta Music Festival. Atlanta: Foote and Davis,
    1909.
Ogren, Kathy J. *The Jazz Revolution: Twenties America and the Meaning of Jazz*. New
    York: Oxford University Press, 1989.
O'Leary, Cecilia Elizabeth. *To Die For: The Paradox of American Patriotism*.
    Princeton: Princeton University Press, 1999.
Olmsted, Frederick Law. *The Cotton Kingdom*. 1861. Reprint, New York: Da Capo
    Press, 1996.
Orr, N. Lee. *Alfredo Barili and the Rise of Classical Music in Atlanta*. Atlanta:
    Scholars Press, 1996.
"Our Atlanta Dudes." *Atlanta Historical Bulletin* 5 (July 1940): 236–37.
Ownby, Ted. *Subduing Satan: Religion, Recreation, and Manhood in the Rural South,
    1865–1920*. Chapel Hill: University of North Carolina Press, 1990.
Parsons, Elsie Clews. "Joel Chandler Harris and Negro Folklore." *Dial* 66
    (May 17, 1919): 491–93.
"Passing of the Minstrels." *Literary Digest* 62 (August 16, 1919): 28–29.
"The Passing of a Picturesque People." *Sky-Land Magazine* 1 (October 1913):
    126–30.
Payne, Lewis. "The Negro in the World of Music." *Etude* 24 (June 1916): 406.
Pendle, Karin, ed. *Women and Music: A History*. Bloomington: Indiana University
    Press, 1991.
Perkins, A. E. "Negro Spirituals from the Far South." *Journal of American Folklore*
    35 (July–September 1922): 223–49.
Peterson, Richard A. *Creating Country Music: Fabricating Authenticity*. Chicago:
    University of Chicago Press, 1997.

Pierce, Edwin H. "The New Social Status of Musicians." *Etude* 32 (July 1914): 529.

Pierson, William D. "Puttin' Down Ole Massa: African Satire in the New World." In *African Folklore in the New World,* edited by Daniel J. Crowley. Austin: University of Texas Press, 1977.

Pike, G. D. *The Jubilee Singers and Their Campaign for Twenty Thousand Dollars.* Boston: Lee and Shepard, 1873.

Pioneer Citizens' History of Atlanta, 1833–1902. Atlanta: Byrd Printing Co., 1902.

"The Plantation Melody." *Colored American Magazine* 11 (July 1906): 59–61.

Plantinga, Leon. *Romantic Music: A History of Musical Style in Nineteenth-Century Europe.* New York: W. W. Norton, 1984.

Porter, Michael Leroy. "Black Atlanta: An Interdisciplinary Study of Blacks on the East Side of Atlanta, 1890–1930." Ph.D. diss., Emory University, 1974.

Postell, Mary Walton. "Tales Told Out of School." *Atlanta Historical Bulletin* 13 (March 1968): 23–63.

Powell, John. "Music and the Nation." *Rice Institute Pamphlet* 10 (1923): 126–63.

———. "How America Can Develop a National Music." *Etude* 45 (May 1927): 349–50.

"A Prison 'Sing' at Jackson." *The Survey,* December 13, 1919, 240.

Proctor, Henry Hugh. "The Atlanta Riot, Fundamental Causes, and Reactionary Results." *Southern Workman* 36 (August 1907): 424–26.

———. *Between Black and White: Autobiographical Sketches.* 1925. Reprint, Freeport, N.Y.: Books for Libraries Press, 1971.

Puckett, Newbell Niles. *Folk Beliefs of the Southern Negro.* Chapel Hill: University of North Carolina Press, 1926.

Pudup, Mary Beth, Dwight Billings, and Altina Waller, eds. *Appalachia in the Making: The Mountain South in the Nineteenth Century.* Chapel Hill: University of North Carolina Press, 1995.

Rabinowitz, Howard N. *Race Relations in the Urban South, 1865–1890.* Oxford University Press, 1978.

"Race Conservation." *Berea Quarterly* 16 (July 1912): 3.

Raine, James Watt. *The Land of Saddle-Bags: A Study of the Mountain People of Appalachia.* New York: Council of Women for Home Missions and Missionary Education Movement of the United States and Canada, 1924.

Ralph, Julian. "Our Appalachian Americans." *Harper's* 107 (June 1903): 32–41.

Randall, Ethel Annis. "The Boys' Recital." *Etude* 42 (February 1924): 86.

Randolph, Harold. "Why Do Not More Men Take Up Music?" *Etude* 41 (May 1923): 299–300.

Rathbun, F. G. "The Negro Music of the South." *Southern Workman* 22 (November 1893): 174.

Raymond, C. Rexford. "British Ballads in Our Southern Highlands." *Berea Quarterly* (November 1899): 12–14.

Richardson, Anna Davis. "Old Songs from Clarksburg, W.VA, 1918." *Journal of American Folklore* (October–December 1919): 497–504.

Richardson, Clement, ed. *The National Cyclopedia of the Colored Race*. Montgomery, Ala.: National Publishing Co., 1919.

Ripley, Frederick H. "The Ideal Supervisor." *Journal of Proceedings and Addresses of the National Education Association* (1907): 851–56.

Roberts, Kate Louise. *The Club Woman's Handybook of Programs and Club Management*. New York: Funk and Wagnall's Co., 1914.

Roberts, Randy. *Papa Jack: Jack Johnson and the Era of White Hopes*. New York: Free Press, 1983.

Robeson, M. Bertha. "Woman's Work in Music." *Etude* 16 (March 1898): 68.

Rodeheaver, Homer. *Rodeheaver's Negro Spirituals*. Chicago: Rodeheaver Co., 1923.

Roediger, David R. *The Wages of Whiteness: Race and the Making of the American Working Class*. Revised. London: Verso, 1999.

Roell, Craig H. *The Piano in America, 1890–1940*. Chapel Hill: University of North Carolina Press, 1989.

Rogers, Joseph M. "Do Men Lack Culture?" *Lippincott's Monthly Magazine* 87 (January 1911): 126–28.

Roosevelt, Theodore. Letter to the Editor. *Berea Quarterly* 2 (May 1897): 2.

———. "Race Decadence." *Outlook* 97 (April 8, 1911): 764.

Rossiter, Frank R. *Charles Ives and His America*. New York: Liveright, 1975.

Roth, Darlene Rebecca. *Matronage: Patterns in Women's Organizations, Atlanta, Georgia, 1890–1940*. Brooklyn: Carlson Publishing, 1994.

Roth, Darlene R., and Andy Ambrose. *Metropolitan Frontiers: A Short History of Atlanta*. Atlanta: Longstreet Press, 1996.

Rotundo, E. Anthony. *American Manhood: Transformations in Masculinity from the Revolution to the Modern Era*. New York: Basic Books, 1993.

Russell, James Michael. "The Chamber of Commerce in the Economic and Political Development of Atlanta from 1900 to 1916." *Atlanta Historical Bulletin* 19 (Fall 1975): 19–33.

———. *Atlanta, 1847–1890: City Building in the Old South and the New*. Baton Rouge: Louisiana State University Press, 1988.

Rydell, Robert W. *All the World's a Fair: Visions of Empire at American International Expositions, 1876–1916*. Chicago: University of Chicago Press, 1984.

Ryder, Georgia A. "Harlem Renaissance Ideals in the Music of Robert Nathaniel Dett." In *Black Music in the Harlem Renaissance*, edited by Samuel A. Floyd Jr. Westport, Conn.: Greenwood Press, 1990.

Sablosky, Irving. *What They Heard: Music in America, 1852–1881*. Baton Rouge: Louisiana State University Press, 1986.

Savage, Kirk. *Standing Soldiers, Kneeling Slaves: Race, War, and Monument in Nineteenth-Century America*. Princeton: Princeton University Press, 1997.

Scarborough, Dorothy. *On the Trail of Negro Folk-Songs*. Cambridge: Harvard University Press, 1925.

Schabas, Ezra. *Theodore Thomas: America's Conductor and Builder of Orchestras, 1835–1905*. Urbana: University of Illinois Press, 1989.

"The School at Rabun Gap." *Outlook* 123 (November 12, 1917): 319–21.

Scott, Anne Firor. *The Southern Lady: From Pedestal to Politics, 1830–1930.* 1970. Reprint, Charlottesville: University Press of Virginia, 1995.

———. *Natural Allies: Women's Associations in American History.* Urbana: University of Illinois Press, 1991.

Seeing Atlanta, Georgia, by the Photograph Route. Atlanta: N.p., 1917.

Semple, Ellen Churchill. "The Anglo-Saxons of the Kentucky Mountains." *Geographical Journal* 17 (June 1901); reprinted in *Appalachian Images in Folk and Popular Culture,* edited by W. K. McNeil. 2d ed. Knoxville: University of Tennessee Press, 1995.

Seroff, Doug. "Polk Miller and the Old South Quartette." *John Edwards Memorial Foundation Quarterly* 18 (Fall–Winter 1982): 147–50.

Seymour, Harriet A. *What Music Can Do for You: A Guide for the Uninitiated.* New York: Harper and Brothers, 1920.

Shaler, Nathaniel S. *The Neighbor: A Natural History of Human Contacts.* Boston: Houghton Mifflin, 1904.

Shapiro, Henry D. *Appalachia on Our Mind: The Southern Mountains and Mountaineers in the American Consciousness, 1870–1920.* Chapel Hill: University of North Carolina Press, 1978.

Sharp, Cecil J. *English Folk-Song: Some Conclusions.* London: Simpkin and Co., 1907.

Shearin, Hubert G. "British Ballads in the Cumberland Mountains." *Sewanee Review* 19 (July 1911): 313–27.

Shearin, Hubert G., and Josiah H. Combs. *A Syllabus of Kentucky Folk-Songs.* Lexington: Transylvania Printing Co., 1911.

Shepherd, John, and Peter Wicke. *Music and Cultural Theory.* Malden, Mass.: Blackwell Publishers, 1997.

Silber, Nina. *The Romance of Reunion: Northerners and the South, 1865–1900.* Chapel Hill: University of North Carolina Press, 1992.

Simms, L. Moody, Jr. "Folk Music in America: John Powell and the 'National Musical Idiom.'" *Journal of Popular Culture* 7 (Winter 1973): 510–15.

Sims, Anastatia. *The Power of Femininity in the New South: Women's Organizations and Politics in North Carolina, 1880–1930.* Columbia: University of South Carolina Press, 1997.

Skowronski, JoAnn. *Women in American Music: A Bibliography.* Metuchen, N.J.: Scarecrow Press, 1978.

Slotkin, Richard. *Gunfighter Nation: The Myth of the Frontier in Twentieth-Century America.* New York: Atheneum, 1992.

Small, Christopher. *Musicking: The Meanings of Performing and Listening.* Hanover, Conn.: Wesleyan University Press, 1998.

Smith, Catherine Parsons. "Inventing Tradition: Symphony and Opera in Progressive-Era Los Angeles." In *Music and Culture in America, 1861–1918,* edited by Michael Saffle. New York: Garland Publishing, 1998.

Smith, Charles Alphonso. "A Great Movement in Which Everyone Can Help."

In U.S. Bureau of Education, *An Opportunity to Help in an Important Work.*
Washington, D.C.: U.S. Bureau of Education Special Inquiry, 1913.

Smith, Fanny Morris. "The Beginning of the Club Year." *Etude* 18 (November 1900): 410.

———. "On the Woman's Club as a Co-Operative Business." *Etude* 19 (November 1901): 412–13.

———. "The Record of Woman in Music." *Etude* 19 (November 1901): 317.

Smith, J. David. *The Eugenic Assault on America: Scenes in Red, White, and Black.* Fairfax, Va.: George Mason University Press, 1993.

Smith, Joseph Hutchison. "Folk Songs of the American Negro." *Sewanee Review* 32 (April 1924): 206–24.

Smith, Reed. *South Carolina Ballads.* Cambridge: Harvard University Press, 1928.

Smythe, Augustine T., et al. *The Carolina Low-Country.* New York: Macmillan, 1932.

Snyder, Franklyn Bliss. "Leo Frank and Mary Phagan." *Journal of American Folklore* 31 (April–June 1918): 264–66.

Sousa, John Philip. *Marching Along: Recollections of Men, Women, and Music.* Revised. Westville, Ohio: Integrity Press, 1994.

Southern, Eileen. *The Music of Black Americans.* 3d ed. New York: W. W. Norton, 1997.

"The Southern Problem." *Berea Quarterly* 9 (October 1905): 3.

Spencer, Jon Michael. *Black Hymnody: A Hymnological History of the African-American Church.* Knoxville: University of Tennessee Press, 1992.

———. *The New Negroes and Their Music: The Success of the Harlem Renaissance.* Knoxville: University of Tennessee Press, 1997.

Squire, Belle. "The Status of the Musician." *Etude* 25 (September 1907): 574.

Stanford, Charles Villiers, and Cecil Forsyth. *A History of Music.* New York: Macmillan, 1918.

Steele, Annie K. "The Music of Our South." *Etude* 34 (April 1916): 263–64.

Steele, Mrs. William D. "The Relation of the Woman's Club to the Musical Life of the Community." *Journal of Proceedings of the Music Supervisors' National Conference* (1919): 123–27.

Stekert, Ellen J. "Tylor's Theory of Survivals and National Romanticism: Their Influence on American Folk Song Collectors." *Southern Folklore Quarterly* 32 (September 1968): 209–36.

Stephenson, Gilbert T. "The Segregation of the White and Negro Races in Cities." *South Atlantic Quarterly* 13 (January 1914): 1–18.

Sternberg, Constantin. "Are Girls Taught Music to the Exclusion of Boys?" *Etude* 12 (March 1894): 66.

Still, William Grant. "My Arkansas Boyhood." Reprinted in *The William Grant Still Reader: Essays on American Music,* edited by Jon Michael Spencer; a special issue of *Black Sacred Music: A Journal of Theomusicology* 6 (Fall 1992): 245–51.

Stone, James H. "Mid-Nineteenth-Century American Beliefs in the Social Value of Music." *Musical Quarterly* 43 (January 1957): 38–49.

Stowe, Harriet Beecher. *Uncle Tom's Cabin.* 1852. Reprint, New York: Penguin Classics, 1986.

Sullivan, Jack. *New World Symphonies: How American Culture Changed European Music.* New Haven: Yale University Press, 1999.

Surette, Thomas Whitney. *Music and Life: A Study of the Relations between Ourselves and Music.* Boston: Houghton Mifflin, 1917.

Sutherland, Pete. "Beware of Old-Time Music Revivals: The Henry Ford Story." *Old-Time Herald* 2 (February–April 1991): 33–7.

"A Talk to Boys Who Don't Want Music." *Etude* 39 (September 1921): 603.

Talley, Thomas. *Negro Folk Rhymes, Wise and Otherwise.* New York: Macmillan, 1922.

Tapper, Thomas. "What Should the Musician Know about Business?" *Etude* 43 (February 1925): 85–86.

Tawa, Nicholas. *Mainstream Music of Early-Twentieth-Century America.* Westport, Conn.: Greenwood Press, 1992.

Thompson, Holland. *From the Cotton Field to the Cotton Mill: A Study of Industrial Transition in North Carolina.* New York: Macmillan, 1906.

Thompson, Samuel H. *The Highlanders of the South.* New York: Eaton and Mains, 1910.

Thurber, Cheryl. "The Development of the Mammy Image and Mythology." In *Southern Women: Histories and Identities,* edited by Virginia Bernhard, Betty Brandon, Elizabeth Fox-Genovese, and Theda Perdue. Columbia: University of Missouri Press, 1992.

Tibbetts, John C., ed. *Dvořák in America, 1892–1895.* Portland, Oreg.: Amadeus Press, 1993.

Tick, Judith. "Passed Away Is the Piano Girl: Changes in American Musical Life." In *Women Making Music: The Western Art Tradition, 1150–1950,* edited by Jane Bowers and Judith Tick. Urbana: University of Illinois Press, 1986.

———. "Women in Music." In *The New Grove Dictionary of American Music,* edited by H. Wiley Hitchcock and Stanley Sadie. New York: Macmillan Press, 1986.

———. "Charles Ives and Gender Ideology." In *Musicology and Difference: Gender and Sexuality in Music Scholarship,* edited by Ruth A. Solie. Berkeley: University of California Press, 1993.

Tischler, Barbara. *An American Music: The Search for an American Musical Identity.* New York: Oxford University Press, 1986.

Toll, Robert. *Blacking Up: The Minstrel Show in Nineteenth-Century America.* New York: Oxford University Press, 1974.

Tompkins, Daniel A. "The Mountain Whites as an Industrial Factor in the South." In *The South in the Building of the Nation,* vol. 10, edited by S. C. Mitchell. Richmond: The Southern Historical Publication Society, 1910.

Trachtenberg, Alan. *The Incorporation of America: Culture and Society in the Gilded Age.* New York: Hill and Wang, 1982.

Traquair, Ramsay. "Women and Civilization." *Atlantic Monthly* 132 (September 1923): 289–96.

"The Triumph of Edward MacDowell." *Etude* 28 (November 1910): 723.

Tucker, Nana. *The Atlanta Music Club: Silver Anniversary History and Record.* Atlanta: John T. Hancock, 1940.

Turbeville, Robert Paul, ed. *Eminent Georgians.* Atlanta: Southern Society for Research and History, 1937.

Turner, Chittenden. "Music and the Woman's Crusade." *Arts and Decoration* 19 (September 1923): 29, 70, 73.

Turner, William H. "The Demography of Black Appalachia: Past and Present." In *Blacks in Appalachia,* edited by William H. Turner and Edward J. Cabbell. Lexington: University of Kentucky Press, 1985.

"The Uncultured Sex." *Independent* 67 (November 11, 1909): 1099–1100.

Upton, George P. *Woman in Music.* 2d ed. Chicago: A. C. McClurg and Co., 1886.

———., ed. *Theodore Thomas: A Musical Autobiography.* 2 vols. Chicago: A. C. McClurg and Co., 1905.

Van de Wall, Willem. *The Utilization of Music in Prisons and Mental Hospitals.* New York: National Bureau for the Advancement of Music, 1924.

———. *Music in Institutions.* New York: Russell Sage Foundation, 1936.

Van Vechten, Carl. "The Folksongs of the American Negro: The Importance of the Negro Spirituals in the Music of America." *Vanity Fair* 24 (July 1925): 52, 92.

"The Voice of the South in American Music." *Current Opinion* 61 (September 1916): 174.

Wallashek, Richard. *Primitive Music.* London: Longmans, Green, 1893.

Waller, Altina L. *Feud: Hatfields, McCoys, and Social Change in Appalachia, 1860–1900.* Chapel Hill: University of North Carolina Press, 1988.

———. "Feuding in Appalachia: Evolution of a Cultural Stereotype." In *Appalachia in the Making: The Mountain South in the Nineteenth Century,* edited by Mary Beth Pudup, Dwight B. Billings, and Altina L. Waller. Chapel Hill: University of North Carolina Press, 1995.

Ward, Ronald David. "The Life and Works of John Powell, 1882–1963." Ph.D. diss., Catholic University of America, 1973.

Washington, Booker T. Introduction to *Twenty-Four Negro Melodies Transcribed for the Piano,* by Samuel Coleridge-Taylor. Boston: Oliver Ditson Co., 1905.

Washington, E. Davidson, ed. *Selected Speeches of Booker T. Washington.* Garden City, N.Y.: Doubleday, Doran, 1932.

Watson, Thomas. "Foreign Missions, Continued." *Watson's Jeffersonian Magazine* 3 (July 1909): 487–509.

Wedell, Marsha. *Elite Women and the Reform Impulse in Memphis, 1875–1915.* Knoxville: University of Tennessee Press, 1991.

Wells, Paul F. "Mellie Dunham: 'Maine's Champion Fiddler.'" *John Edwards Memorial Foundation Quarterly* 12 (Autumn 1976): 112–18.

Welter, Barbara. "The Cult of True Womanhood, 1800–1860." *American Quarterly* 18 (Summer 1966): 151–74.

Weston Woman's Club, ed. *History of Webster County, Georgia.* Roswell, Ga.: W. H. Wolfe Associates, 1980.

Whaley, Marcellus S. *The Old Type Passes: Gullah Sketches of the Carolina Sea Islands.*
  Boston: Christopher Publishing House, 1925.

"When Kreisler Played." *Musician* 22 (March 1917): 223.

"Where to Listen for the American Note in Music." *Current Opinion* 71
  (November 1921): 614.

Whisnant, David E. *All That Is Native and Fine: The Politics of Culture in an American
  Region.* Chapel Hill: University of North Carolina Press, 1983.

———. *Modernizing the Mountaineer: People, Power, and Planning in Appalachia.*
  Revised. Knoxville: University of Tennessee Press, 1994.

White, Deborah Gray. *Ar'n't I a Woman: Female Slaves in the Plantation South.* New
  York: W. W. Norton, 1985.

White, Jack. *Bench and Bar of Georgia.* Atlanta: Franklin Printing Co., 1935.

White, Newman Ivey. "Racial Traits in the Negro Song." *Sewanee Review* 28 (July
  1920): 396–404.

———. *American Negro Folk-Songs.* Cambridge: Harvard University Press, 1928.

———. "The White Man in the Woodpile: Some Influences on Negro Secular
  Folk-Songs." *American Speech* 4 (February 1929): 207–15.

White, Newman Ivey, gen. ed., Henry M. Belden et al., associate eds. *The Frank C.
  Brown Collection of North Carolina Folklore.* 7 vols. Durham, N.C.: Duke
  University Press, 1952–64.

Whitesitt, Linda. "The Role of Women Impresarios in American Concert Life."
  American Music 7 (Summer 1989): 163.

———. "Women as 'Keepers of Culture': Music Clubs, Community Concert
  Series, and Symphony Orchestras." In *Cultivating Music in America: Women
  Patrons and Activists since 1860,* edited by Ralph P. Locke and Cyrilla Barr.
  Berkeley: University of California Press, 1997.

Wiener, Jonathan. *Social Origins of the New South.* Baton Rouge: Louisiana State
  University Press, 1978.

Wiggins, Gene. "Gordon Tanner: Fiddler and Fiddle Maker." *Devil's Box* 12 (June
  1978): 18–26.

———. *Fiddlin' Georgia Crazy: Fiddlin' John Carson, His Real World, and the World of
  His Songs.* Urbana: University of Illinois Press, 1987.

Wilgus, D. K. *Anglo-American Folksong Scholarship since 1898.* New Brunswick, N.J.:
  Rutgers University Press, 1959.

Wilgus, D. K., and Nathan Hurvitz. "'Little Mary Phagan': Further Notes on a
  Native American Ballad in Context." *Journal of Country Music* 4 (Spring 1973):
  17–26.

Williams, Vernon J., Jr. *Rethinking Race: Franz Boas and His Contemporaries.*
  Lexington: University Press of Kentucky, 1996.

Williamson, Joel. *The Crucible of Race: Black-White Relations in the American South
  since Emancipation.* New York: Oxford University Press, 1984.

Williford, William Bailey. *Peachtree Street, Atlanta.* Athens: University of Georgia
  Press, 1962.

———. *Americus through the Years: The Story of a Georgia Town and Its People, 1832–
  1975.* Atlanta: Cherokee Publishing Co., 1975.

Willis, William S., Jr. "Franz Boas and the Study of Black Folklore." In *The New Ethnicity: Perspectives from Ethnology*, edited by John W. Bennett; 1973 Proceedings of the American Ethnological Society. St. Paul: West Publishing Co., 1975.

Wilson, H. J. "The Negro and Music." *Outlook* 84 (December 1, 1906): 823–26.

Wilson, Samuel Tyndale. *The Southern Mountaineers*. 4th ed. Revised. New York: Literature Department, Presbyterian Home Missions, 1914.

Wilson, Shannon H. "Lincoln's Sons and Daughters: Berea College, Lincoln Memorial University, and the Myth of Unionist Appalachia." In *The Civil War in Appalachia: Collected Essays*, edited by Kenneth W. Noe and Shannon H. Wilson. Knoxville: University of Tennessee Press, 1997.

Wilson, William A. "Herder, Folklore, and Romantic Nationalism." *Journal of Popular Culture* 6 (Spring 1973): 819–35.

Wilson, Woodrow. "Berea's Discovery in the Mountains." *Berea Quarterly* 15 (July and October 1911): 5–11.

Winans, Robert B. "The Folk, the Stage, and the Five-String Banjo in the Nineteenth Century." *Journal of American Folklore* 89 (October–December 1976): 407–37.

———. "Black Instrumental Music Traditions in the Ex-Slave Narratives." *Black Music Research Journal* 10 (Spring 1990): 43–53.

Winn, Edith Lynwood. "The Woman as Musician." *Etude* 18 (September 1900): 335.

Wittke, Carl. *Tambo and Bones: A History of the American Minstrel Stage*. Durham: Duke University Press, 1930.

Wolf, William A. "Boys' Week in a Musical School." *Etude* 38 (July 1920): 454.

Wolfe, Charles K. "The Great 1927 Nashville Fiddlers' Convention." *The Devil's Box* 22 (September 1973): 27–31.

———. "Old-Time Fiddling Contests at Knoxville's Market Hall." *Devil's Box* 27 (December 1974): 24–27.

———. "The 1926 Tennessee State Championship Contest." *Devil's Box* 9 (March 1975): 6–10.

———. "Bill Shores and North Georgia Fiddling." *Old Time Music* 25 (Summer 1977): 4–8.

———. *Tennessee Strings: The Story of Country Music in Tennessee*. Knoxville: University of Tennessee Press, 1977.

———. "The Atlanta Fiddling Contests, 1913–1916." *Devil's Box* 14 (June 1980): 12–29.

———. "Rural Black String Band Music." *Black Music Research Newsletter* 4 (Fall 1980): 3–4.

———. "An 1899 Fiddlers' Carnival." *Devil's Box* 14 (December 1980): 50–52.

———. "The Atlanta Contests, 1921–1934." *Devil's Box* 15 (March 1981): 17–25.

———. *Kentucky Country: Folk and Country Music of Kentucky*. Lexington: University Press of Kentucky, 1982.

———. *The Devil's Box: Masters of Southern Fiddling*. Nashville: Vanderbilt University Press, 1997.

Wolfe, Charles K., Peggy Bulger, and Gene Wiggins. "Roba Stanley: The First Country Sweetheart." *Old Time Music* 26 (Autumn 1977): 13–18.

Wolters, Raymond. *The New Negro on Campus: Black College Rebellions of the 1920s.* Princeton: Princeton University Press, 1975.

"Woman and Music." *Etude* 18 (September 1900): 334–35.

"Women as Musicians." *Etude* 18 (November 1900): 411.

Wood, Mary I. *The History of the General Federation of Women's Clubs.* Norwood, Mass.: Norwood Press, 1912.

Woodward, C. Vann. *Origins of the New South, 1877–1913.* Baton Rouge: Louisiana State University Press, 1951.

Work, John Wesley. *Folk Song of the American Negro.* Nashville: F. A. McKenzie, 1915.

———. "Negro Folk Song." *Opportunity* 1 (October 1923): 292–94.

Wyman, Loraine, and Howard Brockway. *Lonesome Tunes.* New York: H. W. Gray Co., 1916.

Zumwalt, Rosemary Levy. *American Folklore Scholarship: A Dialogue of Dissent.* Bloomington: Indiana University Press, 1988.

Index

80; appeal to whites, 69, 70, 71,
72, 74, 75, 76, 79, 84, 94, 95, 96,
97; disgarded by blacks, 69, 71, 75,
77–78; and New South, 70, 103;
and race consciousness, 78; linked
to black inferiority, 78–79; and
Dvořák, 79–80; and Proctor, 88,
90, 94, 97
State Association for the Education of
Georgia Mountaineers, 119
Stereotypes: and Colored Music Festival, 94, 95; of Appalachian culture,
120–22, 123, 136, 141; and old-time
fiddling, 120–23, 131–32
Still, William Grant, 161 (n. 55)
Strikes, 104, 125, 126, 128
Sunday concerts, 40–41, 59, 154
(nn. 137, 138)
Swanson, William, 140
Sylva, Marguerite, 23, 149 (n. 32)

Taft, William Howard, 14
Tallulah Falls Industrial School, 118
Tanner, Gid, 123, 127, 131
Tanner, Gordon, 169 (n. 105)
Tarzan, 27
Tennessee, 111, 135
Textile factories, 8
Thomas, Edna, 74, 75–76
Thomas, Theodore, 29, 151 (n. 85)
Thompson, Samuel H., 124
Tin Pan Alley, 134
Toscanini, Arturo, 29, 151 (n. 87)
Tourism, 48, 58
Turner, E. K., 41
Twain, Mark, 74

Underclass, 104
Union Grove, North Carolina, 135
United Daughters of the Confederacy
(UDC), 129, 170–71 (n. 140)
University of Virginia, 109
Upper-class blacks: and musical

culture, 12; and Colored Music
Festival, 85–86, 87, 96; and First
Congregational Church, 88
Upper-class whites: and musical culture, 12; and Metropolitan Opera
season, 19; and gender roles, 64;
and Colored Music Festival, 97;
and Appalachian culture, 104; and
Georgia Old-Time Fiddlers' Convention, 104, 120–21; and crackers,
123–24; and poor whites, 124; and
minstrel shows, 131. *See also* Elites
Urbanization: and masculinity, 10, 49,
112–14, 138; and gender roles, 16–
17, 115–16, 137; and urban development, 35, 48, 63; and Appalachian
culture, 105, 140–41
U.S. Census Bureau, 53
U.S. Department of Education, 109
U.S. Supreme Court, 70

Victoria of Schleswig-Holstein, Princess, 75
Violence: and race relations, 7, 9, 83,
88, 92; white-on-black violence, 9,
61, 136; and Appalachian culture,
113, 136, 137, 138; and masculinity,
137. *See also* Lynching; Race riots
Virginia, 111
Voting restrictions, 7

Wagner, Richard, 27
Washington, Booker T., 57, 78, 80,
81, 88, 117
Washington, D.C., 135
Watson, James, 4
Webster County, Georgia, 1–2
Wells, Emilia, 137
West Virginia, 111, 124, 135
Wheeler, Anita Sorrells, 174 (n. 193)
White culture: and white supremacy,
18–19; blacks' reputed imitation of,
69–70; and black culture, 71, 72,